Ex Libris
(stolen from)
Wil. Anderson

THE FIRST

SIMON AND SCHUSTER · NEW YORK

TO FLY

Aviation's
Pioneer
Days

SHERWOOD HARRIS

SECOND PRINTING

SBN 671–20474–2
LIBRARY OF CONGRESS CATALOG CARD NUMBER: 79–101875
DESIGNED BY EDITH FOWLER
MANUFACTURED IN THE UNITED STATES OF AMERICA

*The author is grateful for permission from several publishers to quote from
the following works:*

The American Heritage History of Flight, *by the editors of* American Herit-
age. *American Heritage Publishing Co., Inc., New York, N.Y., 1962.*
Claude Grahame-White, *by Graham Wallace. Putnam & Company Ltd.,
London, 1960.*
"Coast to Coast in Twelve Crashes," *by Sherwood Harris.* American Herit-
age, *October, 1964.*
"Early Flying Experiences," *by Major General Benjamin D. Foulois,
U.S.A.F. (Retd.),* Air Power Historian, *April, 1955.*
"Glenn H. Curtiss' First Off-Water Flight," *by George E. A. Hallett.* Aero-
space Historian, *Winter, 1966.*
Men, Women and 10,000 Kites, *by Gabriel Voisin. Putnam & Company
Ltd., London, 1963.*
The Papers of Wilbur and Orville Wright, *edited by Marvin W. McFarland.
McGraw-Hill Book Co., Inc., New York, 1953.*
Santos-Dumont, *by Peter Wykeham. Putnam & Company Ltd., London,
1962.*

FOR LORNA

Contents

1939

Not many pilots will tell you the first time around how they really got interested in flying. If you ask, you will probably hear something like: "There was this field near where I grew up, just a little grass strip, really, and I used to go out there and watch the planes and I finally got so that I wanted to try it myself." Or: "Do you remember those funny little balsa-wood airplane models that kids used to build? Well, I used to make them, too, and one thing just sort of led to another."

This all sounds very natural and reasonable and, if you are talking to a beribboned fighter pilot or a senior airline captain, it is becomingly modest, the stuff that good legends are made of. But I am convinced that the real reason why people become aviators is that their first time up in an airplane is such a stunning experience that they are never satisfied again until they can manage some way of arranging their lives so as to recapture regularly something of the exhilaration of that first ride. Why pilots won't admit this I've never fully understood, unless the experience is unfathomable to some degree and hard to 'talk about until you come to the hours of the night when truth is sought and secrets are told. But this I do know: if a pilot does decide to tell you about his first time up, you will be astonished at the vividness of his recollections of the sights and sounds and smells of his first flight even though he may have long since forgotten just about everything else that happened to him in that year.

My own first flight was prosaic enough—a family trip from

Baltimore to Charleston, South Carolina, in an Eastern Airlines DC-3 in the late 1930's. Only in those days the DC-3 was the bright, modern flagship of the "Great Silver Fleet" and the pilots and stewardesses were godlike in the eyes of a boy from a small rural town. On that flight I saw things beyond imagining: real houses and trees and cars reduced to the size of toys, rivers that flashed like lightning as the sunlight struck them, towering clouds that looked like piles of whipped cream as the afternoon wore on, and finally the most breathtaking happening of the day—another plane about a mile away streaking by us so fast in the opposite direction that I blinked and it was gone!

In time I did the other things too—made the airplane models and hung around the nearest airfield hypnotized by the planes taking off and landing. We were in the midst of World War II then and the field was a naval air station. So no one in my family was at all surprised when I signed up for Navy flight school after I finished college. It wasn't long before I got my wings and thought I knew all there was to know about flying. It seems that everyone who survives the business of learning to land a plane on an aircraft carrier ends up feeling this way until something comes along to jolt that idea out of his head and show him how much he still has to learn.

For me, the jolt didn't come while I was flying full time. I'm sure I had my share of bad landings, black nights and hideous weather. But somehow I managed to complete my Navy tour without any of the serious, sobering moments that make one wonder what it is all about. And when my personal moment of truth finally did arrive, it was in a form that I was hardly prepared for. It came while I was walking around in a museum.

I don't know how many times I have visited the Smithsonian Institution in Washington and looked at the airplanes on exhibit there, nor how many times I walked past the airplane with the improbable name *Vin Fiz* that sits in the entrance of the small building that houses most of the aeronautical collection. We have all heard of the Wright "flyer" and Lindbergh's *Spirit of St. Louis*. But do you know why the *Vin Fiz* is famous enough to have a place of honor at the Smithsonian? It was the plane used by a pilot named Cal Rodgers who made the first coast-to-coast flight across the United States. On the face of it, this doesn't sound particularly impressive. However, Rodgers made his flight in the year 1911. It took him eighty-four days, he had twelve major crashes on the way, and there wasn't much of his original flying machine that hadn't been replaced by the time he reached California. And finally the implications of this flight began to hit me. Rodgers' transcontinental trip took place only eight years after the Wright brothers' first flight. Mankind had dreamed of flying for centuries, going back to the time when the legend of Daedalus and Icarus was conceived on the threshold of recorded history. Then, within an extremely short span of time after man's first flight, we had an airplane flying across the United States.

Clearly there had been a remarkable burst of technological development in the wake of the Wrights' epoch-making flight. How had this come about? I obviously didn't know as much about flying as I thought. And what kind of men had done the pioneering work? Here was the kicker: their dream had been much more powerful than anything I and my contemporaries had known, for there was no stunning first flight with someone else to get these early pilots started. When the Wrights, Glenn Curtiss, Santos-Dumont, Blériot and their contemporaries made their first flights, there were no Eastern Airlines captains to guide them through the clouds on a golden afternoon. They did not know what to expect and were not driven into the sky by the memory of a powerful experience.

Within a dozen years after the Wrights' first flight, sleek, streamlined monoplanes were buzzing around the racecourses of Europe at close to 125 miles per hour. The world altitude record was an astonishing 25,755 feet. A German pilot had won the world endurance record by flying continuously for twenty-four hours and twelve minutes, and in Tsarist Russia a giant, multi-engined plane designed by young Igor Sikorsky had flown with sixteen persons aboard. The first landing and takeoff had been made from a warship, the seaplane was well-developed and the first experimental helicopters had appeared. The English Channel had been flown from France to England, from England to

France, and by a woman; pilots had learned to roll, "loop the loop" and do other fancy maneuvers; and—more ominously—the first bombs had been dropped from an airplane on an enemy in combat.

From our vantage point in the second half of the twentieth century, such rapid technological progress does not seem surprising. But there is an essential difference between now and then. Today, governments mobilize the wealth and ingenuity of entire nations to develop machines for flights in outer space. Giant corporations with resources undreamed of at the turn of the century come up with new lines of computers or new generations of jet aircraft so fast that we can hardly comprehend the changes they bring with them. In the Wrights' time, one man with a vision—or two brothers—could change the world.

Soon after I began to understand these things I discovered that I was having almost as much fun reading about the exploits of the early pilots in old newspapers as I found in the limited amount of flying I still did privately and with the Naval Reserve. To my delight, there were a few early pilots still living who were happy to recall for me what it was really like to learn to fly around 1910. Their experiences were almost incredible and— incredibly—were almost unknown outside of a small circle of dedicated aviation historians. Much has been written about the dashing fighter pilots of World War I, the staggering air battles of World War II and the famous pilots and flights in between the two wars. But the earlier and even more colorful period from 1903 to 1915 seemed to have been forgotten. Not even the achievements of the Wright brothers appeared to be fully understood. The high drama of Louis Blériot's flight across the English Channel, the Cal Rodgers cross-country odyssey, the scandalous (or so it seemed at that time) conduct of our first women pilots and the exploits of Lincoln Beachey, the first American stunt pilot to do a loop, all seemed relegated to the obscurity of yellowing and crumbling newspaper clippings along with many other equally vivid early aviation incidents and personalities. It seemed unfitting that obscurity was the fate of so many of those courageous early pilots, and that those of us who fly today knew so little about the achievements and sacrifices of the very people who made it possible for us to take to the air.

What follows, I hope, will make up for this neglect and help you savor, as I have, that wonderful, far simpler time when mankind first looked up and saw flying machines make their rickety way across the sky.

1900

It was the kind of bright, balmy October day that helps Washingtonians forget their dreadful summers. The wind was high in the morning, but by noon it had veered around to the southeast and was blowing gently. The skies were clear except for patches of summery white cumulus clouds. The temperature climbed steadily until it reached a high of 79 degrees, not a record, but well above the seasonal average.

Forty miles downstream from the nation's capital, at a wide place in the Potomac River just before it bends eastward in its final run into the Chesapeake Bay, an odd-looking houseboat swung at anchor in midstream. From waterline to rooftop the boat was conventional enough and resembled a warehouse floating on a barge. But on the roof was a nestlike wooden superstructure, and poised for flight in this nest was a huge thing that looked very much, from a distance, like a man-made version of the prehistoric pterodactyl.

The houseboat swarmed with mechanics, photographers, reporters and other observers. As midday approached, the tempo of activity stepped up. A tugboat which had been standing by all morning was dispatched farther downstream. Many of the reporters and observers set off from the houseboat in skiffs, and a bespectacled young man, dressed in white duck yachting trousers and a cork-lined jacket, started up a gasoline engine in the strange, winged contraption, then climbed aboard it. It was 1903 and the young man, Charles M. Manly, fervently hoped to be the first human being to make a successful sustained flight in a self-

Samuel P. Langley (right) and his test pilot, Charles M. Manly, confidently expected to demonstrate the world's first airplane.

propelled flying machine. He was taking no chances either: strapped to his leg was a compass that would help him find his way back to the houseboat if the flight was too successful and he got lost.

Meanwhile, awaiting results anxiously in Washington was the flying machine's inventor and builder, Dr. Samuel Pierpont

Langley, who was prevented from attending the launching by the press of business at the Smithsonian Institution, which he headed. The aging, white-whiskered Dr. Langley was almost seventy by now and was recognized as one of the foremost scientists in the United States. A man of great natural gifts, Dr. Langley had never gone to college but had taught himself civil engineering, architecture and astronomy and had worked as an assistant at the Harvard Observatory. After that he had gone on to teach mathematics at the U. S. Naval Academy. While serving subsequently as director of the Allegheny Observatory in Pennsylvania prior to taking up his Smithsonian post, Dr. Langley had become fascinated with the idea of human flight.

From 1891 through 1893, Langley built thirty-one exquisite miniature propeller-driven flying models powered with rubber bands. He called his aircraft "aerodromes," a confusing misnomer incorrectly derived from the Greek word *dromos,* meaning a race or racecourse. With some of the more successful models, Langley made flights of approximately 75 feet. By the end of 1896, the eminent scientist had successfully test-flown large, steam-driven models with wing spans of roughly 13 feet. On the final test flight of the year, in late November, one model flew three quarters of a mile at a speed of approximately 30 miles per hour.

The final design that emerged from these experiments had two pairs of wings, one pair set behind the other in a tandem arrangement much like that of a dragonfly. In August, 1903, a 13-foot version of this design powered by a gasoline engine remained airborne for twenty-seven seconds and covered almost 1,000 feet. Meanwhile, a full-scale gasoline-powered machine with an open oval car for a single pilot was being built by Langley and by October it was ready for a test flight. It seemed that Langley and his young assistant were about to achieve man's centuries-old dream of human flight.

After the engine had been running awhile and Manly felt that it was developing its full 52.4 horsepower, he waved to the spectators and signaled for the launch. A man on the forward part of the superstructure fired two rockets into the air. The tugboat answered with two blasts of its steam whistle. A mechanic cut the cable that restrained the machine on its launching rail and Manly was on his way.

"Easily and rapidly the mechanical bird moved along the 70-foot track," wrote a reporter for the Washington *Evening Star.* "The speed was not great, apparently not more than 40 or 50 feet a second. It took the air fairly well. For a fraction of a second the aerodrome stood up in the face of the five-mile wind then blowing. But when that brief period had passed there had passed also the time when the airship had a chance for successful flight. The next instant the big and curious thing turned gradually downward. The declination, though not abrupt, was positive. . . . It disappeared beneath the waves, but only for a moment."

The Washington *Post*'s description was even more vivid: "There was a roaring, grinding noise—and the Langley airship tumbled over the edge of the houseboat and disappeared into the river sixteen feet below. It simply slid into the water like a handful of mortar."

Miraculously, Manly managed to free himself from the tangle of guy wires, torn canvas and shattered wing ribs and made it to the surface. In some ways, the old scientist waiting for word at the Smithsonian was less fortunate, for the newspapers reacted to the failure of his machine to fly with savage, scornful gibes. "The ridiculous fiasco which attended the attempt at aerial navigation in the Langley flying machine was not unexpected," crowed an editorial in the New York *Times.* "The flying machine which will really fly might be evolved by the combined and continuous efforts of mathematicians and mechanicians in from one to ten million years—provided we can meanwhile eliminate such little drawbacks and embarrassments as the existing relation between weight and strength in inorganic materials," the *Times* went on. "No doubt the problem has its attractions for those it interests, but to ordinary men, it would seem as if the effort might be employed more profitably." The *Times* had obviously made up its mind.

Photographs made at the instant of launch show the frail, poorly braced 42-foot wings bending badly out of shape under the strain of trying to lift the fully loaded 850-pound machine.

But Dr. Langley concluded that the crash had resulted from a failure in the launching device which caused it to snag the machine as it slid toward the takeoff point. And so, with winter approaching and money running out, the old man and his fearless test pilot decided to rebuild their machine and try one more flight.

On December 8, 1903, the second attempt was made from the same houseboat on the Potomac. As the machine left the launching rail, the guy wires connecting its tail and rear wings apparently broke. The craft swooped upward, turned over and fell into the water. This time Manly came close to being trapped for good in the wreckage as it settled in the icy winter water. The experience made a vivid, indelible impression on him, and in recounting the incident later he wasn't quite able to conceal his fright no matter how hard he tried to assume the detachment and objectivity of a good scientist:

The writer can only say that from his position in the front end of the machine, where he was facing forward and where his main attention was directed towards insuring that the engine was performing at its best, he was unable to see anything that occurred at the rear of the machine, but that just before the machine was freed from the launching car he felt an extreme swaying motion immediately followed by a tremendous jerk which caused the machine to quiver all over, and almost instantly he found the machine dashing ahead with its bow rising at a very rapid rate, and that he, therefore, swung the wheel which controls the . . . tail to its extreme downward limit of motion, finding that this had absolutely no effect, and that by this time, the machine had passed its vertical position and was beginning to fall backwards, he swung himself around on his arms, from which he supported himself, so that in striking the water with the machine on top of him he would strike feet foremost. The next few moments were for him most intense, for he found himself under the water with the machine on top of him, and with his cork-lined canvas jacket so caught up in the fittings of the framework that he could not dive downward, while the floor of the aviator's car, which was pressing against his head, prevented him from coming upward. His one thought was that if he was to

Langley's dream came to a bitter end when his aircraft crashed into the icy waters of the Potomac River in December, 1903.

get out alive he would have to do so immediately, as the pressure of the water on his lungs was beginning to make itself seriously felt. Exerting all the strength he could muster, he succeeded in ripping the jacket entirely in two and thus freeing himself from the fastenings which had accidentally held him, he dived under the machine and swam under the water for some distance until he thought he was out from under the machine. Upon rising to the surface his head came in contact with a block of ice which necessitated another dive to get free of the ice.

This time the newspapers were kinder to Langley, though they held out little hope for human flight. Said the New York *Times:* "We hope that Prof. Langley will not put his substantial greatness as a scientist in further peril by continuing to waste his time, and the money involved, in further airship experiments. Life is short, and his is capable of services to humanity incomparably greater than can be expected to result from trying to fly."

And so it seemed, as 1903 drew to a close, that man was not quite ready to fly. Many besides Langley had also tried, and so far all had failed to get off the ground in a powered machine that could do more than just return to earth right away. Not all the early test pilots had been as fortunate as the intrepid Manly. The great German glider pilot Otto Lilienthal was dead, his back broken in a glider crash in 1896. And in England, Percy Pilcher, a promising young disciple of Lilienthal's, had also been killed in a glider accident. The others had simply given up when the solution ultimately eluded them.

Then on December 17, 1903, only nine days after Langley's last failure, came this startling telegram from an obscure sand spit on the North Carolina coast named Kitty Hawk:

SUCCESS FOUR FLIGHTS THURSDAY MORNING ALL AGAINST TWENTY ONE MILE WIND STARTED FROM LEVEL WITH ENGINE POWER ALONE AVERAGE SPEED THROUGH AIR THIRTY ONE MILES LONGEST 57 SECONDS INFORM PRESS HOME CHRISTMAS.

OREVELLE WRIGHT

The message was addressed to Bishop Milton Wright of Dayton, Ohio, and it was from his sons, Orville—whose name got garbled in transmission—and Wilbur.

The telegram arrived late in the afternoon, and after supper

RECEIVED at   *170*

176 C KA CS 33 Paid.   Via Norfolk Va

Kitty Hawk N C Dec 17

Bishop M Wright

            7 Hawthorne St

Success four flights thursday morning all against twenty one mile

wind started from Level with engine power alone average speed

through air thirty one miles longest 57 seconds inform Press

home ~~Xmas~~ Christmas .   Orevelle Wright   525P

Bishop Wright asked an older son, Lorin, to take a copy down to the Dayton reporter for the Associated Press. He did so, but by this time the press was pretty skeptical of man's attempts to fly. A few papers carried announcements of the flight the next day. However, these got their facts so confused that it was hard to tell what had really happened. The consensus was that some sort of airship with a fan beneath to keep it up and one behind to push it along had made a flight of three miles under such perfect control that the pilot was able to select a landing spot and alight gracefully just where he wanted to.

What took place on the real first flight was another matter. To begin with, the homemade gasoline engine aboard the Wright airplane didn't run very well. The Wrights' mechanic, Charles E. Taylor, had to squirt oil around the bearing surfaces by hand before starting it up each time and then the engine would run less than a minute before it began seizing up. The aircraft was also hard to control and had a habit of diving abruptly into sand. It couldn't yet make a turn, much less a precision landing as the newspapers said; it was uncomfortable, dangerous and easily damaged.

But the newspapers were right about one thing. The two shy, straitlaced Wright brothers *were* the first people in the world to achieve powered flight. On December 17 they made four flights —of 120, 175, 180 and 852 feet—and they had photographs to prove it, including perhaps the most dramatic aviation picture of all time, showing the first flight just an instant after it became airborne with Orville at the controls.

The first Wright powered machine may have left a lot to be desired as far as performance went, but it was a thing of unique beauty and grace. And in its lines it foreshadowed all that was to follow until man began to send wingless, unstreamlined machines into space. Looking back over sixty years, it may seem that the family resemblance between the Wright machine and today's sleek, modern aircraft is somewhat vague and indistinct. But the resemblance is real enough, for the underlying principles of flight discovered by the Wrights and applied to the design of their aircraft are the same immutable principles that apply today.

With their first flights on December 17, 1903, the Wright brothers demonstrated that they had mastered the three essential elements of flight. First of all, they had designed wings with sufficient lifting power to sustain their machine in the air. Next, they had built themselves a powerplant consisting of engine and propeller that was capable of moving the craft through the air fast enough so that air rushing over the wings generated enough lift to keep the machine airborne. Finally, they had developed a system of controlling the movement of their machine so that once it was off the ground, they could keep it off the ground until they were ready to land or—as in the case of the first few flights— until their engine quit.

Others before them, such as Langley, had developed wings with lifting power and powerplants capable of driving a machine through the air. In these two areas, the Wrights improved substantially on existing technology. But in the field of aircraft control the Wrights, at the very beginning of their interest in flying, came up with a method of controlling the motion of their aircraft that permitted them to succeed where all others had failed. Arguing, debating, discussing things between themselves

With incredible courage, Otto Lilienthal made successful glider flights in Germany by leaping off a hill with these frail wings.

as the nineteenth century drew to a close, the two brothers made one of those rare intuitive mental leaps that suddenly send the human race surging ahead into undreamed-of realms just when a situation seems stagnant. The Wrights' breakthrough was profound—their control system is used on every fixed-wing aircraft that flies today. And, like most great scientific advances, it was simple. It had to be, for neither brother had gone to college. In fact, neither finished high school.

Prior to the Wrights the most successful man-carrying aircraft had been the gliders of Otto Lilienthal in Germany and Octave Chanute in the United States. Between 1891 and 1896, Lilienthal made some two thousand flights in batlike gliders which he launched from a man-made hill near Berlin. In some of these he covered distances of nearly 1,000 feet. In the Lilienthal glider the pilot flew standing up, with his arms and shoulders supported by

Octave Chanute's most successful glider was flown in Indiana in 1896–97 and foreshadowed the biplane design of the Wright brothers.

a special harness. His hips and legs dangled beneath the glider, and by swinging the weight of the lower part of his body the pilot was supposed to counteract any gusts that tended to upset the glider's delicate balance.

The Chanute glider looked more like a conventional biplane but was also controlled by shifting weight. As in the Lilienthal glider, the pilot of the Chanute glider dangled below the wings and attempted to control his craft by swinging the lower part of his body. Working with test pilots Paul Avery and A. M. Herring, Chanute tested his designs on the sand hills bordering Lake Michigan near Miller, Indiana, in 1896.

In neither case did control by shifting weight work very well. Lilienthal was killed on a routine glide on August 9, 1896, when a gust of wind threw his craft out of control. It fell from an altitude of about fifty feet, breaking Lilienthal's back. He died the next day. Despite the fact that Herring once made a flight of 359 feet in the Chanute machine, experiments with it in the fall of 1896 were generally inconclusive and were soon discontinued.

The problem lay in the fact that a shift of weight—even a large one—was not sufficient to counteract gusts of wind once the Lilienthal and Chanute gliders had been tipped over or nosed down beyond a certain point. The balance of these gliders was something like that of a bicycle. As long as they were upright, level and moving ahead, they were steady. But once they started leaning to one side or the other, they tended to keep right on going over like a leaning bicycle until they passed the point where the shifting of weight would do any good. A boy on a bike can always put his foot out and save himself when he leans over too far, but there was nothing like this to save the pilots of the Lilienthal and Chanute gliders from a crash once they reached the point of no return.

The first thing the Wrights did was solve the problem of control. Many years later, Orville Wright recalled the chain of events that led to their remarkable piece of deductive reasoning:

Our first interest began when we were children. Father brought home to us a small toy actuated by a rubber spring which would lift itself into the air. We built a number of copies of this toy, which flew successfully. By "we" I refer to my brother Wilbur and myself. But when we undertook to build the toy on a much larger scale it failed to work so well. The reason for this was not understood by us at the time, so we finally abandoned the experiments. In 1896 we read in the daily papers, or in some of the magazines, of the experiments of Otto Lilienthal, who was making some gliding flights from the top of a small hill in Germany. His death a few months later while making a glide off the hill increased our interest in the subject and we began looking for books pertaining to flight. We found a work written by Professor Marey on animal mechanism which treated of the bird mechanism as applied to flight, but other than this, so far as I can remember, we found little.

In the spring of the year 1899 our interest in the subject was again aroused through the reading of a book on ornithology. We could not understand that there was anything about a bird that would enable it to fly that could not be built on a larger scale and used by man. At this time our thought pertained more particularly to gliding flight and soaring. If the bird's wings would sustain it in the air without the use of any muscular effort, we did not see why man could not be sustained by the same means. We knew that the Smithsonian Institution had been interested in some work on the problem of flight, and accordingly, on the 30th of May 1899, my brother Wilbur wrote a letter to the Smithsonian inquiring about publications on the subject.

Dr. Langley had done considerable work of his own by this time, had already flown his steam-powered models and was well informed on the work of other people. Thus the Smithsonian sent the Wrights several monographs by Langley as well as papers by Lilienthal, Chanute and other scientific writers of this period who had explored the problem of flight. The Wrights studied this material and were immediately struck by a fact that everyone else had missed. As Orville put it when he continued his account:

On reading the different works on the subject we were much impressed with the great number of people who had given thought to it, among these some of the greatest minds the world has produced. But we found that the experiments of one after another had failed. Among those who had worked on the problem I may mention Leonardo da Vinci, one of the greatest artists and engineers of all time; Sir George Cayley, who was among the first of the inventors of the internal combustion engine; Sir Hiram Maxim, inventor of the Maxim rapid-fire gun; Parsons, the inventor of the turbine steam engine; Alexander Graham Bell, inventor of the telephone; Horatio Phillips, a well-known English engineer; Otto Lilienthal, the inventor of instruments used in navigation and a well-known engineer; Thomas A. Edison; and Dr. S. P. Langley, Secretary and head of the Smithsonian Institution. Besides these were a great number of other men of ability who had worked on the problem. But the subject had been brought into disrepute by a number of men of lesser ability who had hoped to solve the problem through devices of their own invention which had all of them failed until finally the public was led to believe that flying was as impossible as perpetual motion. . . .

After reading the pamphlets sent to us by the Smithsonian we became highly enthusiastic with the idea of gliding as a sport. We found that Lilienthal had been killed through his inability to properly balance his machine in the air. Pilcher, an English experimenter had met with a like fate.

We found that both of these experimenters had attempted to maintain balance merely by the shifting of the weight of their bodies. Chanute, and I believe all the other experimenters before 1900, used this same method of maintaining the equilibrium in gliding flight. We at once set to work to devise a more efficient means of maintaining the equilibrium. . . .

The first method that occurred to us for maintaining the lateral equilibrium was that of pivoting the wings on the right and left sides of the shafts carrying gears at the center of the machine which, being in mesh would cause one wing to turn upward in front when the other wing was turned downward. By this method we thought it would be possible to get a greater lift on one side than on the other so that the shifting of weight would not be necessary for the maintenance of balance. However, we did not see any method of building this device sufficiently strong and at the same time light enough to enable us to use it.

In other words, the brothers reasoned that if a gust of wind struck a glider and tilted it over to the point of instability, the thing to do was to increase the lift of the low wing so that it would rise, while simultaneously decreasing the lift of the high wing so that it would drop back to a stable level position. This was the breakthrough that was needed. The next step was to figure out a practical way to apply this solution to the control problem. Again Orville tells how Willbur worked it out:

A short time afterward, one evening when I returned home with my sister and Miss Harriet Silliman, who was at that time a guest of my sister's in our home, Wilbur showed me a method of getting the same results as we had contemplated in our first idea without the structural defects of the original. He demonstrated the method by means of a small pasteboard box, which had two of the opposite ends removed. By holding the top forward corner and rear lower corner of one end of the box between his thumb and forefinger and the rear upper corner and the lower forward

27

corner of the other end of the box in like manner, and by pressing the corners together the upper and lower surface of the box were given a helicoidal twist, presenting the top and bottom surfaces of the box at different angles on the right and left sides. From this it was apparent that the wings of a machine of the Chanute double-deck type, with the fore-and-aft trussing removed, could be warped in like manner so that in flying the wings on the right and left sides could be warped so as to present their surfaces to the air at different angles of incidence and thus secure unequal lifts on the two sides.

Miss Silliman, an Oberlin College classmate of Orville and Wilbur's younger sister Katharine, visited the Wright family at Dayton in late July, 1899, thus pinpointing with some precision the date on which the Wright breakthrough was conceived.

Wilbur was then thirty-two years old and Orville almost twenty-eight. Up until this time they had led serene but somewhat threadbare lives as part of a Midwest minister's large, close-knit family. Their father, Bishop Milton Wright, was one of the leaders of the United Brethren Church. For almost fifty years since his ordination as a minister in 1850, he had taught in church schools or preached in a string of small communities in southeastern Indiana. The three older Wright sons, Reuchlin, Lorin and Wilbur, were all born in Indiana. Orville and his sister Katharine were born in Dayton, where the family had moved in 1869. The Wrights moved back to Indiana once more after that, then settled permanently in Dayton in 1884. Mrs. Wright, the mother, died in Dayton on July 4, 1889.

The first time the younger brothers Wilbur and Orville teamed up on a major enterprise was in the publication of a Dayton neighborhood newspaper, *The West Side News*, which made its debut in March, 1889. It was a four-page, three-column weekly which the two brothers and a friend wrote, edited, solicited advertising for and printed themselves on a press which they had built. Orville was the driving spirit behind this venture; since he was twelve years old he had been interested in printing as a hobby and had worked his way up through more and more ambitious equipment—most of it homemade. He had even

Wilbur (left) and Orville Wright

worked two summers in a Dayton printing plant. *The West Side News* prospered, and in April, 1890, Orville and Wilbur became equal partners in a much more ambitious daily paper, *The Evening Item*. However, *The Evening Item* lasted only four months before it succumbed to stiff competition from the four other Dayton dailies, which were much larger and had much greater circulations.

At about this time a minor technological revolution was going on in the bicycle world. For many years the "ordinary" bike with the huge front wheel and tiny back one had dominated the scene. But then in 1885 the "safety" bike was introduced. This was a forerunner of the modern bicycle and had two wheels of the same size with the familiar chain-and-sprocket drive linking back wheel and pedals. Pneumatic tires were introduced in 1889, and within five years "safety" bikes with pneumatic tires had virtually driven the old "ordinary" off the market.

Orville Wright bought his first safety bike with pneumatic tires in 1892 and paid $160 for it, a considerable sum of money in those days. Then Wilbur bought one. Sensing the great potential popularity of the new bikes, the brothers promptly went into the business of selling several well-known makes in Dayton. In their first year in their new enterprise they also added a repair shop to their salesroom. Before long they were manufacturing their own line of bikes, the most popular of which was the "Wright Special," which sold for eighteen dollars. As a foundation for the brothers' aeronautical researches, the bicycle business was to prove ideal, for it provided them with both the income they needed to support their experiments and a well-equipped machine shop that could turn out just about anything they needed to make an airplane.

The Wrights' first attempt at flight was decidedly casual. A day or two after Wilbur conceived his wing-warping idea, while Miss Silliman was still visiting, the two brothers began building a large kite to test their new theory. Its design was simple enough: it consisted of two 5-foot wings mounted in biplane fashion, one above the other. These wings were trussed and braced in such a way that they could be warped in the desired fashion by four control lines leading to two sticks, one in each hand. The kite also had a small rigid wooden tail which was supposed to steady it in the air.

Orville was not present when the kite was first tested, and

neither brother was ever able to recall exactly when Wilbur first tried it out. But the kite was very definitely a success. According to Wilbur's accounts to his family, the model responded very well to the warping control. "We felt," said Orville later, "that the model had demonstrated the efficiency of our system of control."

With this intriguing experience behind them, the brothers began hatching more ambitious plans during the long winter days they spent in their bicycle shop building up their inventory for the heavy spring sales season. "We decided to experiment with a man-carrying machine embodying the principle of lateral control used in the kite model already flown," said Orville. "We expected to fly the machine as a kite and in this way we thought we would be able to stay in the air for hours at a time, getting in this way a maximum of practice with a minimum of effort."

Figuring correctly that a man-carrying kite would require quite a breeze to keep it aloft, the brothers began making inquiries about locations with strong, dependable winds. In late 1899 Wilbur wrote to the U. S. Weather Bureau and asked about prevailing winds in the Chicago area in August, September, October and November. This information was duly provided. But the Wrights wanted something more; for, like most dreams spawned during a Northern winter, this one also included a vision of warmth and sunshine and a chance to relax in pleasant surroundings after a busy working season.

Accordingly, Wilbur addressed a letter in May, 1900, to Octave Chanute, the American glider enthusiast whose works the brothers had studied. Wilbur began: "For some years I have been afflicted with the belief that flight is possible to man. My disease has increased in severity and I feel that it will soon cost me an increased amount of money if not my life. I have been trying to arrange my affairs in such a way that I can devote my entire time for a few months to experiment in this field." He went on to describe his and Orville's ideas for a man-carrying kite and how to control it and asked Chanute's advice about where they might find a locality with prevailing winds of about 15 miles an hour without rain or "too inclement weather."

Chanute responded to Wilbur's letter with great interest, listed several published papers for them to read, and suggested they head for the sand hills on the Atlantic coast of South Carolina or Georgia. On August 3 the Wrights got off another letter, this time to the weather station at Kitty Hawk, North Carolina. On the basis of the replies to this letter, Wilbur set out from Dayton for the North Carolina Outer Banks on September 6, carrying with him all the material needed for their man-carrying glider except some spruce spars which he hoped to purchase en route. Orville planned to follow as soon as the kite was ready to test.

It was quite a trip for Wilbur, enough almost to discourage a less determined man right from the beginning. Wilbur left Dayton on a 6:30 P.M. train and rode all night and all the next day, down to the end of the Chesapeake and Ohio line at Old Point Comfort, Virginia, near the mouth of the Chesapeake Bay. Then he took a steamer across Hampton Roads to Norfolk, where he spent the night of Friday, September 7. On Saturday morning he shopped for the spruce spars he needed for the kite but was unsuccessful and finally settled for white pine. That afternoon he set out for Elizabeth City, North Carolina, which, he thought, was the jumping-off point for the Carolina Outer Banks.

The low, thin sand spits that comprise the Outer Banks begin a few miles to the southeast of Norfolk and continue down the North Carolina coast in a meandering line that sometimes sticks close to the mainland and other times sweeps far out toward the ocean. In spots, the banks are high and wide enough to support sizable towns. In other places the beach is barely above water at high tide. The easternmost limit of the banks is Cape Hatteras, which juts out into the warm water of the Gulf Stream and is so temperate in climate that such southern flora as Spanish moss and scrub palmetto trees flourish there despite the fact that they normally do not occur north of South Carolina. In the summertime, a strong prevailing wind sweeps in off the ocean from the southeast and drives the sand across the dunes in stinging, shifting swirls during the day. When the wind dies down there are mosquitoes.

At Elizabeth City, Wilbur found it difficult to book passage for the 40-mile trip by boat to Kitty Hawk. "No one seemed to know anything about the place or how to get there," Wilbur commented in a notebook he was beginning to keep. Apart from the weather station, the settlement at Kitty Hawk consisted of no more than a score of scattered houses about halfway down the Outer Banks. But Kitty Hawk did have a post office, or at least a postmaster, and, in the absence of any roads or bridges to the place, was visited once a week by a boat that brought mail and supplies from Elizabeth City. To his dismay Wilbur discovered he had just missed the regular boat and would have to wait six days before it made the trip again. But he soon located another boat. He continued with his tale:

At last on Tuesday left. I engaged passage with Israel Perry on his flat-bottom schooner fishing boat. As it was anchored about three miles down the river we started in his skiff which was loaded almost to the gunwale with three men, my heavy trunk and lumber. The boat leaked very badly and frequently dipped water, but by constant bailing we managed to reach the schooner in safety. The weather was very fine with a light west wind blowing. When I mounted the deck of the larger boat I discovered at a glance that it was in worse condition if possible than the skiff. The sails were rotten, the ropes badly worn and the rudderpost half rotted off, and the cabin so dirty and vermin-infested that I kept out of it from first to last. The wind became very light, making progress slow. Though we had started immediately after dinner it was almost dark when we passed out of the mouth of the Pasquotank and headed down the sound. The water was much rougher than the light wind would have led us to expect, and Israel spoke of it several times and seemed a little uneasy. After a time the breeze shifted to the south and east and gradually became stronger. . . .

The strain of rolling and pitching sprung a leak and this, together with what water came over the bow at times made it necessary to bail frequently. At 11 o'clock the wind had increased to a gale and the boat was gradually being driven nearer and nearer the north shore, but as an attempt to turn round would probably have resulted in an upset there seemed nothing else to do but attempt to round the North River light and take refuge behind the point. In a severe gust the foresail was blown loose from the boom and fluttered to leeward with a terrible roar. The boy and I finally succeeded in taking it in though it was rather dangerous work in the dark with the boat rolling so badly. By the time we had reached a position even with the end of the point it became doubtful whether we would be able to round the light which lay at the end of the bar extending out a quarter of a mile from the shore. The suspense was ended by another roaring of the canvas as the mainsail also tore loose from the boom, and shook fiercely in the gale. The only chance was to make a straight run over the bar under nothing but a jib, so we took in the mainsail and let the boat swing around stern to the wind. This was a very dangerous maneuver in such a sea but was in some way accomplished without capsizing. The waves were very high on the bar and broke over the stern very badly. Israel had been so long a stranger to the touch of water upon his skin that it affected him very much.

After rounding Powell's Point, the battered schooner anchored in North River for the rest of the night and most of the next day. Finally, at nine o'clock in the evening of September 12, more than six days outbound from Dayton, Wilbur reached Kitty Hawk. He boarded at the home of the Kitty Hawk postmaster, William J. Tate, until Orville arrived on September 28. After this the brothers pitched a tent and camped out among the dunes. Almost a year had gone by since Wilbur tested the controllable kite in Dayton, and the brothers' concept of what the next step should be had undergone an important modification. Instead of simply experimenting further with a larger, man-carrying kite, they planned and built a craft which they hoped would not require a line to hold it into the wind as a kite does, but which would be capable of gliding freely for short distances in a good breeze. And in fact they went even beyond this development in their thinking. A letter from Wilbur to his father, written shortly before Orville arrived in Kitty Hawk, provides the first hint that the brothers had at least considered the problems of powered flight. "I have my machine nearly finished," Wilbur wrote home. "It is not to have a motor and is not expected to fly in the true sense of the word. My idea is merely to experiment and practice with a view to solving the problem of equilibrium. I have plans which I hope to find much in advance of the methods tried by previous experimenters. When once a machine is under proper control under all conditions," Wilbur added confidently, "the motor problem will be quickly solved."

The first glider built and flown at Kitty Hawk was a biplane design like the Dayton kite and had two 17-foot wings. The ribs of the wings were made of ash and provided a shallow curvature to the wing which, the brothers knew from reading about Lilienthal's experiments, would enhance the lifting power of the wings. Both wings were covered with panels of French sateen fabric which had been sewn to size in Dayton ahead of time.

In this early glider, the control problem was not completely solved. The wings and their struts and braces were designed so that they could be warped and the glider tilted, or banked, to counteract any gusts that threatened to upset its equilibrium. But in addition the Wrights anticipated, correctly, that some sort of control would be needed over the up-and-down motion of the craft in order to make the transition between tethered kite and free-flying glider. Once again they rejected the method used by Lilienthal and Chanute of control by shifting the weight of the pilot. Instead, they designed a movable horizontal "rudder" which they placed out in front on a separate frame. This rudder (in modern aviation terminology it would be called an elevator) resembled a small wing and when the front edge was tilted downward, this tended to force the craft toward the ground. Conversely, when tilted upward it pointed the craft toward the sky.

The forward rudder was operated by handles extending from the sides of the flat surface backward to within reach of the pilot who stretched out on his stomach. As bicycle experts the brothers well knew the value of reducing the amount of air resistance offered by a body sitting upright. Wing warping was controlled by a foot bar. The brothers quickly found out when they actually began testing the glider that the pilot couldn't manipulate both handles and foot bar and still hang on. "As we had neither the material nor the tools to change these so as to correct the trouble, we were compelled to test them separately," Wilbur later reported to Octave Chanute in a long, detailed letter. "Two minutes trial

The Wright 1900 glider, flying here like a kite on strings, was controllable, but wouldn't glide very far.

was sufficient to prove the efficiency of twisting the planes to obtain lateral balance. We also found our system of fore-and-aft balancing quite effective, but it was only when we came to gliding that we became positive of this."

The new craft was first flown as a kite a few feet off the ground. The brothers conducted several experiments with different loads in different winds and found that it took a fairly stiff breeze of about 25 miles per hour to keep their craft in the air with a man aboard. They were somewhat puzzled by the inability of their new wings to generate as much lift as some of the Lilienthal theoretical tables said they should, but their vacation ended on an eminently satisfying note. As Wilbur wrote to Chanute:

After we found the difficulty of simultaneously maintaining both fore-and-aft and lateral balance we almost gave up the idea of attempting to glide, but just before returning we went down to the big hill which was about three miles from our camp and spent a day in gliding. Our plan of operation was for the aeronaut to lie down on the lower plane while two assistants grasped the ends of the machine and ran forward till the machine was supported on the air. The fore-and-aft equilibrium was in entire control of the rider, but the assistants ran beside the machine and pressed down the end which attempted to rise. We soon found that the machine could soar on a less angle than one in six and that if the machine was kept close to the slope (which was one in six by measurement) the speed rapidly increased until the runners could no longer keep up. The man on the machine then brought the machine slowly to the ground, so slowly in fact that the marks of the machine could be seen for twenty or thirty feet back from the point where it finally stopped. We had intended to have the operator turn his body to an upright position before landing but a few preliminary tests having shown that it was feasible to let the machine settle down upon its lower surface with the operator maintaining his recumbent position, we used this method of landing entirely. And although in appearance it was a dangerous practice we found it perfectly safe and comfortable except for the flying sand, and the machine was not once injured although we sometimes landed at a rate of very nearly thirty miles per hour. The operators did not receive a single bruise. With the conditions which obtain at Kitty Hawk there is no need at all of using the upright position. The distance glided was between three and four hundred feet at an angle of one in six and the speed at landing was more than double that of starting. The wind was blowing about twelve miles. We found no difficulty in maintaining fore-and-aft balance. The ease with which it was accomplished was a matter of great astonishment to us. It was so different from what the writings of other experimenters led us to expect.

1903

O ctave Chanute was impressed at
Wilbur's report of their successful gliding flights and wrote back
a week later to ask for more details and to get the brothers' permission to use the information they furnished him in a magazine
article he was working on. A lively correspondence then ensued
between Chanute and Wilbur Wright. Acting as a sounding
board, the old engineer drew out the ideas of the brothers, con-
stantly testing and querying and supplying them with information
from his own gliding experience and the studies he had made of
the works of others such as Lilienthal. Wilbur, in turn, took full
advantage of Chanute's interest and reported on their work and
problems at great length in letters that reveal a considerable
talent. Wilbur obviously enjoyed writing and Orville was content
to let his brother speak for both of them. Chanute, with a life-
time's experience as an engineer behind him, was equally obviously delighted to be included in what he very quickly sensed
was a serious and very exciting undertaking.

By the end of October, 1900, the brothers were back in
Dayton. They left their glider behind at Kitty Hawk, where it
was soon destroyed by the elements. Mrs. William J. Tate, wife
of the Kitty Hawk postmaster, made dresses for her daughters
out of the sateen fabric that had covered the wings. But this was
no great loss; already the Wrights had begun thinking about the
next aircraft they would build.

Chanute was graciously included in the brothers' plans for the
next session at Kitty Hawk and visited the Wright family in

Dayton on June 25 and 26. The return to Kitty Hawk was imminent, and Chanute made arrangements to visit the Wright camp during the summer himself and to have an experimental machine of his own tested by two protégés, Edward C. Huffaker, who had formerly worked with Langley, and George A. Spratt. On Sunday, July 7, Wilbur and Orville left together for the Carolina beaches. The trip was much easier this time and in four days' time they had begun making a camp at Kill Devil Hills, near Kitty Hawk. The biggest of the dunes at Kill Devil Hills was about 100 feet high; it was from this hill that the Wrights made their successful glider flights just before returning home in 1900.

Since they were expecting company, the Wrights' camp was a bit more elaborate this time. For living quarters they had a large tent. They also built a wooden shed to house their new glider. "The building is a grand institution, with awnings at both ends; that is, with big doors hinged at the top, which we swing open and prop up, making an awning the full length of the building at end," Orville wrote home to his sister Katharine. "We keep both ends open almost all the time and let the breezes have full sway."

But this arrangement left them defenseless against a natural hazard—mosquitoes. On this subject Orville waxed eloquent in his letter to Katharine:

Mr. Huffaker arrived Thursday afternoon, and with him a swarm of mosquitoes which became a mighty cloud, almost darkening the sun. This was the beginning of the most miserable existence I ever passed through. The agonies of typhoid fever with its attending starvation are as nothing in comparison. But there was no escape. The sand and grass and trees and hills and everything was fairly covered with them. They chewed us clear through our underwear and socks. Lumps began swelling up all over my body like hen's eggs. We attempted to escape by going to bed, which we did at a little after five o'clock. We put our cots out under the awnings and wrapped up in our blankets with only our noses protruding from the folds, thus exposing the least possible surface to attack. Alas! Here nature's complicity in the conspiracy against us became evident. The wind, which until now had been blowing over twenty miles an hour, dropped off entirely. Our blankets then became unbearable. The perspiration would roll off us in torrents. We would partly uncover and the mosquitoes would swoop down upon us in vast multitudes. We would make a few desperate and vain slaps, and again retire behind our blankets. Misery! Misery! The half can never be told. We passed the next ten hours in a state of hopeless desperation. Morning brought a little better condition, and we attempted on several occasions to begin work on our machine, but all attempts had to be abandoned. We now thought that surely our enemy had done its worst and we could hope for something better soon. Alas, "how seldom do our dreams come true."

The next night we constructed mosquito frames and nets over our cots, thinking in our childish error we could fix the bloody beasts. We put our cots on the sand twenty or thirty feet from the tent and house, and crawled in under the netting and bedclothes, and lay there on our backs smiling at the way in which we had gotten the best of them. The tops of the canopies were covered with mosquitoes till there was hardly standing room for another one; the buzzing was like that of a mighty buzz saw. But what was our astonishment when in a few minutes we heard a terrific slap and a cry from Mr. Huffaker announcing that the enemy had gained the outer works and he was engaged in a hand-to-hand conflict with them. All our forces were put to complete rout. In our desperate attacks on the advancing foe our fortifications were almost completely torn down, and in desperation, we fled from them, rushing all about the sand for several hundred feet around trying to find some place of safety. But it was of no use. We again took refuge in our blankets with the same results as in the previous night. Affairs had now become so desperate that it began to look as if camp would have to be abandoned or we perish in the attempt to maintain it.

Hope springs eternal; that is, it does the next morning when we begin to recover from the attack of the night before. Remembering the claim of the U. S. Army that safety is in "a superior fire," we proceeded to build big fires about camp, dragging in old tree stumps which are scattered about the sands at about a quarter mile from camp, and keeping up such a smoke that the enemy could not find us. Mr. Spratt [who had just arrived], after getting in bed with the smoke blowing over him, before long announced that he could no longer stand the fire, and dragged his cot out into the clear air. A few minutes later he returned, saying the mosquitoes were worse than the smoke. He spent the balance of the night in retreat from mosquito to smoke and from smoke to mosquito. However, the mosquitoes this night were small in number as compared with any previous night or even our fires would probably have been of no avail. Mr. Huffaker, Will, and I had passed the night in comparative comfort, but Mr. Spratt in the morning announced that that was the most miserable night he had ever passed through. Of course we explained to him what we had gone through, and that we were expecting a repetition of it every night. We nearly scared him off after the first night, but as every night since affairs have been improving, he is now a little less uneasy, and has hopes of enduring the agony a few weeks longer.

Yesterday most of the mosquitoes had disappeared and we had a fine day and wind for testing the new machine. We took it off to the Big Hill, about a thousand feet distant, and began our experiments. Our first experiments were rather disappointing. The machine refused to act like our machine last year and at times seemed to be entirely beyond our control.

The 1901 glider was similar in design to the aircraft that had been such a success the previous year, but larger. Its biplane wings had a span of 22 feet and a total area of roughly 300 square feet. (The earlier glider had a wing span of 17 feet and a total wing area of 165 feet.) The system of control was the same as on the earlier craft. Despite its apparent success, the previous year's glider had failed to produce as much lift as Lilienthal's tables indicated it should have; thus the Wrights gave the wings of their 1901 machine a greater curvature to produce a shape more nearly like that used by Lilienthal. All in all, the 1901 glider was a well-built, carefully thought-out aircraft and it should have performed well.

But it didn't. The first time the brothers tried it out on the big dune at Kill Devil Hills, it nosed into the sand after going only a few yards. A second test flight yielded the same results. Believing that there was too much weight forward, the Wrights tried shifting the position of the pilot farther aft for their third

Back in Kitty Hawk for another season, the Wrights again made initial flights with their 1901 glider tethered as a kite.

attempt. "The machine then sailed off and made an undulating flight of a little more than 300 feet," Wilbur noted. "To the onlookers, this flight seemed very successful, but to the operator it was known that the full power of the rudder had been required to keep the machine from either running into the ground or rising so high as to lose all headway. In the 1900 machine one fourth as much rudder action had been sufficient to give much better control. It was apparent that something was radically wrong, though we were for some time unable to locate the trouble."

The brothers resumed experiments with the machine tethered as a kite in winds of approximately 17 miles per hour. Even though they had meticulously designed the wings so their curvature corresponded with that used by Lilienthal when he worked out his tables, they found that the lifting power of their wings was far less than it should have been. They reasoned that the curvature, or camber, of their wings was too great, despite the fact that it was exactly what Lilienthal recommended. But the Wrights figured that if the top surface of a wing were curved too much, the airflow over the top surface would strike the forward, or leading, edge of the wing at such an angle as to force it down.

So they changed the shape of the wings on their glider and flattened out the curvature.

Wilbur wrote:

On resuming our gliding, we found that the old conditions of the previous year had returned; and after a few trials, made a glide of 389 feet. The machine with its new curvature never failed to respond promptly to even small movements of the rudder. The operator could cause it to almost skim the ground, following the undulations of its surface, or he could cause it to sail out almost on a level with the starting point, and passing high above the foot of the hill, gradually settled down to the ground. The wind on this day was blowing 11 to 14 miles per hour. The next day, the conditions being favorable, the machine was again taken out for trial. This time the velocity of the wind was 18 to 22 miles per hour. At first we felt some doubt as to the safety of attempting free flight in so strong a wind, with a machine of over 300 square feet, and a practice of less than five minutes spent in actual flight. But after several preliminary experiments we decided to try a glide. The control of the machine seemed so good that we then felt no apprehension in sailing boldly forth. And thereafter we made glide after glide, sometimes following the ground closely, and sometimes sailing high in the air.

Chanute arrived at the camp on August 4 and spent a week there observing the Wright glider in action in numerous flights, the longest of which was 366 feet. There was also a Chanute glider in the camp all this time, but no one quite got up the nerve to give it a good workout. Its design was similar to that of the machine flown by Chanute in 1896. But Chanute's protégé Huffaker had come up with a novel way of constructing the new glider with paper tubes for the main structural members. The tubes were then put together so that they could be folded and unfolded easily to make a sort of portable flying machine. Fortunately for all concerned, the Chanute-Huffaker glider got left out in the rain accidentally. The paper tubes came apart when they got soaked and the machine collapsed in a heap before it could hurt anybody.

The weather continued rainy and unpleasant as the end of August approached, and camp was abandoned. The Wrights left their glider locked up in the shed at Kill Devil Hills. They had a vague notion to return for a couple of weeks in October when it might be more pleasant, but for the time being they had had enough of camp life, mosquitoes and bad weather.

The Wrights' experience with the 1901 glider's poor performance in its first few flights made them thoroughly skeptical of the data developed by Lilienthal, and they returned to Dayton determined to run some tests and find out for themselves what kind of wing produced the greatest lift. The first testing device they constructed was a turntable, made out of a bicycle wheel. A flat plane, like a weathervane, was attached to the rim of the wheel. When wind blew over this device, the wheel tended to turn. By attaching a model wing section to another part of the rim so that its lifting power counteracted the tendency of the wheel to turn, the Wrights believed they could find out how various wing sections performed in comparison to the Lilienthal data. However, this device proved unsatisfactory in a natural wind. To get better results, the brothers mounted the turntable on a bicycle and pedaled it through calm air at a speed of 12 to 15 miles an hour. Again they were suspicious of the results they obtained.

Next they built a highly successful wind tunnel in their Dayton workshop. It was small, measuring 6 feet in length and having a cross section of 16 square inches. At one end, a two-bladed fan, driven by a gasoline engine used in their bicycle shop to power a lathe, drill press and band saw, developed a wind of 25 to 35 miles per hour. This blast passed through a honeycomb which straightened out the air current generated by the whirling blades of the fan. The wing section to be tested was mounted in the other end of the wind tunnel so that it could move back and forth in the airstream, the amount of movement indicating the amount of lift a particular shape developed. A direct reading of the amount of drag, or resistance to the airflow, was also possible.

The Wright wind tunnel was not the first ever used to test wing shapes. As early as 1871 English scientist Francis Herbert Wenham had experimented with a wind tunnel, and several others since then had worked with wind tunnel devices. But none achieved as spectacular results as did the Wrights. In their work with their homemade wind tunnel, these two untrained, self-educated engineers demonstrated a gift for pure scientific research that made the more eminent scientists who had studied the problems of flight look like bumbling amateurs.

By early October, 1901, the Wrights had their wind tunnel set up and operating well. In the next month they tried out more than a hundred model wings of various shapes, including models of bird wings. The letters between Wilbur and Octave Chanute flew thick and fast as Wilbur went into detail on the experiments, and the older man, somewhat doubtful at first, was gradually won over to the Wrights' conviction that previous research on wing design was misleading.

"I am now absolutely certain that Lilienthal's table is very seriously in error, but that the error is not so great as I had previously estimated," Wilbur wrote on October 6 in a long letter about the first wind tunnel experiments.

"I have read with great interest your letter of the 6th and greatly esteem your ingenious experiments on air reactions," Chanute replied. "I can find no fallacy in your methods," he went on, but it was clear he wasn't convinced. "I find, however, that Lilienthal's coefficients were obtained in natural wind, which he claims to give much greater values than for the same surfaces driven in still air. . . . Whether there is any other cause for the discrepancies you have found, I will now proceed to inquire."

To which Wilbur answered: "It would seem that still air is as effective as natural wind in actual practice and I can see no theoretical reason why it should not be." The brothers were now well along in their experimental work, and Chanute was deluged with data from their observations and astute theoretical reasoning from this data. The delighted Chanute responded in kind, pointing out obscurities and inconsistencies in the brothers' conclusions and countering their results with those obtained by others. But the evidence the Wrights accumulated in their tests was overwhelming and Chanute finally capitulated. On November 18 he wrote: "It is perfectly marvelous to me how quickly you get results with your testing machine; the checks on Langley's curve having been sent almost by return mail. You are evidently better equipped to test the endless variety of curved surfaces than anybody has ever been. I hope that you will do so, and tabulate the results as you go along."

The bicycle business could stand only so much neglect; consequently Wilbur and Orville began a series of systematic tabulations of the behavior of forty-eight different model wings which they could finish by the end of the year. They varied in curvature from flat planes to an odd hook-shaped model which was thought to have originated in Russia. Some of the model wings had rounded or pointed tips; others were squared off. In one experiment three model wings were mounted together in a triplane arrangement. Other experiments were conducted with variations on birds' wings.

The Wrights emerged from this series of experiments with several notebooks full of data, mankind's first good grasp of the complex theoretical formulas required to predict the lifting power and behavior of different types of wings, and a clear idea of which wing designs would work and which ones were useless. As their busy manufacturing season wore on, they completed their plans for an improved glider for the next trip to Kitty Hawk. By August 20, the activity in the normally quiet Wright household had reached fever pitch. As Katharine Wright wrote to her father, who was away on a trip:

They really ought to get away for a while. Will is thin and nervous and so is Orv. They will be all right when they get down in the sand where the salt breezes blow, etc. They insist that, if you aren't well enough to stay out on your trip, you must come down with them. They think that life at Kitty Hawk cures all ills, you know.

The flying machine is in the process of making now. Will spins the sewing machine around by the hour while Orv squats around marking the places to sew. There is no place in the house to live but I'll be lonesome enough by this time next week and wish that I could have some of their racket around. . . .

The brothers arrived at the site of their previous camp on Thursday, August 28, and began drilling a well and tidying up their old storage shed. Their old 1901 glider was still there, too, but it was obsolete now and the Wrights unsentimentally took it apart to make room for the new machine. Some of the wooden uprights used to brace the wings of the old machine were salvaged, however, and were used in the construction of the new glider. As guests were being expected, a more elaborate extension was built onto the shed to serve as living quarters in place of the tent used during the previous year.

The 1902 glider resembled the Wrights' previous machine in its general biplane design, but was a great improvement in aerodynamic efficiency. It was bigger, with wings that measured 32 feet 1 inch, and more graceful-looking due to the fact that the wings were narrower. The curvature of the upper surface of each wing was also much less pronounced than in the previous year's model. This change in wing configuration was a direct result of the Wrights' wind tunnel experiments and represented the most efficient wing design that they had come up with so far. The design of the control system was refined somewhat in order to permit the pilot, again lying prone, to handle everything and still have a hand left over to hang on with. Up-and-down control was once again effected with a forward horizontal "rudder" that could be tilted by working handles jutting back just in front of the pilot. However, the wing-warping wires were led into a wooden cradle which fitted around the pilot's hips as he lay on the lower wing. By moving his hips from side to side he also moved the cradle from side to side and manipulated the wires that warped the wings.

In their last flights with the 1901 glider, just before the rainy weather set in and they returned to Dayton, the Wrights had experienced some difficulty with a tendency of the glider to slew around toward the low wing when the wing-warping controls were used. Time did not permit sufficient testing during the previous summer to pin down what the trouble was. However, the Wrights reasoned that the addition of a fixed vertical tail would stabilize the aircraft when the wings were banked. As it turned out, they were only partly right. And their miscalculation resulted in their first serious gliding accident.

The glider was finished and ready for testing on Friday, September 19. It was first flown as a kite, without anyone aboard. Orville noted in his diary that tests of the highly important wing-warping control were not completely satisfactory, "but we are convinced that the trouble with the 1901 machine is overcome by the vertical tail." The next day they took their aircraft to the big dune and tested it as a glider. Right from the start they began making glides of over 200 feet, and Orville noted: "It was apparent that the machine would not swing around the higher wing as it did last year." But a new problem had developed. Every time the glider got into a steep bank, its nose pitched up.

Rain and light winds plagued the brothers for the next few days and it was difficult for them to judge just how serious the new problem was. Wilbur seemed to be able to keep the slewing under control by his quick and skillful manipulation of the wing-warping controls and the up-and-down forward rudder. But Orville wasn't so fortunate when it was his turn to test-fly the new glider:

On my third or fourth glide, I was sailing along smoothly without any trouble at all from the fore-and-aft control, when I noticed that one wing was getting a little too high and that the machine was slowly sidling off in the opposite direction. I thought that by moving the end [wing] control mechanism an inch or so I would bring the wing back again to its proper position and, as I was going so smoothly with no need of changing the front rudder, I attempted to make the change. The next thing I knew was that the wing was very high in the air, a great deal higher than before, and I thought I must have worked the twisting apparatus the wrong way. Thinking of nothing else than the end control, after assuring myself as to what was the proper

The standard way of launching the Wright 1902 glider was to station helpers at each wing tip and have them run downhill into the wind.

motion, I threw the wing tips to their greatest angle. By this time I found suddenly that I was making a descent backwards toward the low wing, from a height of 25 or thirty feet, as a result of the machine having turned up at an angle of nearly 45° in front, which fact I had not noticed at all while occupied in the manipulation of the wing ends. . . . The result was a heap of flying machine, cloth, and sticks in a heap with me in the center without a bruise or a scratch. The experiments suddenly came to a close till repairs can be made.

The soft sand had saved Orville from injury, but it took the two men three days to rebuild their glider. This was quite a job—they had to disassemble the glider, remove the cloth covering from the broken wings, splice the broken ribs and spars, stretch the fabric over the wings again and tack it down, then finally reassemble their machine and readjust all the braces and control wires. They made no changes, however, concluding that the control difficulty still lay in their lack of proficiency in piloting the new machine.

For the next week or so Wilbur and Orville took turns practicing with the glider, flying farther and farther all the time until

As the 1902 season wore on, the Wrights consistently made flights of more than 200 feet, among them this high ride with Wilbur aboard.

Wilbur could consistently sail more than 500 feet. In the meantime, their older brother Lorin had arrived for a vacation, as well as George Spratt, their guest of the previous summer. Chanute also visited the Wrights with A. M. Herring who test-flew a Chanute glider with disappointing results. Life in the camp on the Outer Banks had become considerably more congenial, but the Wrights were still not satisfied with the performance of their glider.

At this point, Orville had an inspired thought. Why not make the vertical tail movable, instead of fixed? He noted, simply, in his diary: "While lying awake last night, I studied out a new vertical rudder." Bad weather—a mixture of rain and high winds —plagued the Wrights after they redesigned the rudder and made it movable. But then, as October, 1902, drew to a close, they made more than 375 flights, including their best: a breathtaking flight of 622½ feet that lasted twenty-six seconds. Control was no longer a problem, the wings they had designed on the basis of scientific data from their wind tunnel experiments proved to be powerful lifting surfaces, and, as time and time again they soared out from the top of the "Big Hill," they put on a marvelous show. Though the guests were all gone and the brothers were by themselves in camp, their performances were not entirely unappreciated. As Orville noted briefly in his notebook one day, "Steamer came in to watch exper."

Orville wrote home to Katharine:

The past five days have been the most satisfactory for gliding that we have had. In two days we made over 250 glides, or more than we had made all together up to the time Lorin left. We have gained considerable proficiency in the handling of the machine, now, so that we are able to take it out in any kind of weather. Day before yesterday we had a wind of 16 meters per second or about 30 miles per hour, and glided in it without any trouble. That was the highest wind a gliding machine was ever in, so that we now hold all the records! The largest machine we handled in any kind of weather, made the longest distance glide (American), the longest time in the air, the smallest angle of descent, and the highest wind!!! Well, I'll leave the rest of the "blow" till we get home.

Wilbur sails out from the sand dunes on another long glide with the 1902 craft.

Rations are getting low again, and we are dropping back on beans. I'm cooking up a lot of them tonight, trying to do two things at once—cooking for tomorrow and writing letters. We are running a fire all night now so as to keep warm, and have managed to keep comfortable in bed, but on one or two mornings we found it a little chilly downstairs. Well, I can't think of anything else to say until I get home, so good-bye.

Now all the Wrights needed to do was obtain a lightweight engine, hook it up to a set of propellers and, in addition to the other records Orville was so proud of, they would have the world's first true airplane. They had solved the problem of control, they knew better than anyone else how to design and build efficient wings, and they could construct an aircraft strong enough to fly in the face of a 30-mile-an-hour wind and take the shocks and bumps of hundreds of landings without falling apart. In all the world, no one had yet come as close to attaining man's age-old desire to fly as these two self-taught scientists. There had been a flurry of activity in France at about the same time the Wrights began their glider work, but it was not related to the experiments at Kitty Hawk and had been spectacularly unsuccessful. In the United States, Langley was moving steadily and innocently toward the disasters of 1903, completely in the dark, as was everyone except the Wrights' immediate family, about the significance of the developments on the remote North Carolina beach.

Within a few weeks after their return to Dayton, the Wrights began trying to locate a small engine, weighing around 180 pounds, that might develop eight or nine horsepower. They wrote to at least ten well-known American engine manufacturers, but nothing turned up that seemed promising. This was not too surprising. The automobile and motorcycle industries were still in their infancy in 1902 (the Ford Motor Company was not even founded until 1903) and the early gasoline engines were mostly crude affairs that were weak, heavy and unreliable—all qualities that ruled them out for the Wright flying machine.

So the brothers decided to build their own engine, counting heavily on the skill and ingenuity of Charles E. Taylor, the top mechanic in their bicycle factory. Here in Taylor's words is the way they went about it:

The first thing we did as an experiment was to construct a sort of skeleton model in order that we might watch the functioning of the various vital parts before venturing with anything more substantial. Orv and Will were pretty thorough that way—they wouldn't take anything for granted but worked everything out to a practical solution without too much haste. I think this had a lot to do with their later success.

When we had the skeleton motor set up we hooked it up to our shop power, smeared the cylinder with a paint brush dipped in oil and watched the various parts in action. It looked good so we went ahead immediately with the construction of a four-cylinder engine. I cut the crank shaft from a solid block of steel weighing over a hundred pounds. When finished it weighed about 19 pounds. We didn't have spark plugs but used the old "make and break" system of ignition [in which a spark is produced by the opening and closing of contact points inside the combustion chamber]. The gas pump was geared on to the cam shaft and the gas was led in and made to spread over the chamber above the heated water jackets and this immediately vaporized it. . . . I must admit there wasn't much to that first motor—no carburetor, no spark plugs, not much of anything but cylinders, pistons and connecting rods, but it worked.

The Wrights started building the engine in December, 1902, and had it ready for test runs in their shop by the following February. The first trials were not successful. The bearings froze on an early run, cracking the main body of the engine. A lighter casting was ordered to replace the cracked body, new bearings were installed, and the rebuilt engine was tested successfully in May.

Meanwhile, they went to work on the ribs and spars for the wings of their next machine. They had already decided to make it bigger than anything they had tried before. The wings were to be 40 feet 4 inches long and 6 feet 6 inches wide. Instead of making the larger wing ribs out of one solid piece of wood they made them out of two thin strips, with the long spars sandwiched in between in order to save weight. They also conducted wind tunnel experiments to see what shape they should make the struts and braces of the new machine to cut drag to a minimum. To their surprise a square cross-section with the corners slightly rounded off proved to be the design that would slow down their aircraft the least. It was even more efficient than a teardrop shape advocated by Chanute—another case of expert opinion proved wrong by the Wrights' handy wind tunnel.

Propellers to drive the new craft were expected to present little problem. Since 1816, when the British experimenter Sir George Cayley thought of the idea of using them on steerable balloons, propellers had become part of the design of every powered aircraft, fanciful and otherwise, that had been seriously advanced, except for the flapping-wing, or ornithopter, variety. In France in the 1870's, Alphonse Pénaud had built little flying models in which a twisted rubber band powered a tiny fan. Another Frenchman, Clément Ader, tried to fly in an odd, bat-winged craft with a big four-bladed propeller up front and actually succeeded in making a short but controversial hop of a few feet. In America, Langley's unmanned steam-driven models had proven successful by the time the Wrights were ready to add power to their glider design. The only difficulty was that none of the Wrights' predecessors, including Langley, seemed to understand what the problems were when they designed their propellers.

Consequently, the Wrights soon discovered that all the previous aircraft propeller designs were little more than windmills of various sizes and shapes that beat the air ineffectually, generating little thrust or pull, despite the horsepower that made them turn.

In a letter later written to George Spratt, Orville described their situation as they went about designing a propeller after their return from Kitty Hawk in 1902:

Our motor on completion turned out a very pleasant surprise. Instead of the eight horsepower, for which we had hoped but hardly expected, it has given us 13 horsepower on the brake, with a weight of only 150 lbs. in the motor. During the time the engine was building we were engaged in some very heated discussions on the principles of screw propellers. We had been unable to find anything of value in any of the works to which we had access, so that we worked out a theory of our own on the subject.

The Wrights began experimenting with propeller designs by hooking up the shop engine that ran the lathe, drill press and band saw—and the wind tunnel—so that it turned their experimental propeller at a measurable number of revolutions per minute. Then they measured the velocity of the wind current generated by the propeller. From the first the Wrights realized something that previous experimenters had missed. For decades, seagoing ships had been pushed through the water by the action of the rear surfaces of their propellers shoving the water behind them. But the Wrights reasoned that aircraft propellers would have to behave differently. They felt that the propeller should be designed like a set of whirling wings in which the forward surface developed thrust along the aircraft's flight path, just as the top surface of a wing produced lift.

This piece of reasoning was every bit as important as the thinking that produced the wing-warping idea and the movable-rudder concept of 1902. But the Wrights were in a hurry now. There was much to do before the next summer and too little time to devote to debate with Octave Chanute or to record the mental process by which their minds grasped a fact that had eluded many others. So they simply jotted down in a notebook the results of two tests, worked out a formula on the basis of this data that enabled them to predict propeller performance with amazing accuracy, then made themselves a pair of propellers. These were carved from spruce laminations consisting of three pieces of wood glued together. Rough shaping was done with a hatchet. The brothers used a drawknife to whittle the blades to the final degree of precision.

It was almost the end of September before all was packed up and ready for the return to Kitty Hawk. The Wrights were aware from the newspapers that Langley was about to make his first attempt at flight with his big, man-carrying machine, but they weren't particularly concerned. Earlier, Wilbur had even expressed some doubt that the Langley machine would work. "Prof. Langley seems to be having rather more than his share of trouble just now with pestiferous reporters and windstorms," he commented in a letter to Chanute. "It would be interesting to attempt a computation of the possible performance of his machine in advance of his trial, but the data of the machine as given in the newspapers are so evidently erroneous that it seems hopeless to attempt it. It is a sure thing that the speed will not be from 60 to 90 miles per hour with an expenditure of 25 horsepower as the papers have reported its prospective flight. I presume that you are to be one of the guests of honor at the launching festivities. Our invitation has not yet arrived," Wilbur added ironically.

"I have no invitation from Langley either," Chanute answered in a letter the next day.

Soon after the brothers arrived at their campsite at Kill Devil Hills, Orville wrote home this full report to Katharine:

We reached camp Friday noon, having come over from Manteo in a small gasoline launch. We found everything in pretty good shape. The building, however, is several feet nearer the ocean than when we left last year, and about a foot lower in places. We had supposed two years ago when the wind at a speed of 107 miles per hour took the anemometer cups away with it (beating anything within the memory of the oldest inhabitant), and when the mosquitoes were so thick as to dim the very brightness of the sun, exceeding in numbers all excepting those that devoured the whole of Raleigh's settlers on Roanoke, and last year when lightning turned night into day, and burned down every telegraph pole between here and Kitty Hawk, we had supposed that nature had reached her limit; but far from it! Dan says this year has been one continuous succession of storms of unprecedented severity; the rain has descended in such torrents as to make a lake for miles about our camp; the mosquitoes were so thick that they turned day into night, and the lightning so terrible that it turned night into day. Really it paralyses the mind to try to think of all these things at once. . . .

We have started the new building and will probably have it

pretty well up by the end of this week. We will have the old machine ready for practice on days of good winds, and will work on the new machine on rainy and calm days. The hills are in the best shape for gliding they have ever been, and things are starting off more favorably than in any year before.

As October wore on, the clear days and steady winds prevailed which were ideal for glider flights with the 1902 machine. Instead of going for distance, the Wrights added a new twist to their glider work and began trying to see how long they could remain airborne by "soaring." By this they meant taking off into a wind strong enough to sustain them in a hovering position a few feet from their point of takeoff. In previous summers at Kitty Hawk they had marveled at the ability of buzzards and hawks to do this and had spent many hours watching them hover almost motionless above the dunes. They now found their 1902 machine well suited for soaring and by the end of the month were so proficient at this type of flight that they consistently remained airborne more than a minute each time they went up. Orville finally set the record with a flight of one minute, eleven and four-fifths seconds. This, of course, was a world record—and one which stood unchallenged until October 24, 1911, when Orville again made a record-breaking soaring flight of nine and three-quarter minutes. The 1911 record was not broken for ten years.

Meanwhile, the new aircraft that would soon change history was beginning to take shape. By October 15, with the assistance of their friend George Spratt, the Wrights had completed the upper wing and covered it with cloth. Another friend sent them a sobering account of Langley's first disastrous attempt at a man-carrying flight and Wilbur commented in a letter to Chanute: "I see that Langley has had his fling and failed. It seems our luck to throw now, and I wonder what our luck will be."

The transition from glider to powered flying machine was a tremendous step; the 1903 airplane reflected this in almost every detail. The pilot was still going to lie prone on the bottom wing, but with him stretched out like this, the only place for the engine had to be to one side of him. However, the engine weighed 34 pounds more than either potential pilot; thus the airplane was

The Wright airplane stands in front of its "hangar" at Kill Devil Hills shortly before its famous first flight.

unbalanced. The Wrights corrected this by adding four inches more to the wing on the heavy side. The additional wing span was expected to create additional lift on that side and cancel out the extra weight of the engine.

Instead of a single propeller, the brothers decided to use a pair of propellers rotating in opposite directions. In addition to producing thrust, a whirling propeller produces torque, or a twisting force that tends to turn an airplane to one side. The Wrights figured correctly that they could cancel out this sidewise pull by mounting two propellers that would turn, and thus pull, in opposite directions. Connecting the propellers to the engine was the only feature on the machine that betrayed its humble bicycle shop origins—a chain-and-sprocket drive.

As in the 1902 glider, a hip cradle controlled the warping of the wings and caused the aircraft to bank. The vertical movable surface in the rear was also connected to the hip cradle. The front horizontal rudder, which made the plane climb and dive, was once again controlled by a line that ran back to a lever within reach of the pilot's left hand. The engine was essentially uncontrollable. Once it had been started and adjusted on the ground, the only thing the pilot could do to the engine was stop it by moving a stick-and-string system that shut off the fuel.

The lower wing, the rudder and the tail surfaces were completed toward the end of October and most of the uprights and wire braces had been installed between the two wings. On November 2, they began hooking up the engine and the propellers. Two days later, Orville optimistically noted in his diary: "Have machine now within half day of completion." Chanute was due for a visit any day now and Spratt had to leave soon, so the brothers pushed hard for an early test flight. But now, after such a long period of success, they ran into a frustrating series of setbacks.

First two propellers came loose on their shafts the first time the engine was started up. The shafts were sent via Spratt back to Charlie Taylor in the Dayton shop to be made stronger. Then the weather turned dismal, very cold and rainy. Chanute arrived, but throughout his six-day stay the brothers were unable to get much done because of the cold and the lack of rebuilt propeller shafts. They puttered around with their engine some, tuning until it ran smoothly at high speeds.

The new shafts arrived on November 20. This time the sprockets for the chain drives from the engine began to slip. No amount of tightening seemed to help. In desperation the two men turned to a tire cement known as "Arnstein's" which, Orville claimed, would fix anything from a stopwatch to a threshing machine. It must have been a remarkable compound, for after the brothers had filled the threads of the sprocket screws with Arnstein's and let it set awhile, they had no more difficulty with loose sprockets.

On November 25, just as the brothers were getting ready to take the new machine out for their first trial flight, it began to rain. Before the skies cleared up again, a crack developed in one of the propeller shafts. Orville left for Dayton on November 30 to make new, hopefully foolproof propeller shafts. He arrived back at the camp Friday, December 11. The shafts were installed and the machine was hauled out on Saturday for another attempt at flight, but the brothers judged that there was not sufficient wind to take off from the level ground right near their camp and not enough time to try for a launching down the Big Hill, almost half a mile away. The next day the weather was perfect, but it was Sunday and that, to the Bishop's sons, meant no flying.

The Wrights' activities in four seasons at Kitty Hawk had generated considerable interest among the few residents there. The brothers had consequently acquired a set of loyal fans who didn't want to miss the final act. The Wrights arranged to hoist a signal on a small flagstaff on their larger building when they were about to make their first attempt at flight, so that the men at the Kill Devil Hills Life Saving Station just about a mile away would have enough warning to walk over in time for the attempt.

At half past one on the afternoon of Monday, December 14, the Wrights hoisted their signal and started walking their machine toward the Big Hill. There they were met by six men from the lifesaving station, who helped them lug the 605-pound aircraft up the slope.

Since the new aircraft was so heavy—the 1902 glider weighed only 112 pounds—the Wrights were concerned about the possibility of its skids digging into the sand during the takeoff run and failing to lift off. So they build a 60-foot track composed of four 15-foot two-by-four pieces of wood to the top of which was nailed a metal strip. A small wooden truck ran along this track on rollers made from bicycle hubs. The sledlike skids of the aircraft rested on this little truck.

Unfortunately the attempt on Monday was a flop. This is Orville's account of what happened:

After testing the engine, with help of men (Bob Wescott, John T. Daniels, Tom Beacham, W. S. Dough, and Uncle Benny O'Neal), we took machine 150 ft. uphill and laid track on 8° 50′ slope. A couple of small boys, who had come with the men from the station, made a hurried departure over the hill for home on

Wilbur does a belly flop attempting to make the first powered flight and loses his turn to Orville.

hearing the engine start. We tossed up coin to decide who should make first trial, and Will won. After getting adjustments of engine ready I took right end of machine. Will got on. When all was ready Will attempted to release fastening to rail, but the pressure due to weight of machine and thrust of screws was so great he could not get it loose. We had to get a couple of men to help push machine back till rope was slipped loose. While I was signaling man at other end to leave go, but before I myself was ready, Will started machine. I grabbed the upright the best I could and off we went. By the time we had reached the last quarter of the third rail (about 35 to 40 feet) the speed was so great I could stay with it no longer. I snapped watch as machine passed end of track. (It had raised from track six or eight feet from end.) The machine turned up in front and rose to a height of about 15 feet from ground at a point somewhere in the neighborhood of 60 feet from end of track. After thus losing most of its headway it gradually sank to the ground turned up at an angle of probably 20° incidence. The left wing was lower than the right so that in landing it struck first. The machine swung around and scraped the front skids so deep in sand that one was broken, and twisted around until the main strut and brace were also broken, besides the rear spar to lower surface of front rudder.

Some early aviators might have been tempted to call this first 60-foot hop a "flight," but not the Wrights. However, they were now confident of ultimate success. They got off a telegram to their father telling him ". . . success assured keep quiet."

It took them a day to repair the damaged front rudder and rudder frame. Then the weather failed to cooperate again. In his diary for Wednesday, December 16, Orville notes: "We completed repairs by noon and got the machine out on the tracks in front of the building ready for a trial from the level. The wind was gradually dying and by the time we were ready was blowing only about 4 to 5 meters per second (about 10 miles per hour). After waiting several hours to see whether it would breeze up again we took the machine in."

The next day, Thursday, December 17, was perfect for flying, though seasonably cold. The wind was blowing from the north 20 to 25 miles an hour and the puddles near camp were covered with ice. The two brothers waited awhile to see whether the wind would hold. By this time they had been at their camp eighty-four days, their food was mostly beans, it was beginning to be bitterly cold, and they knew their machine would work. So they hoisted their signal and were soon joined by several men from the lifesaving station. They must have been moved by an uncanny sense of history that morning, for they painstakingly adjusted their cumbersome glass-plate camera so that it could snap a picture at the precise moment of lift-off.

Again Orville's diary preserves the flavor of the historic occasion:

After running the engine and propellers a few minutes to get them in working order, I got on the machine at 10:35 for the first trial. The wind, according to our anemometers at this time, was

This is one of the most extraordinary photographs in the annals of aviation. With remarkable clarity it shows the moment of lift-off of the Wright brothers' historic first powered flight on December 17, 1903. Orville is at the controls, and Wilbur, who ran alongside the right wings during takeoff (see footprints in the sand), is stepping back to get a better view of the marvelous event that has just taken place. The picture was snapped by John T. Daniels of the Kill Devil Hills Life Saving Station with a camera that the Wrights set up before the flight and aimed at the end of the launching rail. The first flight lasted 12 seconds and covered 120 feet. It was followed later in the day with three more successful flights, the longest of which was 852 feet.

blowing a little over 20 miles (corrected) 27 miles according to the Government anemometer at Kitty Hawk. On slipping the rope the machine started off increasing speed to probably 7 or 8 miles. The machine lifted from the truck just as it was entering on the fourth rail. Mr. Daniels took a picture just as it left the tracks. I found the control of the front rudder quite difficult on account of its being balanced too near the center and thus had a tendency to turn itself when started so that the rudder was turned too far on one side and then too far on the other. As a result the machine would rise suddenly to about 10 ft. and then as suddenly, on turning the rudder, dart for the ground. A sudden dart when out about 100 feet from the tracks ended the flight. Time about 12 seconds (not known exactly as watch was not promptly stopped). The lever for throwing off the engine was broken, and the skid under the rudder cracked.

Then it was Wilbur's turn again. Orville continues his narrative:

After repairs, at 20 min. after 11 o'clock Will made the second trial. The course was like mine, up and down but a little longer over the ground though about the same in time. Dist. not measured but about 175 ft. Wind speed not quite so strong. With the aid of the station men present, we picked the machine up and carried it back to the starting ways. At about 20 minutes till 12 o'clock I made the third trial. When out about the same distance as Will's, I met with a strong gust from the left which raised the left wing and sidled the machine off to the right in a lively manner. I immediately turned the rudder to bring the machine down and then worked the end control. Much to our surprise, on reaching the ground the left wing struck first, showing the lateral control of this machine much more effective than on any of our former ones. At the time of its sidling it had raised to a height of probably 12 to 14 feet.

The last flight, made by Wilbur, was the most spectacular and satisfying of all. Again Orville describes it in his diary:

At just 12 o'clock Will started on the fourth and last trip. The machine started off with its ups and downs as it had done before, but by the time he had gone over three or four hundred feet he had it under much better control, and was traveling on a fairly even course. It proceeded in this manner till it reached a small hummock out about 800 feet from the starting ways, when it began its pitching again and suddenly darted into the ground. The front rudder frame was badly broken up, but the main frame suffered none at all. The distance over the ground was 852 feet in 59 seconds. The engine turns was 1,071, but this included several seconds while on the starting ways and probably about half a second after landing. The jar of landing set the watch on the machine back so that we have no exact record for the 1,071 turns. Will took a picture of my third flight just before the gust struck the machine. The machine left the ways successfully at every trial, and the tail was never caught by the truck as we had feared.

After removing the front rudder, we carried the machine back to camp. We set the machine down a few feet west of the building and while standing about discussing the last flight, a sudden gust of wind struck the machine and started to turn it over. All rushed to stop it. Will who was near one end ran to the front, but too late to do any good. Mr. Daniels and myself seized the spars at the rear, but to no purpose. The machine gradually turned over on us. Mr. Daniels, having had no experience in handling a machine of this kind, hung onto it from the inside, and as a result was knocked down and turned over and over with it as it went. His escape was miraculous as he was in with the engine and chains. The engine legs were all broken off, the chain guides badly bent, a number of uprights and nearly all the rear ends of the ribs were broken. One spar only was broken.

The historic first successful airplane was never to fly again. The brothers packed it up in the next couple of days and brought it back to Dayton with them as they hurried home for Christmas. It was later reassembled and exhibited a couple of times in New York and once at the Massachusetts Institute of Technology. For many years it languished in a shed at Dayton; then, in 1928, it was sent to the Science Museum in London after the Smithsonian Institution repeatedly refused to recognize it as the first aircraft capable of sustained free flight with a man aboard, giving Langley's ill-fated machine that honor. In 1942, after many years of controversy, the Smithsonian belatedly reversed its position and Orville Wright asked the Science Museum to return the aircraft to the United States when it would be safe to do so after the war. After Orville Wright's death in January, 1948, the 1903 machine came back from twenty years' exile, was painstakingly restored and was placed on exhibit on December 17, 1948, the forty-fifth anniversary of its first flight.

1905

Now that the Wrights had learned to build a successful flying machine, their next step was to learn how to fly it. As the year 1904 opened, the world's first aviators had less than two minutes' total flight time between them in their powered aircraft and they wanted to build something that would stay up a little longer.

The first problem was the engine. The crude but successful four-cylinder motor built for the 1903 flyer lost power rapidly after a few minutes' operation, because of overheating. The engine had a radiator of sorts, but water circulation in the cooling system was not efficient enough to keep the engine temperature under control.

On the first day of the new year, the Wrights sent some patterns for their next engines to a local Dayton foundry. They planned to build two engines with four cylinders each. A third design with eight cylinders in a V arrangement was worked out but put aside. One of the four-cylinder engines was the same size as the 1903 model; the other was slightly larger. In the design of both these new engines, the Wrights solved the cooling problem by greatly increasing the amount of space around the cylinders through which the cooling water circulated. Other improvements were made in the fuel and lubrication system.

The brothers pushed the construction of the new engines throughout the month of January and, in the meantime, began work on the structure of a new aircraft. The bicycle business does not appear to have suffered during the brothers' preoccupation with airplanes. At one point Orville notes in his diary that $3,900 was deposited in one Dayton savings institution and $1,000 in another. But he was required to spend some time bringing the business' books up to date, a fact he noted in his diary with some vexation.

Toward the end of May both engine and aircraft were ready for testing. The new flying machine was a little heavier than the first one and its wings had a slightly different curvature to increase the lift; but otherwise the airframe and controls were almost identical to the first machine.

Instead of returning to North Carolina, the Wrights obtained permission to conduct their test flights in a 90-acre pasture about eight miles east of Dayton known as Huffman Prairie. The brothers had offered to lease the field from its owner, Dayton banker Torrence Huffman, but he let them use it for nothing, provided they chased his cows and horses out of the way before they tried anything.

The field was convenient. The Dayton–Springfield interurban trolley ran along one edge, and Orville and Wilbur soon became regular riders as they commuted back and forth from Dayton. But convenience, it seemed for a time, was just about the only good feature to the place, as Wilbur reported to Chanute:

We are in a large meadow of about 100 acres. It is skirted on the west and north by trees. This not only shuts off the wind somewhat but also probably gives a slight downtrend. However, this matter we do not consider anything serious. The greater troubles are the facts that in addition to cattle there have been a dozen or more horses in the pasture and as it is surrounded by barbwire fencing we have been at much trouble to get them safely away before making trials. Also the ground is an old swamp and is filled with grassy hummocks some six inches high so that it resembles a prairie dog town. This makes the track-laying slow work. While we are getting ready the favorable opportunities slip away, and we are usually up against a rain-storm, a dead calm, or a wind blowing at right angles to the track.

The first flight of the 1904 season was planned as something of an occasion. Bishop Milton Wright, then seventy-five years old, made the trolley trip out to Huffman's field with his older son Lorin and his family. Several reporters from the Dayton and Cincinnati newspapers were invited to attend and actually showed up despite the general skepticism about man's ability to fly that prevailed in the press after the Langley failures.

Unfortunately, the Wrights' performance with their new machine did little to cure the reporters' skepticism. On three different days in the last week of May, the Wrights attempted to get off the ground. First the wind, never as reliable in southwest Ohio as on the North Carolina Outer Banks, died out and prevented the brothers from taking off. Then it rained. And the new engine began acting up. As the frustrations mounted, the two men attempted one flight. The aircraft ran the length of the starting rail, but failed to pick up enough airspeed to take off and plopped down ignominiously at the end of the track. Finally, on the third day, they managed a short hop in which they got up six or eight feet, then came right back down due to a loss of power in the engine.

Compared to what other would-be aviators of the day were accomplishing, this abortive flight of the Wrights was impressive in itself. But for the two brothers, it was a pretty dismal beginning to what had promised to be an exciting season. "We certainly are having more than our usual share of trouble," Wilbur wrote later to his father, who was out of town for a few days.

Gradually, however, their luck improved. On June 21, Wilbur reported the first really significant activity of the season to Chanute:

Today we had our first decent chance, but as the margin was very small, we were not skillful enough to really get started. The first two flights were for a distance of a little more than a hundred feet and the third two hundred and twenty-five feet. On this one Orville almost got away, but after about 200 ft. he allowed the machine to turn up a little too much and it stalled it. He had a speed of about 18 miles on leaving the track, but the rise necessary to gain a little room for maneuvering reduced this to about 16 miles, and as the wind was blowing only 8 miles, and unsteady at that, the resistance was too high to permit rapid acceleration, owing to the great angle of incidence required. To get started under such conditions requires perfect management. We are a little rusty. With a little more track and a little more practice we hope to get a real start before long and then we will see what the machine can really do in the way of flying. The machine landed nicely each time without any injury at all.

Wilbur probably didn't realize it, but when he said that Orville had "stalled" the machine, he introduced a term that would stick and become a vivid part of the experience of every person who has since learned to fly. In modern aviation usage, a stall occurs when a wing loses its lift. In many cases a stall will lead quickly into the wild gyrations of a tailspin; in all cases an aircraft in a stalled condition begins to fall out of the sky as Orville did. This mention of a stall in Wilbur's letter to Chanute is the first recorded instance in which the term was used in reference to a loss of wing lift. But the Wrights had already gotten to know a good bit about this aerodynamic condition. In June, 1903, Wilbur reported some interesting findings to a Chicago meeting of the Western Society of Engineers in an address about their glider experiments:

On two occasions we observed a phenomenon whose nature we were not able to determine with certainty. One day my brother noticed in several glides a peculiar tapping as if some part of the machine were loose and flapping. Careful examination failed to disclose anything about the machine that could possibly cause it. Some weeks later, while I was making a glide, the same peculiar tapping began again in the midst of a wind gust. It felt like little waves striking the bottom of a flat-bottomed rowboat. While I was wondering what the cause could be, the machine suddenly, but without any noticeable change in its inclination to the horizon, dropped a distance of nearly ten feet, and in the twinkling of an eye was flat on the ground.

Wilbur had simply "stalled out," as we would say today, and all aviators will recognize the "tapping" that preceded his descent as "buffeting," which is one of the classic symptoms of an impending stall. The Wrights did not know exactly what they

The warping wings of the Wright 1904 airplane show up clearly here as the two brothers prepare it for flight at Huffman Prairie near Dayton.

had discovered, but their notes on the subject and their terminology provide further evidence of their clearheadedness and the scientific validity of their early experimental work.

Throughout July and August of 1904, the Wrights made a large number of short, generally unsatisfying flights. Three times, however, they remained aloft for more than thirty-five seconds and covered distances ranging from 1,304 to 1,738 feet. The performance of their new plane on these three long flights was excellent, and the Wrights concluded that if they could develop some better way of taking off in light and unreliable winds, they might consistently be able to make very long flights. Already they were beginning to ponder their next major problem: how to make a turn. The pasture was getting smaller and smaller, it seemed, on these long flights, and unless they could figure out a way of making their machine turn around they would be faced with the problem of landing outside Huffman's property. And this meant lugging the aircraft a long way back to their home base before trying another flight.

With characteristic inventiveness the Wrights designed a simple catapult launching device that would speed their plane down the launching rail fast enough to become airborne in even a dead calm. The starting device consisted of a tower, a 1,600-pound weight, and ropes and pulleys rigged so that when the weight descended it exerted a strong pull on the launching car as it slid down the first 50 feet of track. The first time the catapult was tested, the Wrights got airborne in three out of three attempts in a wind that registered only about two miles an hour—virtually a calm.

Now they could fly whenever they wanted to on a clear day, and the tempo of their activity quickened. In the two weeks following the first test of the catapult, they made ten flights, staying up once for almost half a mile. They began their first uneven, halting efforts to make the plane turn by working the clumsy hip cradle that warped the wings into a bank and moved the vertical rudder.

All the 1904 flights were conducted openly and with no attempt to discourage visitors, although these were few. As the brothers rode back and forth to town on the trolley, they talked modestly about their work. Even though the local newspapers continued to ignore the excitement in their own back yard, the word began to get around. Clear across the state in Medina, a remarkable man named A. I. Root heard about what was going on and set off on a pilgrimage by car to visit the Wrights. Root had sort of a professional interest in what the Wrights were doing: he was a beekeeper by trade and naturally curious about things that flew. When he reached Huffman Prairie he arranged to board with a farm family that lived across the road from the field. Root seemed to hit it off well with the Wrights, and because of this he enjoys a rather special place in the history of aviation.

On the morning of September 20, Wilbur climbed aboard the 1904 machine. It was cloudy and with a hint of rain in the air, not too promising a day. But he got off on a beautiful flight anyway, one that S-turned some 2,500 feet across the field in the space of little over a minute.

In the afternoon Wilbur decided to try it again. With a chill, damp northeast wind blowing he got a big push by the catapult, sped down the launching rail and sailed into the air. He leveled off just a few feet above the grass, then eased his left wing down and began a wide turn. Somehow he managed to hold the aircraft steady as he swung around through the points of the compass until he had completed a full, perfect circle and returned to his starting point. The flight lasted a minute and a half and was witnessed by Mr. Root. The beekeeper didn't quite grasp all the technical fine points of this achievement, but he knew it was important. And when he got back home, he wrote up the event in *Gleanings in Bee Culture,* a modest professional journal that he edited. This was the first published eyewitness account of man's conquest of the air:

Dear friends, I have a wonderful story to tell you—a story that, in some respects, outrivals the Arabian Nights fables—a story, too, with a moral that I think many of the younger ones need, and perhaps some of the older ones too if they will heed it. God in his great mercy has permitted me to be, at least somewhat, instrumental in ushering in and introducing to the great wide world an invention that may outrank the electric cars, the automobiles, and all other methods of travel, and one which may fairly take a place beside the telephone and wireless telegraphy. Am I claiming a good deal? Well, I will tell my story . . .

It was my privilege, on the 20th day of September, 1904, to see the first successful trip of an airship, without a balloon to sustain it, that the world has ever made, that is, to turn the corners and come back to the starting-point . . .

At first there was considerable trouble about getting the machine up in the air and the engine well up to speed. They did this by running along a single-rail track perhaps 200 feet long. . . . The operator takes his place lying flat on his face. This position offers less resistance to the wind. The engine is started and got up to speed. The machine is held until ready to start by a sort of trap to be sprung when all is ready; then with a tremen-

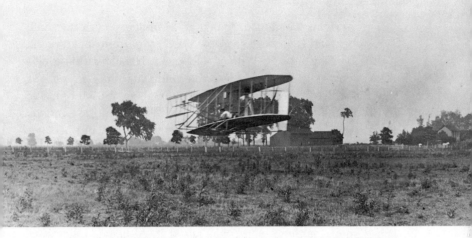

With Orville aboard, the 1904 machine makes a grass-cutting flight of 356 feet.

dous flapping and snapping of the four-cylinder engine, the huge machine springs aloft. When it first turned that circle, and came near the starting-point, I was right in front it; and I said then, and I believe still, it was one of the grandest sights, if not the grandest sight, of my life. Imagine a locomotive that has left its track, and is climbing up in the air right toward you—a locomotive without any wheels, we will say, but with white wings instead . . . Well, now, imagine this white locomotive, with wings that spread 20 feet each way, coming right toward you with a tremendous flap of its propellers, and you will have something like what I saw. The younger brother bade me move to one side for fear it might come down suddenly; but I tell you, friends, the sensation that one feels in such a crisis is something hard to describe.

When Columbus discovered America he did not know what the outcome would be, and no one at that time knew; and I doubt if the wildest enthusiast caught a glimpse of what really did come from his discovery. In a like manner these two brothers have probably not even a faint glimpse of what their discovery is going to bring to the children of men. No one living can give a guess of what is coming along this line, much better than any one living could conjecture the final outcome of Columbus' experiment when he pushed off through the trackless waters.

The Wrights continued flying at Huffman Prairie on into November and bested their September 20 performance several times. On November 9 Wilbur celebrated Theodore Roosevelt's election by exuberantly circling the field four times in a flight that lasted five minutes and four seconds. A month later Orville did the same thing, making four circles in five minutes. But the world continued to ignore them, and except for Root's account their magnificent display of airmanship and technical achievement went almost completely unnoticed.

There was some aeronautical activity in other parts of the world during this time. In Europe, free ballooning had been going on for over a century and was now a respectable, established sport for those who could afford it. Although Lilienthal's death had put a damper on glider experiments, there was some work being done by a group of Frenchmen who had heard of the Wright experiments through Chanute. But they merely copied what they believed to be the Wright design without understanding the rationale behind it and they had little success.

By the 1880's in France, the first clumsy self-propelled airships had put in an appearance, the forerunners of the blimp and the dirigible. And by 1904, a dapper little Brazilian pioneer named Alberto Santos-Dumont had thrilled Paris time and time again with flights over the city in a series of airships he had designed and built himself.

America's first significant airship flights also took place in 1904. During the summer of that year, Thomas S. Baldwin, an extraordinary airman and showman who specialized in parachute jumping from free balloons, assembled a 54-foot airship powered by a gasoline engine that was built by a rising young motorcycle racer and builder named Glenn Curtiss. Baldwin tested his airship in Oakland, California, in August, then brought it to St. Louis that fall to take part in an international exposition. He christened it the *California Arrow*. The airship made its debut rather spectacularly on October 25 with Roy Knabenshue aboard as pilot.

One of America's earliest airships was the lumbering *California Arrow,* which made its debut, with Roy Knabenshue trying to control it, at the St. Louis Fair.

Knabenshue once summed up the first flight of the *California Arrow* in St. Louis this way for a St. Louis newspaper:

It was a very harrowing experience. For the first few minutes we narrowly missed the fence and then we headed straight for the Brazilian building and missed it by inches, then headed straight for the Ferris wheel and I had visions of sliding down one of its spokes.

By experimenting with the tiller rope I found it was possible to steer. . . . I then described a very wide circle and headed back towards the grounds . . . When I got to within a thousand feet of the landing place, or the starting place, the engine just coughed and died and then we became a balloon ascension—it became a free balloon and drifted across the city and landed over in Illinois.

At one point the Wrights themselves considered taking one of their machines to St. Louis to compete for a $100,000 prize for a 10-mile flight around the fairgrounds, but they thought the conditions laid down for the prize flight were unrealistic and, after much debate and even a trip to St. Louis to look over the course, they decided not to enter.

As it turned out anyway, the St. Louis Fair provided the Wrights with their first nibble of interest from a commercial point of view. One of the visitors to the fair was Lieutenant-Colonel John E. Capper of the British Army, who came to the United States expressly to find out what was going on here in the field of aeronautics. He and his wife visited the Wrights in Dayton after they left the fair. Although Colonel Capper did not see an actual flight, he was astute enough to feel that the Wrights were on to something and he invited them to submit a proposal to furnish aircraft to the British government.

In January, 1905, the brothers wrote to Colonel Capper asking him to confirm the British government's interest in receiving a proposal from them. They also wrote to their Congressman, Robert M. Nevin, and asked him to find out whether the United States government might be interested in their invention:

The series of aeronautical experiments upon which we have been engaged for the past five years has ended in the production of a flying-machine of a type fitted for practical use. It not only flies through the air at a high speed, but it also lands without being wrecked. During the year 1904, one hundred and five flights were made at our experimenting station on the Huffman prairie, east of the city; and though our experience in handling the machine has been too short to give any high degree of skill, we· nevertheless succeeded, toward the end of the season in making two flights of five minutes each, in which we sailed round and round the field until a distance of about three miles had been covered, at a speed of thirty-five miles an hour. The first of these record flights was made on November 9th, in celebration of the phenomenal political victory of the preceding day, and the second, on December 1st in honor of the one hundredth flight of the season.

The numerous flights in straight lines, in circles, and over 'S'-shaped courses, in calms and in winds have made it quite certain that flying has been brought to a point where it can be made of great practical use in various ways, one of which is that of scouting and carrying messages in time of war. If the latter features are of interest to our own government, we shall be pleased to take up the matter either on a basis of providing machines of agreed specification, at a contract price, or of furnishing all the scientific and practical information we have accumulated in these years of experimenting, together with a license to use our patents; thus putting the government in a position to operate on its own account.

If you can find it convenient to ascertain whether this is a subject of interest to our own government, it would oblige us greatly as early information on this point will aid us in making our plans for the future.

The Wrights were offering the United States government a good deal and Congressman Nevin realized this. He tried to get the new Secretary of War, William Howard Taft, to take them up on their offer. But the country's most eminent scientist, Dr. Langley, had tried and, even with a Congressional appropriation of $50,000 to back him, had failed to fly. Therefore it was unlikely that man could fly. Ergo, the Wrights were charlatans, or so the line of reasoning went in the War Department's Board of Ordnance and Fortification, where the Wright letter finally ended up. And that was that. The Department's response to Congressman Nevin is a classic example of the closed mind in action:

I have the honor to inform you that, as many requests have been made for financial assistance in the development of designs for flying machines, the Board has found it necessary to decline to make allotments for the experimental development of devices for mechanical flight, and has determined that, before suggestions with that object in view will be considered, the device must have been brought to the stage of practical operation without expense to the United States.

It appears from the letter of Messrs. Wilbur and Orville Wright that their machine has not yet been brought to the stage of practical operation, but as soon as it shall have been perfected, this Board would be pleased to receive further representations from them in regard to it.

The Board had either not taken the trouble to read the Wrights' letter or had been unable to understand what it had said.

The British response was much more interesting. In February the brothers received a letter inviting them to submit terms. On March 1 they answered that they were ready to sign a contract to build an airplane capable of carrying two people 50 miles at a speed of no less than 30 miles per hour. The price: $2,500 per mile for each mile flown in a trial flight, with the British government under no obligation to buy if they couldn't fly more than 10 miles. With the benefit of hindsight, it is easy to see what a bargain this would have been for the British. Even if the Wright plane went the full 50 miles at its trial flight, the price would have been only $125,000 for a head start on the rest of the world. But the British government, like the American, was still not ready to take to the air. And as visionary as the Wrights were, they were unable, at this point, to conceive of anything other than a military use for their invention. Airmail, passengers, freight, sport—these developments would have to wait for new men with other ideas.

In the meantime, the brothers were planning their work for the 1905 summer and fall flying season. Even though they were far ahead of the field, they still were not satisfied with the performance of their aircraft. After working so hard to get their 1904 machine to make turns, they found several times that they were then unable to stop it from turning and it had gone down, striking the ground in a tilted, wing-down position that, more often than not, was accompanied by the noise of cracking spars and struts and wire braces letting go. As Wilbur put it: "The cause of the difficulty proved to be very obscure and the season of 1904 closed without any solution of the puzzle."

While the Wrights had been working out with their 1904 machine, they had also begun building two others, very similar in design. One of these became their 1905 flyer. The other ultimately wound up as a 1907 model. When they stopped flying for the season in December, 1904, they removed the engine from the 1904 plane and put it in one of their new machines. This engine was rather remarkable in that it became more powerful as it grew older. When first installed in the 1904 machine, it developed between 15 and 16 horsepower. By January, 1905, the Wrights measured its horsepower at 16.64, and by the end of the 1905 season it was putting out more than 20 horsepower. They attributed this phenomenon to the smoothing of the pistons and cylinders due to wear.

The brothers felt that the turning problem they encountered in their 1904 machine was due to their lack of skill in controlling the aircraft rather than any flaw in its basic design. Thus the airframe of the 1905 machine was almost identical to the 1904 version, and very similar to the 1903 flyer. However, the new airplane carried fuel and water sufficient for an hour's flight, which the brothers confidently expected to make. By the end of May the new plane was assembled at Huffman Prairie and ready to go. The Wrights delayed testing it until June 23, expecting a visit by a British representative who never did show up. Then they began a wild and wonderful three months of flying. The notes from their diaries tell the story of the forty-nine flights they made in 1905:

First flight . . . 272 ft. over ground. The left wing was struck in landing and four ribs were cracked at rear left corner. [Power insufficient. Missing explosions.]

. . . While getting ready . . . the anchor stake was pulled from the ground and the machine ran down the track with O.W.

doubled over the front handle riding backwards. Fortunately no serious damage to man or machine.

. . . 136 ft. over the ground. Machine suddenly turned to left and struck left wing tip, breaking rear spar of left lower wing and cracked end bow.

Distance 664 feet . . . Machine acted very queerly in side steering and Orville was compelled to shut off power and land to avoid running into fence.

Distance 774 feet. Machine refused to steer properly, and while attempting to shift rear rudder, W.W. shut off power by mistake. The machine turned up and came almost to a standstill, and dropped very hard, breaking rear center spar and front left spar . . . [Pulled engine loose. Broke several wires.]

. . . Distance 568 feet. Time about 12 sec. The machine seemed to steer all right laterally, but after attaining high speed began to undulate somewhat and suddenly turned down and struck at a considerable angle. . . . The machine rolled over on front edge. O.W. was thrown violently out through the broken top surface but suffered no injury at all.

. . . Owing to very hard rain the field became flooded and delayed us several weeks.

. . . 1,556 ft. over the ground. Found it impossible to make turn in time and so shut off engine and landed within a few feet of stump.

. . . W.W. 690 meters in 45⅘ sec. Awkwardness in handling side steering devices made it necessary to land to avoid going over fence. Landing made at high speed. (Landed in ditch.) The machine jumped the ditch. . . . Nothing broken.

. . . Made complete circle and landed at starting point. Found the rear tail apparently too small. Geo. Feight and 6 farmers present.

. . . 170 meters in 12 sec. This was first trial of O.W. with new rudder. A very comical performance.

. . . 1,041 meters in 1′ 5⅘ sec. Circle. Mr. Huffman and three children and Mr. Morley and two daughters present.

By the end of 1905, the Wrights were making long flights of up to 39 minutes' duration.

. . . Large tail was put on just before this flight. It proved awkward to handle and machine was stopped at far end of field.

. . . O.W. 4,730 meters. 4′ 54 sec. Four rounds of field, and landed at starting point.

. . . O.W. 2,700 meters. 2′ 48⅗ sec. Two complete circles. Two pictures.

. . . W.W. 4,751 meters in 4′ 45⅗ sec. Four complete circles. Twice passed over fence into Beard's cornfield. Chased flocks of birds on two rounds and killed one which fell on top of upper surface and after a time fell off when swinging a sharp curve.

. . . Made one complete circle to the left, and on second round made a figure eight but let the machine run into the ground while attempting the circle to the right. The landing was very rough, but except one screw, one rear skid stick and a few wires, nothing was broken. Chain jumped the sprocket while landing.

. . . 5,056 meters in 5′ 31 sec. 4½ rounds of field. Stalled from turning too short circles.

. . . 17,961 meters 18′ 11⅖ sec. O.W. About 16 rounds of field. Count lost. Flight lasted till gasoline was exhausted.

. . . During last minute the engine almost stopped at one time, but started up again and ran fairly well for another half minute but with reduced power. The machine at the slow speed could not be stopped from circling and made a very rough landing, breaking one skid stick and several ribs. The trouble proved to be due to a chunk of rubber lodging in the gasoline pump. We removed it next day and inserted a screen in the supply pipe.

. . . O.W. 19,570 meters in 20′ 49⅘″. Fourteen rounds of field 12 pictures. Gasoline exhausted. Mr. Huffman witnessed flight.

. . . O.W. 24,535 meters in 26′ 11⅕ sec. Rear thrust bearing heated again. Two traction cars passed during flight. Three-gallon tank fitted to machine.

. . . O.W. 33,456 meters in 34′ 39⅘″? We had fitted oiler to rear bearing on axle under chains but not on front bearing. Front bearing heated. 12 pictures. 40–60 ft. high.

The forty-eighth and next-to-last flight of 1905 was the best of all and smashed all records. Here is how the Wrights laconically recorded it!

(48.) 2nd trial. W.W. Speed through air 17.05 meters per sec. 38,956 meters in 39′ 23⅘″. About 30 rounds of field. Gasoline exhausted. Ellis, Theodore Waddel, Huffman, and about a dozen others present, including Beard of the *Journal*.

The solution to the problem encountered the previous year of the aircraft failing to come out of a turn proved to be a simple matter once the brothers understood what the trouble was. Years later, Wilbur told what they had found out in 1905 that enabled them to stay airborne more than half an hour:

For a long time we were unable to determine the peculiar conditions under which this trouble was to be expected. But as time passed we began to note that it usually occurred when we were turning a rather short circle. We, therefore, made short circles sometimes for the purpose of investigating and noting the exact conduct of the machine from the time the trouble began until the landing was made.

At one time we thought it might be due to the fact that the machine, in circling, did not face exactly in the line of motion. To test this point we disconnected the rudder wire from the warping wire and operated the rudder by an entirely different handle. The trouble, however, continued as before. A flight . . . was made on the 28th of September, 1905, with the rudder wires entirely disconnected from the warping wires. When it was noticed that the machine was tilting up and sliding toward the tree, the operator turned the machine down in front and found that the apparatus responded promptly to the lateral control.

The remedy was found to consist in more skillful operation of the machine and not in a different construction. The trouble was really due to the fact that in circling, the machine has to carry the load resulting from centrifugal force, in addition to its own weight. . . . The machine in question had but a slight surplus of power above what was required for straight flight, and as the additional load, caused by circling, increased rapidly as the circle became smaller, a limit was finally reached beyond which the machine was no longer able to maintain sufficient speed to sustain itself in the air. . . . When we had discovered the real nature of the trouble, and knew that it could always be remedied by tilting the machine forward a little, so that its flying speed would be restored, we felt that we were ready to place flying machines on the market.

But the market was not ready for the Wrights. A few days after their record thirty-nine-minute flight, they decided to try the U. S. government again. A new general had been appointed to the Army's Board of Ordnance and Fortification and they thought their luck might be better the second time around. So they wrote, on October 9, 1905, and stated that they were prepared to furnish an aircraft capable of flying 100 miles with one person aboard. "We do not wish to take this invention abroad, unless we find it necessary to do so, and therefore write again, renewing the offer," they said.

Back came the answer: "I have the honor to inform you that, as many requests have been made for financial assistance in the development of designs for flying machines . . ." It was practically word for word the same kind of form letter Congressman Nevin had received earlier in the year when he made his pitch. The personnel had changed at the Board of Ordnance and Fortification all right, but the closed minds remained. The Wrights tried once more and, in a letter remarkable under the circumstances for its restraint and patience, they once again offered to build a machine to whatever specifications the Board cared to state and to furnish proof of their claims to have built a flying machine whenever the Board desired.

Within a week they had their reply: "It is recommended that the Messrs. Wright be informed that the Board does not care to formulate any requirements for the performance of a flying machine or take any further action on the subject until a machine is produced which by actual operation is shown to be able to produce horizontal flight and to carry an operator."

Clearly, the world just wasn't ready yet to accept the fact that the airplane had been invented. So the two remarkable men who created the airplane calmly and deliberately decided to quit flying until the world *was* ready.

1906

Across the Atlantic and several years before the Wrights' first flights, it had seemed a simple matter to two teen-age French brothers to convert a big box kite into a free-flying glider capable of carrying a passenger. These two, Gabriel and Charles Voisin, had already achieved some success with a 16-foot 5-inch kite which was so stable that it stayed tethered aloft for days at a time while they watched in fascination from the terrace of their home near Lyon. They had followed this in 1899 with a slightly smaller box kite which could lift them off the ground when they clung to it in a good strong breeze. A simple modification to make it easier to hang on to was all they felt this latter craft needed to soar away with one of them aboard.

When the wind was favorable they took their fledgling glider out to a nearby slope and ran downhill with it some twenty times without getting off the ground. Obviously the slope was too gentle to give them a good start. So they took their glider to a quarry and got ready to jump off a 200-foot cliff. Gabriel was to be first, but when he got to the edge of the cliff he just stood there. Then Charles tried, but he too had second thoughts. "If there had been the slightest sign of a spectator, one of us would assuredly have smashed himself to pieces at the foot of the cliff, but our solitude saved us," Gabriel recalled many years afterward.

Two years later, Louis Blériot, a prospering French automobile headlight manufacturer, built his first flying machine. He reasoned, logically enough, that if birds could fly by beating their wings, why not man? But when Blériot started up the motor for the first test of his flapping-wing design, the machine flapped and flapped but failed to get off the ground. This was the last flapping-wing design for M. Blériot. Clearly there had to be a better way.

Though the men involved in these abortive attempts to fly were later to exert a profound influence on aviation, their early efforts were conducted in merciful obscurity. In 1901, however, there was nothing at all obscure about the activities of Alberto Santos-Dumont, the dapper little heir to a Brazilian coffee fortune who lived in Paris. For this was the year that he finally succeeded in piloting a lumbering hydrogen-filled airship from a park in the Paris suburb of St.-Cloud to the Eiffel Tower and back, a distance of seven miles, in a few seconds under thirty minutes. It had taken Santos-Dumont three different airships, four separate attempts, one serious crash and several minor accidents to accomplish the Eiffel Tower round trip, and all Paris was acclaiming the audacious feat. With things like this going on, France confidently expected to be the first nation to conquer the air. No one seemed to have heard of the Wright brothers on that side of the Atlantic.

By all rights, the French should have been first. They had a glorious tradition of aeronautical pioneering that stretched back to the launching of the world's first balloon by the Montgolfier brothers in 1783. The list of French triumphs that followed was impressive: the first humans to make a balloon ascension, the first manned balloon flight across the English Channel, the first dirigible, the first rapid-sequence photographs of birds' wings in flight. French experimenters had developed model helicopters many years before Bishop Milton Wright brought home for his sons that "small toy actuated by a rubber spring which would lift itself into the air."

And in 1890, a flying machine built by French engineer Clément Ader became the first powered heavier-than-air craft to get off the ground with a man aboard. Powered by a 20-horsepower steam engine and looking like an overgrown bat on wheels, Ader's machine hopped about 160 feet, but was out of control all

Obviously inspired by a bat, one of innumerable early French efforts tries—and fails—to get off the ground.

the way. Unable to duplicate this leap, he built two more machines which either did or did not make similar jumps, depending on the bias of the person telling the story. Those anxious to establish Ader as the inventor of the first airplane insist that he made hops of 300 feet. Others claim that he never left the ground.

Unlike the United States, where unsuccessful attempts to fly were greeted with derision, the French press and French public opinion were sympathetic to those who were trying to advance the science. There was something about man's efforts to conquer the air that appealed to the French sense of gallantry, and men like Ader were treated with respect even though they failed to accomplish what they set out to do. In this favorable climate, it was inevitable that the challenge of flying would attract many other talents, and in 1898 the Aéro Club of France was founded by a group of prominent and wealthy citizens including Prince Roland Bonaparte and Gustave Eiffel, the builder of the tower.

The objective of the Aéro Club was to promote all aeronautical activities, and to this end the Club sponsored competitions for prize money put up by some of its members. The first was a whopping 100,000 francs (approximately $20,000), which was won by Santos-Dumont on his Eiffel Tower round trip. The Club next put up a 1,500-franc ($300) prize for the first heavier-than-air machine to fly 100 meters (328 feet). Though it was hard to tell from the efforts of the Voisins, Blériot and Santos-Dumont precisely what direction heavier-than-air aviation would take in the future, it seemed just a matter of time before someone in France would come forward with a machine that could win the Aéro Club prize.

But then, in April, 1903, Octave Chanute visited Paris, and thoroughly upset the French aeronautical world with an address to the Aéro Club in which he described the latest work of Langley and the Wright brothers in America. Ernest Archdeacon, a wealthy and very influential member of the Aéro Club, reported on Chanute's talk in the French magazine *La Locomotion*, offered a new prize of 3,000 francs ($600) for the first flight of only 25 meters (82 feet), and sounded the alarm:

From all this it results, my very dear colleagues in locomotion, that the solution is approaching and approaching even very quickly; but also that France, this great homeland of inventors, assuredly does not hold the lead *in the special science* of AVIATION, even when the majority of good minds are today convinced that that alone is the true way.

Will the homeland of the Montgolfiers have the shame of allowing the ultimate discovery of aerial science, which is assuredly imminent, and which will constitute the greatest scientific revolution that has been seen since the beginning of the world, to be realized abroad?

Gentlemen scholars, to your compasses! You, you Maecenases, and you too, gentlemen of the government, your hand in your pocket . . . or else we are beaten!

There were three distinct approaches to the problem of heavier-than-air flight that emerged from the French activity of this period. The Voisins—especially Gabriel—continued to work with

Alberto Santos-Dumont.

aircraft based on the box-kite principle which Lawrence Hargrave, working in Australia in virtual isolation from the aeronautical mainstream, had discovered and developed in the 1890's. Ultimately, a very successful biplane design emerged from the Voisins' work. On the other hand, Louis Blériot, now an active member of the Aéro Club, concentrated on adapting powerful, lightweight engines for use in relatively unsophisticated monoplane airframes.

The third approach was that of Santos-Dumont and it defies description. While the Voisins and Blériot were experimenting with designs that at least bore a faint family resemblance to airplanes as they have come to be known, the design worked out by Santos-Dumont resembled nothing seen before or since. Ironically, it was the first powered aircraft to fly in France.

After his triumphant flight around the Eiffel Tower in airship No. 6, Santos-Dumont built five more airships of varying size, shape and success before turning to heavier-than-air flight in 1905. Then he tried a monoplane glider equipped with floats that was towed down the Seine behind a motorboat. It managed to lift off the water a couple of times, but it was uncontrollable and it plopped right back in. Santos-Dumont's next design was for a helicopter with a double set of rotors, but this was abandoned after a mock-up was constructed.

Meanwhile, Gabriel Voisin had been lured to Paris by the racy living in the *fin-de-siècle* French capital. Voisin was an architect and it wasn't long before he had acquired his first Parisian mistress and a full-time job helping put up the buildings for the great 1900 Exhibition. One day he came upon a group of workers setting up one of Ader's aircraft for exhibition. This encounter reawakened all of Voisin's boyhood dreams of flying:

I had been completely ignorant of the work of this engineering genius. I had never seen a flying machine and I had no idea of the wonders which can be achieved by inspiration when it is associated with advanced techniques.

I knew the men who were doing the installation work. One of Ader's colleagues, who was directing them, acceded to my request and let me sit in the cabin.

Often I have been moved; but on that day I was overcome by an enthusiasm which I had never known before. In my hands were the mysterious controls which could give life to this incomparable creation. To my right and to my left I saw the mechanism which would drive the airscrew blades. The steam generator only needed to be lit to animate this marvel. The wings of the aircraft were spread in the gallery. Suspended on a tackle, the huge bird was lifted and gently swung from side to side. Why was it in this place? Why was it not up in the sky flying over us and our petty activities?

Voisin later sought out Ernest Archdeacon of the Aéro Club and was hired to pilot a small biplane glider that had been built for the wealthy sportsman. The tests were successful. "For the first time in France, a Frenchman had been seen by members of the public in a machine flying between earth and sky, and this above the level of the point of departure," Voisin claimed.

The design of Archdeacon's glider was based on the familiar box-kite principle and this, of course, was something that Voisin knew all about from the experiments he and his brother conducted in Lyon. Consequently, when Voisin built a second glider it was also based on the box kite. This craft crashed while being towed behind a car on its first trial with, luckily, no one aboard. Voisin then built another big box kite for Archdeacon, this one equipped with floats for trials on the Seine. On its first run down the river behind a high-speed motorboat it rose off the water with Voisin aboard and remained airborne for a distance of from 150 to 600 meters, depending on the enthusiasm of the reporter.

It was a heady experience for Voisin, and one he treasured throughout the rest of his long life. In his autobiography, published when he was eighty-four, he recalled:

The big Panhard engine of the racing boat was idling. Tellier was an expert helmsman. Gradually and cautiously he took up the slack of my towing cable. Now, fifty-five years later, as I write these lines, I hear once more the lapping of the water against the sides of the floats . . . I had the controls ready. I waited for a time and then I applied the elevator. My lovely glider instantly left the water.

Donkey power failed to give Santos-Dumont enough speed to test the controls of his first airplane, *No. 14-bis.*

In a few seconds I was as high as the tops of the poplars along the quay. I went along without oscillation either in pitch or roll . . . I alighted on the water without incident.

Everybody in Paris who was interested in heavier-than-air craft had been at our trial, which had been photographed. Santos-Dumont was there. He had not, until then, begun to think about aviation. Yet on the same day as we did our experiment, he dismantled his last dirigible and began the work which eventually brought him to the aircraft of 1906. The comparison of the two machines and of the dates, which can be readily checked, proves immediately that my old friend was inspired by my glider of the Seine experiment.

Louis Blériot was so excited by what he witnessed that he ordered a similar glider from Voisin on the spot. Two months later it was ready. But it swerved sideways on its first trial run, dipped a corner into the water and crashed, dunking Voisin and slashing him painfully in a tangle of piano-wire bracing.

As summer gave way to fall and it became too cold for further work on the river, Voisin went to work full time for Blériot. In the closing months of 1905, while the Wrights were chasing birds and doing figure eights with their plane three thousand miles away, Santos-Dumont began to plan a radically different machine behind closed doors at his workshop.

There has never been anything quite as marvelous as the Santos-Dumont machine that was trundled out for its first work-out in the spring of 1906. The box-kite principle, popularized by Voisin, was obviously the basic feature of the design. In fact, the machine resembled a whole gaggle of box kites all heading in the same general direction at the same time. The 33-foot wing consisted of six box-kite cells set side by side and angled sharply upward from the center of the wings to the tips in a pronounced dihedral or V-shape. This angle was supposed to give the craft the stability it needed in flight to keep from tipping over on its side.

Another box-kite cell stuck out on the fuselage about 30 feet *ahead* of the wing. The cell could be tilted up, down and sideways and provided the only flight control for the strange machine. A pusher-type propeller at the rear was driven by a fine 24-horsepower engine manufactured by Léon Levavasseur. This awkward, tail-first configuration soon came to be called a *canard* (duck) design, because the aircraft resembled a wild duck in flight with its neck thrust forward—and because of a French *double-entendre* in the word *canard*, which also means a hoax.

Santos-Dumont first checked the balance of his machine by dangling it from a cable stretched between two heavy steel poles. Next he rigged up a pulley on the tightrope and hired a man with a donkey to haul him back and forth while he tested the movement of the control and its effect on the aircraft—which was nil, since the donkey couldn't trot fast enough to produce any response in the control surfaces.

Further trials called for slinging the aircraft under his latest dirigible, the *No. 14*. With this arrangement, Santos-Dumont felt that the airship would provide the margin of lift needed to sustain him safely when he applied power to the heavier-than-air machine for the first time and attempted to pilot it. But this hybrid was a failure, too. When the engine was started up with Santos-Dumont aboard, the heavier-than-air part of the combination lunged forward, dragging the gasbag along behind with such violent lurches that no control was possible. Santos-Dumont's experienced airship ground crew was able to hang on to the mooring lines, however, and the monstrosity was brought to earth again, its plucky pilot uninjured.

Santos-Dumont now separated the two craft, christened the heavier-than-air machine the *No. 14-bis*, replaced the 24-horsepower engine with one of 50 horsepower and, on September 13, 1906, summoned the members of the Aéro Club for a demonstration at Bagatelle field in the Bois de Boulogne. His first attempt was a long and unsuccessful full-speed run across the grass in which his wheels never left the ground. On the second run, the machine was seen to lift off the grass for a few seconds as Santos-Dumont, standing awkwardly upright amidship, moved the control wheel that operated the forward box kite to the full up position. Before he could reverse the wheel, *No. 14-bis* staggered, stalled and fell heavily to the ground, collapsing the undercarriage and shattering the propeller.

Santos-Dumont had the damage repaired, made the forward control more sensitive to quick changes and was ready to try again a month later. On October 23 the official witnesses met once more at Bagatelle. From early morning until late afternoon Santos-Dumont was plagued by a series of minor malfunctions and tried, without success, to get off the ground several times. But finally he made it. Among those watching was Captain Ferdinand Ferber, an aviation enthusiast of several years' standing, who had made a few unsuccessful aircraft himself. "At 4:45 in the afternoon, his airplane left the ground smoothly and without shock," said Ferber. "The crowd watched, spellbound, as though witnessing a miracle; it remained mute with astonishment, but immediately afterward, at the moment of landing, gave vent to a roar of enthusiasm and carried the aviator shoulder high in triumph."

The Santos-Dumont flight was officially agreed to be about 60 meters and the Aéro Club announced that the little Brazilian had won the Archdeacon prize. In the excitement, the vaguer reports emanating from the United States about the work of the Wrights were conveniently forgotten and Santos-Dumont was hailed as the conqueror of the air, the first man to fly.

But Santos-Dumont's *No. 14-bis* was an airplane with no future. He succeeded in making two more flights with it—one of them 220 meters, lasting twenty-one and a third seconds—but the craft was awkward and essentially uncontrollable. After his last flight in *No. 14-bis*, a short hop in April, 1907, Santos-Dumont abandoned the *canard* design and proceeded along more conventional lines, finally coming up with a highly successful monoplane, the Demoiselle, in 1909. Although *No. 14-bis* exerted no lasting influence on aircraft design, it did accomplish two things: it stimulated French aeronautical activity to an even greater fever pitch than had Chanute's reports about American work, and it established Santos-Dumont as a man of rare courage. Almost from the start he realized his machine was uncontrollable, yet he was willing to push it to its limits knowing full well that the big 50-horsepower engine thrashing away inches behind him would crush him if he ever crashed.

For a while after the trials on the Seine, Gabriel Voisin and Louis Blériot teamed up to build airplanes. Blériot had some radical design ideas which he wanted to test, while Voisin felt sure that success lay in the direction of a more sophisticated box kite. Though the two men became great friends and passed many a pleasant hour working together in their shop, they began to split up over a Blériot-inspired design for a sort of flattened flying cylinder which failed to do anything in trials on a lake near Paris. Blériot compromised in the next design, allowing Voisin his box-kite arrangement for the main wing structure but insisting on the cylindrical design for the tail. This machine had a tremendous powerplant and two propellers. It was tried on floats and then on wheels, but showed no inclination to leave the ground and the two men parted company. Gabriel Voisin painted out the name "Blériot-Voisin" above the doorway to his shop and made it "Les Frères Voisin," for his brother had just come to Paris to work with him.

Things were pretty desperate at first at the Voisin aircraft factory. Their first customer was a man who wanted a flapping-wing machine. Though the Voisins knew it wouldn't fly, their client was able to pay cash, so they followed his plans and gave him what he wanted. "This machine had varied fortunes," said Gabriel Voisin. "It ended its career hanging from a wheel from a kind of mountain railway built at Massy Palaiseau, all without results."

The Voisins' first successful true airplane was built for a well-to-do Parisian sculptor, Léon Delagrange. He had worked up a fanciful multiwinged design of his own, but the Voisins talked him out of it and got him to agree to buy a box-kite type. The order was placed in December, 1906, and the craft was completed in February of the following year. On March 30, 1907, Charles Voisin made a fine, controlled flight of about 260 feet with the Delagrange machine. Gabriel Voisin proudly claimed: "Our machine was far from being some kind of apocalyptic monster, but was a well-knit structure, thoroughly well thought out and not open to adverse criticism."

The orders began to pour in. A wealthy member of the Aéro Club asked the Voisins to build the gondola and engine assembly for a large and very successful dirigible. A Dutchman and a Russian prince came through with orders for eccentric designs that were built and paid for but were not successful. In the spring of 1907, the brothers were approached by Henri Farman, a well-known bicycle and automobile racer who was one of three sons of the Paris correspondent for the London *Daily Telegraph*. Farman gave the Voisin brothers the opportunity they were now ready for. Unlike their previous customers, Henri Farman had no eccentric designs in mind. He simply ordered an airplane with a 50-horsepower engine that could fly one kilometer.

On October 7 the new airplane made its first flight with

With his box-kite Voisin biplane, Henri Farman made the first circular flight in Europe more than three years after the Wrights' first circle.

Farman at the controls, and by the end of the month he was making flights of more than 2,000 meters. Delagrange was learning to fly his plane also and had gotten to the point where he was attempting his first turns when bad weather set in during the first week of November. But more competition was beginning to spring up. Santos-Dumont was working on the prototype of his famous Demoiselle monoplane, and Louis Blériot and three other designers—Trajan Vuia, a Hungarian engineer living in Paris, and Frenchmen Robert Esnault-Pelterie and Alfred de Pischof— all succeeded in getting into the air by the end of the year.

Voisin aircraft, however, continued to dominate the French scene on into 1908. On January 13, Henri Farman made the first circle in French aviation with his Voisin biplane. He flew slightly more than one kilometer in one minute and twenty-eight seconds, thus winning 50,000 francs ($10,000) in prize money put up by two wealthy members of the Aéro Club for the first plane to fly

Louis Blériot finally got off the ground—briefly—at a field in Paris with his sixth aircraft, *La Libellule*.

one kilometer. Once again, the Wright brothers were conveniently forgotten. "At this moment none of our competitors was worrying us," said Gabriel Voisin triumphantly. "We were indeed the only people in the world able to offer, to those wanting to fly, an airplane capable of flying more or less correctly, and although an army of plagiarists tried their best to equal us, not one could claim to approach the results we obtained."

The one person whom the Voisins could not accuse of plagiarism was Gabriel's old colleague, Louis Blériot. After the flying cylinders, Blériot doggedly persisted in building and trying out strange, original designs which he discarded, one after the other, when they failed, until he hit upon the monoplane which he was soon to make famous. He followed the flying cylinders with a tail-first *canard* monoplane which had wings modeled after those of a dove. It was powered by a 24-horsepower engine with a propeller in the rear. On its first trial it turned over, frightening so badly the man Blériot had hired to pilot it that he refused to have anything further to do with it and warned everyone else to stay away. Consequently, Blériot himself began trying to fly it. He actually made a few short leaps with this machine in April, 1907, before he abandoned it for his next brainstorm.

Blériot's sixth aircraft showed some kinship to Langley's tandem-wing "aerodrome," though it was much smaller. With its two pairs of wings, one set behind the other, it was quickly nicknamed *La Libellule* (The Dragonfly). It was powered by the same 24-horsepower engine used before, but the propeller was in front this time. It had rudimentary movable control surfaces on a vertical stabilizer. On the wing tips there were other movable surfaces that functioned like rudimentary ailerons. But Blériot didn't trust these control surfaces completely and installed a sliding seat in the aircraft so that he might get extra control by shifting his weight.

La Libellule made its debut in July, 1907, and was able to get off the ground for short flights of 25, 150 and 140 meters. All it needed to be a complete success, Blériot felt, was a more powerful engine. He installed a larger powerplant in it, broke his existing record with a hair-raising, uncontrollable flight of 184 meters on September 17, then crashed, fortunately without injury.

The next Blériot aircraft was also a tandem-wing design with the engine in front. It was considerably streamlined and was the first aircraft to have its fuselage completely covered with fabric. With this plane, Blériot made several short hops. He also experimented with the position of the rear set of wings, gradually moving them farther aft and cutting them down in size until they began to resemble a modern horizontal stabilizer assembly. This machine was demolished in a crash on December 18, 1907, before Blériot could completely resolve the role of the rear wings.

Despite the consistent lack of success with his first seven designs, Blériot believed that he was finally moving in the right direction toward a solution to the problem of powered flight. He sold his automobile-headlight business and concentrated all his money, talent and energy on airplanes. And in 1908 he finally came up with the world's first successful true monoplane, a design that ultimately would prevail over all others as the years passed and provide Blériot with a fortune and enduring fame.

In the Blériot VIII, as it was simply called, many modern features emerged clearly for the first time. There was a long, dominant single wing, for example, and a true tail with both vertical and horizontal surfaces. The big 50-horsepower engine was mounted in the nose and drove a four-bladed propeller. There were movable control surfaces similar to modern ailerons on the wing tips to make the aircraft bank, and the tail contained a movable horizontal plane, similar to a modern elevator, to make the aircraft climb and descend. Neither the propeller nor the wings were very efficient in an aerodynamic sense and the plane was slow and awkward. But as seen in flight, its clean and simple lines clearly marked it as the sire of many thoroughbred generations of fighter aircraft.

Blériot made numerous successful short flights with No. VIII in the summer and early fall of 1908. On October 31 he flew a very satisfying cross-country hop of about 30 kilometers from the little town of Toury to neighboring Artenay and back. But much of Blériot's thunder was stolen by Henri Farman, who had flown 27 kilometers in his Voisin biplane near Reims the previous day.

One of the remarkable things about these achievements in French aviation is that they were carried out by men who understood next to nothing about the principles of aerodynamics. Not only had the French ignored reports of the Wrights' successful flights, but the brothers' pioneering work in aerodynamic theory and the results of their wind tunnel test had likewise failed to make it across the Atlantic. Consequently, French aircraft, including the most successful Voisin and Blériot types, were deficient in three important respects: lift, control and propeller design. Since no one in France knew how much curvature would produce the most lift, the wings were designed by guess and could not sustain very heavy loads. Stability in flight was also a matter of guesswork and, with inefficient and sometimes nonexistent lateral controls, once a wing got down on early French airplanes, it was sometimes quite a job to bring the plane back to level flight. In a remarkable interview tape-recorded by the Columbia University Office of Oral History, J. T. C. Moore-Brabazon, holder of the first pilot certificate issued by the British Aero Club, described his own unforgettable experience with control difficulties in a Voisin he bought in France in 1908:

I took the machine back to England, and on May 3, 1909, I made a flight at the Isle of Sheppey in my Voisin, which ranks as the first flight ever made in England by an Englishman.

I flew, I suppose, half a mile at about forty feet. The Voisin machine had no side control, you know. The left wing started going down, and the only way to restore that was to turn around to the right so as to accelerate the wing that was down. Well, when I turned the wheel for the rudder, I found that nothing happened because the pin had gone from the shaft. There was nothing to do but land as quickly as I could at an angle of 45 degrees. Well, that, as you can imagine, busts a machine very much. The engine was at the back, and it shot past me, luckily, and didn't catch fire. But I was pinned down to the ground by a lot of wires. I have a keen recollection of the fact that my two Irish terrier dogs had chased this machine. They were licking my face in the middle of that wreckage, which was rather odd.

French propeller design, by 1908, had not progressed much beyond the small and inefficient windmills that Santos-Dumont had used on his airships. Blériot favored four fairly flat paddles set at an angle to the airstream; others worked with two- and three-bladed paddles, some made of wood, others fabricated from aluminum. Some of these were curved rather than flat, but none worked on the Wright principle that the propeller was like a rotating wing and therefore should have a winglike curvature capable of developing lift.

These disadvantages were offset to a considerable extent by the marvelous engines available to French aircraft designers. While the Wrights were experimenting with engines of 12 to 20 horsepower—and having to build more efficient wings to compensate for the low power available—the French designers had excellent powerplants available to them by the time they first took to the air. Foremost of these was the Antoinette series of engines built by Léon Levavasseur. Levavasseur was both an engineer and an artist, having spent some time at the École des Beaux-Arts in Paris. Thus everything he set his hand to was not only practical, from a mechanical point of view, but beautiful to behold. A big V-8 Antoinette engine of 100 horsepower, built in 1910, had stylishly wrought and highly polishable copper water jackets, for example. Levavasseur also designed and built a slim, graceful monoplane in 1909 which captured the French fancy immediately, although it didn't fly very well. (The name "Antoinette" was not the romantic fancy of an artist, however, but a practical step by a shrewd businessman. The Antoinette after whom Levavasseur named everything he manufactured was the daughter of his principal financial backer.)

Levavasseur specialized in lightweight water-cooled V-8 engines. His first Antoinettes were manufactured for racing motorboats—it was an Antoinette-powered launch, for example, that was doing the towing when Blériot's floatplane glider crashed on the Seine with Gabriel Voisin aboard in 1905. On the basis of his motorboat engines, Levavasseur was selected to build the powerplants for Santos-Dumont's *No. 14-bis*. He furnished both 24- and 50-horsepower engines for this aircraft. These weighed between three and four pounds per horsepower, a thoroughly respectable ratio for aircraft engines on up until World War I. Blériot used the 24-horsepower Antoinette in his *canard*, installed both the 24- and the 50-horsepower models in *La Libellule* and also powered the Blériot VIII with the larger engine. The Voisin brothers selected the 50-horsepower model for the important work they did for Léon Delagrange and Henri Farman. And of course Levavasseur used an Antoinette powerplant in his own Antoinette monoplane.

Though Levavasseur engines dominated the scene during the early years of French aviation, other manufacturers soon began to come forward with promising designs. In 1907 aviator Robert Esnault-Pelterie and motorcycle builder Alessandro Anzani, working independently of each other, developed air-cooled engines in which the cylinders were arranged fanwise across the top of the engine. Esnault-Pelterie's design had five cylinders and was used in the aircraft he built and flew in 1907. Anzani's first engine had three cylinders and was later adopted by Louis Blériot. This fan-shaped arrangement ultimately gave way to the full radial air-cooled engine in which the cylinders are spaced evenly around the crankcase.

A strange new design, which turned out to be very practical for medium powered engines up to 230 horsepower, was introduced by the Séguin brothers in 1908. This was the Gnome rotary engine. In this type, the propeller *and* the engine itself rotated about a stationary crank shaft attached to the airframe of the plane. (This type of engine is obsolete now and hard to visualize, but if automobiles had rotary engines, one would lift the hood and find the whole engine spinning instead of stationary when running.) Rotary engines had the advantage of being light and simple, most of them weighing less than three pounds per horsepower.

But it takes more than a powerful engine to make an airplane. Given enough horsepower, it *is* possible to get a barn door airborne, but it will handle like a barn door and not an airplane. This was roughly the position of French aviation in the summer of 1908: many different aircraft had become airborne in France, but none of them was really safe, reliable or practical yet. The British were even farther behind. An American expatriate, Samuel Franklin Cody, made some short hops in 1908 in a plane that he designed and built himself, but it was not until 1909 that he made sustained, controllable flights. The only other activity outside the United States at this time was in Denmark, where J. C. H. Ellehammer had built a monoplane and flown it for 42 meters in September, 1906. Ellehammer continued his aeronautical experiments and is credited with making the first airplane flight in Germany, in June, 1908.

European, and particularly French, aviators were soon to find out, with a jolt, just how far they had been outdistanced by the American developments they had been inclined to discount. For in a crate in a customs warehouse in Le Havre a new Wright airplane was waiting to be tested.

1908

$\mathbf{A}$fter the Wright brothers' discouraging attempts to interest the United States Army in an airplane in 1905, they began a complex series of negotiations with various people representing different French interests. Once again, they believed that their best approach was through the military. Their first contact was with Captain Ferber, who had learned about the Wrights' work through Octave Chanute. Chanute in turn had kept the Wrights posted on Ferber's interest. On October 9, 1905, the same day the Wrights made their last effort to wake up the U. S. War Department, Wilbur also wrote to Ferber, describing their plans for marketing their invention. "It is our present intention to first offer it to the governments for war purposes, and if you think your government would be interested, we would be glad to communicate with it," he said.

Ferber responded immediately and asked the Wrights to quote a price. They asked for one million francs ($200,000), payable only after putting their machine through its paces in a flight of 50 kilometers in less than an hour. Negotiations dragged on inconclusively through 1906, however, and the Wrights finally engaged a New York banking and investment company with representatives in Europe to act as their business agent outside the United States. The firm would receive a commission of twenty percent on all sales.

At the urging of the company's European agent, Wilbur sailed for France, with all expenses paid, in May, 1907. He was joined by Orville, Charles Taylor and the demonstration machine in late summer when it appeared that some flights might help clinch a deal with the French government. But once again nothing came of the negotiations, and the Wrights and Taylor returned to Dayton. The situation in France was not entirely hopeless; so, in the hope they could return soon, they left their new plane behind without having uncrated it.

In 1908, after a lapse of two and a half years, the Wrights resumed their flying. In the meantime, a personnel rotation in the U. S. War Department brought a young balloon racer, Lieutenant Frank P. Lahm, into Signal Corps headquarters in Washington. Lahm had won the prestigious James Gordon Bennett balloon race in France in 1906 by flying from Paris to England. Through his father, who lived in Paris and was a member of the Aéro Club, young Lahm knew many of the prominent French aviators of the day and understood clearly the implications of their work. When Wilbur Wright called on the officers on the Board just before Thanksgiving, 1907, on his way home from France, he thus found a considerable change in the climate. The Wrights were invited to bid on a contract and won it with a proposal to build a plane for $25,000 that would carry a pilot and a passenger for a 10-mile demonstration ride at an average speed of no less than 40 miles per hour. A short time later, a syndicate of prominent French businessmen also reached a highly profitable agreement with the Wrights to market their invention in France after making demonstration flights there. The French contract called for a cash payment of 500,000 francs plus one half the stock in the syndicate and one quarter of its profits if they could make two flights of 50 kilometers in an hour or less.

The Wrights returned to Kitty Hawk in the spring of 1908 and rebuilt their 1905 aircraft, which was shipped down from storage in Dayton. They installed a larger, 30-horsepower engine and added upright seats to make it suitable for a passenger in the U.S. Army trials. Since the hip-cradle control for wing warping could no longer be used with the upright seats, they re-rigged their control system and installed levers to work the forward elevator and the wing-warping and rudder controls. After several short flights, Wilbur took up their first passenger, Dayton mechanic Charles W. Furnas, on May 14. Later that day, while flying by himself, he lost control of the plane and darted into the ground at a speed of about 54 miles per hour. The plane was badly smashed, but Wilbur got out of it with minor cuts and bruises and a good shaking up that left him stiff for a couple of days.

This accident failed to undermine Wilbur's confidence in either the aircraft or his flying abilities and, rather than wait around for further practice until the plane was repaired, he left camp for France within a few days. His arrival in Paris stirred up speculation in the French press, the gist of which was that the Wrights couldn't possibly make good on their commitment to the French syndicate to make the required flights of 50 kilometers. French aviators were still measuring their achievements in meters —the first cross-country flights of Farman and Blériot would not take place until October.

After looking over several possible sites for his demonstrations, Wilbur finally settled on Le Mans, 125 miles from Paris, which had a big race track, a nearby military parade ground and the added advantage of an automobile factory owned by Léon Bollée, who placed all his facilities at Wilbur's service. The airplane was shipped down from Le Havre, but when the crates arrived in mid-June and were opened, there was little left that resembled an airplane. Wilbur was furious and wrote to Orville:

I opened the boxes yesterday and have been puzzled ever since to know how you could have wasted two whole days packing them. I am sure that with a scoop shovel I could have put things in within two or three minutes and made fully as good a job of it. I never saw such evidences of idiocy in my life. Did you tell Charlie not to separate anything lest it get lonesome? Ten or a dozen ribs were broken and as they are scattered here and there through the surfaces it takes as much time to tear down and rebuild as if we could have begun at the beginning. One surface was so bad that I took it completely down. . . . The cloth is torn in almost numberless places and the aluminum has rubbed off the skid sticks and dirtied the cloth very badly. The radiators are badly mashed; the seat is broken; the magneto has the oil cap broken off, the coils badly torn up [and] the tubes of the screw support are mashed and bent . . . It is going to take much longer for me to get ready than it should have done if things had been in better shape.

Wilbur worked night and day to rebuild the aircraft. He astounded the French by keeping the same hours as his workmen and by living simply and unostentatiously at a nearby hotel. He just didn't act like an aviator, at least not the dashing, flamboyant kind the French were used to.

Further progress on the aircraft was delayed by a serious scalding suffered by Wilbur when a rubber hose came loose from the engine while it was running, spewing boiling water over his side and left arm. These difficulties, plus the fact that he didn't seem like an aviator, heightened the skepticism in the French press. Many bets were made about whether or not he would ever get off the ground, much less fly the specified distance.

Finally, on August 8, Wilbur was ready for a trial flight. Among the spectators at the Le Mans race track for this event

Wilbur Wright set up shop at a race track near Le Mans in 1908 for his first demonstrations in France.

was an adventurous American named Ross Browne who was working for Louis Blériot at the time. In a tape-recorded Columbia oral history interview in 1960, Mr. Browne, who has since died, recalled the excitement of that day:

The newspapers in Paris were calling Wilbur Wright a four-flusher, and said he was bluffing, that he just had the derrick and the rails set up there but wasn't going to fly. Roland Garros, the famous French pilot, told me he asked Blériot, "What's the matter with Wright? Why doesn't he fly?" And Blériot said, "He knows what he's doing."

This went on for two months. Even the London papers were saying that he was a fake, that he couldn't get off the ground, and all that. Sure enough, in August, he decided he was going to fly it. Blériot got word of it; so he and Garros and one of his mechanics and myself all got on a train and went to Paris. At Paris, Blériot got a car and we drove over, about a hundred twenty-five miles, to this race track where Wright was. We met Mr. Wright, and Blériot was all excited. He looked over the machine and he felt the wings. Mr. Wright showed him how the wing warping worked and everything.

To make a long story short, he got into the machine that afternoon, got off into the air and made a beautiful circular flight. You should have seen the crowd there. They threw hats and everything. The Voisins and Delagrange and Santos-Dumont, oh, practically everybody in the country who was interested in flying at the time was there. Everybody was for him then. The next day, too, he made two or three flights.

Naturally all the newspapers came out, and Mr. Wright said, "I'll tell you, with all these crowds here, naturally I want to exhibit my machine, because of potential buyers, and so forth. But this race track is a little too small." You see, in those days those motors were anything but perfect. You couldn't stay in the air very long. Sometimes you might stay ten minutes, or you might stay ten seconds—you couldn't tell. Well, you had to have a place to come down; you couldn't fly across country. So Wright moved to Auvours, the military field, where there was plenty of room. And he made many flights there, the next day and the day after that, the longest over two hours. That was the longest flight made that year, 1908.

Everybody was excited. Well, that's what gave the impetus to all the flying. Everybody was interested overnight, it seemed. And Blériot was just tickled to death. He said, "I'm going to use a warped wing. To hell with the aileron." He was just like a young boy, because it was really marvelous. While he was there, Wright won a prize of twenty thousand francs—the Michelin Prize. That was for the duration—almost two and a half hours. Everybody was tickled about that. But there was another thing that he had in mind. He was forming a French company. Naturally, all these financiers were there, and up till that time they weren't sure, and he wanted them to be sure. So he made that flight for two and a half hours. This clinched everything. The day the papers were signed for that, he also signed papers with an Englishman for the rights for England. So his financial worries then were practically over.

From August 8, 1908, through January 2, 1909, Wilbur Wright made over a hundred flights in France. By the time he was through, he had established the following world records:

Duration: 2 hours 20 minutes 23$\frac{1}{5}$ seconds.
Duration with passenger: 1 hour 9 minutes 45$\frac{1}{5}$ seconds.
Altitude: 115 meters (377.2 feet).

Business was booming and five more airplanes were on the way to fill orders. Wilbur was hailed throughout the country with a warmth and enthusiasm that overwhelmed him. "I have been received in France with a friendliness scarcely to be realized," he wrote to his old friend Octave Chanute. "I never hoped for such treatment. In the reaction from former abuse they seem trying to make up for lost time. No American would think of giving so much time and trouble to assist a stranger as . . . given me here."

French aviation circles were riding the crest of a tremendously exciting wave. In material from the Columbia Oral History Collection never published before, Ross Browne tells how he came to be in France and what life was like in the Blériot crowd in 1908 and 1909:

I was very much interested in aviation, reading a great deal about it. But never having actually come into contact with it, I wanted to see. Through fortunate circumstances, I had a few thousand dollars that I could spend loosely, as it were—I had half a ticket in the Panamanian lottery, which was $15,000 silver, which would be $7,500 in our money. I had half of that, so it gave me a little over $3,000. So after spending several months in the West Indies, chasing around, enjoying myself, I at last arrived in Paris. I had letters of introduction, one of which was to Mr. Blériot. He was not in Paris—he was at Pau in the southern part of France. But I stayed in Paris three or four days. I went to Issy-les-Moulineaux, where the Voisins and the Farmans were getting together planes to fly. There was very little flying there; I just saw one flight. So I got on the train and went to Pau, in the Pyrenees, to Mr. Blériot's factory.

An artist friend of mine, who knew him very well, gave me a personal letter to him. So when I arrived at Pau, I went over to the factory and called up Mr. Blériot to show him the letter. He

The fashionable set still preferred horses, but they turned out in great numbers to see Wilbur Wright fly in France in 1909.

could speak very little English, and I could speak less French. But, fortunately, there was a young chap there, who proved to be just my age, named Roland Garros. He became quite well known as an aviator in later years. Garros and I seemed to take to each other immediately, and he was my main man to get through in French. So I explained to Mr. Blériot that I would like to learn to fly and I didn't know whether I would stay there or not, so I gave him $100 deposit, which he accepted and told me it was all right, that any time I could quit. Garros very kindly got me a very lovely little home—a place to stay—at the beautiful price of about twenty-five francs a week, which was a little less than five dollars. I could have gotten it cheaper even, but they did my laundry.

The fee for the course was $250—that is, in our money. I put down $100. Naturally, after getting settled in the house, and everything, and getting a bicycle—I was all excited. I couldn't get out to the field quick enough. I met Garros, and we rode out and he explained thoroughly the manipulation of the machine, which to me at the time seemed very simple. And, as a matter of fact, the controls were very simple. He put me in a machine and told me to run around. You couldn't get off the ground if you wanted to, the way they had the gas fixed, so I went back and forth three or four times, and it felt very natural. Of course, I had driven a car, so it didn't seem too new to me. So I made two or three runs across the field, and I even turned around at the other end without any help whatsoever. And Garros was quite excited about that; he said everyone else had to be turned around. As I say, I was all excited.

He took me through the factory after that and all through the hangars, showing me the different machines and the motors, and introduced me to several of the fellows. I was surprised how many of them could speak English. As a matter of fact, where I was living, the gentleman had lived in St. Louis for two years and could speak very good English. And the meals there made a gourmet out of me—they were marvelous.

And so, I got into the stride in two or three days. Every morning I'd go out. Mr. Blériot asked Garros how I was doing and Garros had said, "Oh, he'll be able to fly in no time." Fortunately, Mr. Blériot seemed to like me, and I was very fond of him—a lovely gentleman, very warmhearted, and he took an interest, it seemed, in everybody. This went on for two or three

111

Crash! In a rare and unusual sequence, photographer J.-H. Lartigue captures the moment of impact and the rescue of an unknown early French pilot who piled up at Issy-les-Moulineaux near Paris. The pilot survived.

days. I was anxious to get into the air. Garros said, "Don't be too damned anxious—you'll get there quick enough!" About the fourth or fifth day—I think it was on a Sunday morning—we went out, and Garros said, "I'm going to fix the carburetor—give it a little more gas."

So we went down one end of the field; of course, it was an enormous field, even as fields go today. He said, "If you feel your tail going down, let it go very, very casually, and it'll lift itself. But don't go high—just a foot, even—just to feel that you're off. You can tell when you're off the ground. And then just let it sag back. Don't turn your controls; leave your controls as you have them, but shut off your gas." And I did. And I was amazed; I felt like going right on up, but I realized that the landing was the hardest part of it, because the Blériot landing gear was a very tricky affair. The center of gravity was so fine that working your wheel back and forth even an inch would make a big difference and it would be very easy to turn on your nose. Of course Garros explained that to me, and I always was very careful. He said, always pancake—that wasn't the word he used, but that's what he meant—pancake rather than come down. He said, "Always let your tail down. Gradually your front wheels will go down. But for God's sake never put your front wheels down first."

At that time they had a wheel at the end of the fuselage. So, even after you landed, you would run for some distance, because you had no brake at all. Later on, they took the wheel off and put on a skid, and that was a great help in stopping. So I did this for some time, and that afternoon we went home, had lunch, and came back. He said, "Now go a little more." So I did. I went off the ground about four or five different times—going down, then turning around. The next time I went about two or three feet off. So he kept admonishing me to be sure to keep my tail down. He said, "The last time you came down, I thought you were going to have it up. And you did." I said, "Well, you told me to hold it and just sit it down." So he said, "That's the idea." So I felt very proud, and he was very elated. He told me I was doing remarkably well. Of course, in those days I was only about twenty or twenty-one years old, and it was something.

These were all single-seat machines; Blériot didn't have any two-seaters. It was sometime after that—I think it was after 1910—before they had the two-seater; in fact, the machine that he used to fly across the Channel was only a one-seater. You see, the little two-cylinder Anzani we started with was only about seventeen horsepower. Whereas the three-cylinder Anzani, which you graduated to from the smaller one, was around thirty horse-power. That was a three-cylinder Anzani—a stationary, air-cooled motor. That and the Antoinette and the Gnome motors were about the only ones used in those days.

Anyway, a week later, I got a three-cylinder Anzani, and Garros told me, "Do not go up high. Just do the same as you did. Only you know you've got more power. You can go up." So I went up about twenty feet, and I started down and everything went—not exactly black—a blur in my eyes. The only thing I can compare it to, if you've ever been constipated, it will cause the same thing at times. It only lasted two or three seconds. I couldn't imagine what it was, although it had happened to me on several other occasions previously, but never in the machine. So I spoke to Garros about it, and he said, "Well, if I were you, I'd see a doctor and have your eyes examined." Which I did, the following morning. The doctor explained to me that it was a condition that couldn't very well be helped. But he said, "If I were you, I wouldn't fool around flying." He said it might happen while I was coming down, there might be a crowd there, or something like that, and it only takes one or two seconds to cause a very serious accident. Well, I realized that, and I was heartbroken. I said, "Oh, my goodness, after all this."

So I went to a little town about ten miles from Pau, where there was supposed to be a good doctor—I can't remember the name of the town right now. The doctor examined my eyes and told me practically the same thing. And he said there was nothing that he knew that could correct it. But he said it wasn't serious, but it could be if I were caught with that condition in a tight place. So, as I say, I was heartbroken. I thought, "Well, this is the end." Then I spoke to Garros, and Garros said, "You can still fly. It won't affect you at all when you're in the air, because one or two seconds don't mean anything when you're up high enough. The only trouble is in landing. If you feel that, just go up again until it's over and then come down. You can turn around." I said, "Yes, but if you're on these small race tracks, and so forth, with a crowd around you, you can't do that." He said that was true. So I decided that I wouldn't take a license—which

I could easily have done. As a matter of fact, I didn't even tell Mr. Blériot about it, and Garros and I kept it to ourselves.

So I just gave it up. I wouldn't take a license, and never did take a license. And for that reason. Later on, when we were at a meet at Reims, I said, "Oh, damn it, I'd like to get into that." You felt that way. Garros said, "Do what you want to, but I wouldn't if I were you." So I didn't. I decided I wouldn't fly in meets and things like that. I did fly in some exhibitions—but not in any sanctioned meet, where there were other fliers flying. Because it was too much of a risk, not only for me, but for other people as well. The funny thing is, that thing might go on for a year and not happen, and then again it has happened to me a couple of times in a month—right there on the field. And when that did happen to me, then I decided definitely that I wouldn't go ahead.

When I first met Blériot in 1908 he was experimenting on machines. Blériot originally had ailerons on his wings—at the tip of his wings—and, as a matter of fact, I found out that Santos-Dumont was the first one to have ailerons on a machine, and Blériot got it from him. Before that time, he'd had a control in front. He got rid of that entirely, and he was building these machines with ailerons. He'd been experimenting all along, but the machine he had at this time was serviceable; there was no question about that. But he was always looking for something new. I knew the Voisins, the Farman boys—Maurice and Henri Farman. It seemed all those people who were building machines and experimenting were giving each other notes of what they were doing.

So after the flights of Wilbur Wright we jumped back to Pau—Blériot, the mechanic, Garros and I. Right away Blériot said, "Look, we're going to throw out all those aileron things and start warping." And he got his mechanics busy on the warping wing. He was all for it; no more ailerons. So I told Garros, "What's he going to do with all these old airplanes?" He said, "I don't know." I said, "Suppose you ask him how much he wants for them. We can buy four or five of them if we can get them cheap enough. We can fix them up and sell them."

Anyway, after we got back to Pau, Wilbur organized the French company and also sold the English rights. When Wright got all that straightened up, he came down to Pau—in January, 1909—and he brought his machines with him. He was there for some time, flying and demonstrating his machines. And, oh, there were hundreds of people there. Saturdays and Sundays it was crowded. As a matter of fact, I had a little financial deal there, with a friend of the person with whom I was living. He had a taxicab that wasn't big enough; so I lent him a thousand francs to buy another one and I made three hundred francs in a month out of it. There were crowds coming out there, from the train out to the field. Wright was very helpful with Blériot. Blériot then immediately got all of his patents covered by the Wright patent. He paid Wright a bonus, but I believe that Blériot got a very liberal contract, because Wright was very fond of him. Wright could be liberal—but not often.

All this time, Blériot had his mind set on flying the English Channel, and he was working toward that end. But he wanted to get a new machine ready. It was called No. XI. He had that in a special hangar and he was nursing it along while the other work was going on.

The No. XI that Blériot was readying for the Channel attempt became his most famous model. In the next few years he was to build and sell hundreds of these. When World War I broke out, the Blériot No. XI was still going strong and became the principal French training aircraft. There are still a handful of the original No. XI's around today that have been restored to flying condition by museum and antique-aircraft buffs.

The design of the new craft was a refinement of the successful No. VIII monoplane. Wright-type wing warping was substituted for the rotating wing tips, which had not proven very effective on the earlier plane. A fully developed stick-and-rudder system of controls in the pilot's cockpit made its appearance for the first time in No. XI. The stick controlled the wing warping and the up-and-down motion of the elevators. To make the plane go up, the stick was pulled back; to nose over, it was pushed forward. Sidewise motion of the stick banked the plane gently (and not always very effectively) in the direction in which the stick was moved. There were two rudder pedals—one for each foot. Pressure on the left pedal tended to move the plane's nose toward the left; kicking the right slewed the nose to the right. There was a little wheel rigidly fixed to the top of the stick to make the control column easy to grasp with either hand. Except for this wheel, the control system Blériot perfected for No. XI subsequently became the most widely adopted of all the many varieties that sprang up with the different inventors. Although most modern aircraft use a yoke instead of a stick, the movements are still the same as those developed by Blériot.

In 1908 the London *Daily Mail* offered a prize of £500 (approximately $2,500) for the first flight across the English Channel. With this prize, Lord Northcliffe, owner of the *Daily Mail,* hoped to stimulate interest in aviation in his country, which then lagged far behind France and the United States. No takers came forward that year, and in 1909 Lord Northcliffe upped the ante to £1,000.

The first to make a bid for this prize was Hubert Latham, a dashing young Frenchman of English descent, who had just learned to fly an Antoinette in April. Latham was backed heavily by the Antoinette's builder, Léon Levavasseur, who saw in the Channel crossing a good opportunity to popularize his airplane. They went to Calais in the first week of July and set up headquarters in the nearby village of Sangatte.

Summer weather in the Straits of Dover, where the English Channel narrows between Dover and Calais, is notoriously nasty and unpredictable. The big, graceful-looking Antoinette was strictly a fair-weather aircraft. No one dared to fly if there was the merest whisper of a wind, because of its lack of control. For two weeks after Latham and Levavasseur arrived on the coast it was either windy and raining or locked in with fog. There was nothing they could do.

Blériot was apparently in no great hurry to go up to Calais and wait for good weather. On July 13, he made a long 25-mile cross-country flight from Étampes to Orléans which won him a $900 Aéro Club prize. However, his engine caught fire en route and his left leg was badly burned by the flaming gasoline that blew back into the cockpit.

To the great disappointment of holiday crowds that had gathered at Calais on July 14 to celebrate Bastille Day with a glimpse

The first attempt to fly the English Channel resulted in this safe, but damp and ignominious, ditching for Hubert Latham.

of Latham conquering the Channel, it was raining again. A second contestant, Count Charles de Lambert, now arrived on the scene with two Wright biplanes that he had just purchased and the excitement began to mount among the contestants and their entourages, although the throng of spectators had begun to melt away. But many remained, confident of some action before too long.

At dawn on the morning of July 19, the weather finally began to break. Rain gave way to drizzle, which tapered off by 5 A.M. The wind died down, the Channel was calm, and a French Navy ship headed out to sea to stand by for any emergencies along the route of the flight. At 6:42 Latham took off and just at that moment the sun broke through, bathing his graceful Antoinette in golden light.

" 'Thankful to be able to start at last.' That was my thought," Latham later told the *Daily Mail* in a long and colorful exclusive interview:

There also came into my mind the idea that it would have been better had there been fewer spectators—in case of failure. My ear told me that the motor, which had been started a minute or so before, was working splendidly. And then I was away.

There was a short, swift run down the slope towards the sea, and I launched myself into the air. My last thought was one of confidence that my motor would not leave me in the lurch. The start could not have been more auspicious. I left the ground in infinitely better style than was the case with my trial flight on the previous Tuesday. Instead of wobbling on getting into the air, I went up with perfect steadiness. I flew so well, indeed, that I altered my plans. Instead of describing a circle, as I had meant to do, I went straight off over the edge of the cliff. First, however, so as to judge my height from the ground, I steered over the ruined Channel tunnel workings. I estimated that I was then six hundred feet above the level of the water and . . . my motor was showing signs of breaking down. I could hear that more than one of the eight cylinders were misfiring.

I did everything I could to remedy the defect. I examined all the electrical connections that were within my reach. I tried also to alter the carburetion and ignition of the engine. But it was all in vain; in a few seconds my engine had stopped entirely. It was maddening, but I was helpless. Never before had the engine played me such a trick. After so short a flight.

At the moment my motive power was taken from me I estimate that I was quite 1,000 ft. up in the air . . . I took a quick glance ahead and calculated that the torpedo-boat destroyer was about a mile away. Then I glided down to the surface of the water. There was nothing else to be done. I came down, not in a series of short glides, but in one clean, straight, downward slope. It seemed quite a long time to me before I struck the water. My speed at the moment of impact was about forty or forty-five miles an hour.

The machine was under perfect control during the descent. Instead of diving into the sea at an angle I skimmed down so that I was able to make the contact with the sea with the aeroplane practically in a horizontal position. It settled on the water and floated like a cork. I swung my feet up on to a cross-bar to prevent them getting wet. Then I took out the cigarette case, lit a cigarette, and waited for the torpedo-boat destroyer to come up. The wings and tail of the machine supported it in the water. It floated almost flat, although the weight of the motor made the front part tilt down a little. I did not even get wet; only a splash of water flew over me at the moment of impact with the sea. The torpedo-boat destroyer was alongside me in less than five minutes.

Latham's plane was salvaged, but it was so badly damaged in the process that it could not be repaired right away. Levavasseur wired his factory to send another Antoinette to Calais immediately. It was ready for Latham by July 23. In the meantime, Louis Blériot, on crutches and recovering slowly from his burn, had arrived and was tuning up his No. XI monoplane in another nearby little town, Les Baraques. The third contestant, Count de Lambert, dropped out of the race after wrecking one of his Wright airplanes on a test flight.

A gale kept Latham and Blériot on the ground on July 24 and it looked very unlikely that a break would come the next day. For some reason, Alfred Le Blanc, a business associate of Blériot who had come along to help, had a sleepless night and finally got up in the early hours of the morning of July 25. It seemed to him that the weather was improving, so he awakened Blériot. While Latham and his crew slept on, Blériot and Le Blanc drove from the hotel in Calais where they stayed to Les Baraques, where the plane was kept in a garage. At 4 A.M. Blériot threw down his crutches and was helped into his plane. "I won't want them again until I come back from England," he told his crew. A few minutes later he took off. He made a fifteen-minute trial flight around Calais, then landed at the jumping-off spot for England and waited for the sun to come to fulfill the conditions laid down by the *Daily Mail*, which were that the flight had to take place between sunrise and sunset. What happened next was routine—almost uneventful—but it thrilled the world and meant that things could never again be the same. Here, in Blériot's own words, is his exclusive account for the *Daily Mail* of the first flight across the English Channel:

At 4:30 we could see all around. Daylight had come. M. Le Blanc endeavored to see the coast of England, but could not. A light breeze from the southwest was blowing. The air was clear.

Everything was prepared. I was dressed as I am at this moment, a khaki jacket lined with wool for warmth over my tweed clothes and beneath engineer's suit of blue cotton overalls. My close-fitting cap was fastened over my head and ears. I had neither eaten nor drunk anything since I rose. My thoughts were only upon the flight, and my determination to accomplish it this morning.

4:35! *Tout est prêt!* Le Blanc gives the signal and in an instant I am in the air, my engine making 1,200 revolutions—almost its highest speed—in order that I may get quickly over the telegraph wires along the edge of the cliff. As soon as I am over the cliff I reduce my speed. There is now no need to force my engine.

I begin my flight, steady and sure, towards the coast of England. I have no apprehensions, no sensations, *pas du tout.*

The *Escopette* has seen me. She is driving ahead at full speed. She makes perhaps 42 kilometers (about 26 miles per hour). What matters? I am making at least 68 kilometers (42 miles per hour).

Rapidly I overtake her, travelling at a height of 80 meters (about 260 feet).

The moment is supreme, yet I surprise myself by feeling no exultation. Below me is the sea, the surface disturbed by the wind, which is now freshening. The motion of the waves beneath me is not pleasant. I drive on.

Ten minutes have gone. I have passed the destroyer, and I turn my head to see whether I am proceeding in the right direction. I am amazed. There is nothing to be seen, neither the torpedo-destroyer, nor France, nor England. I am alone. I can see nothing at all—*rien du tout!*

For ten minutes I am lost. It is a strange position, to be alone, unguided, without compass, in the air over the middle of the Channel.

I touch nothing. My hands and feet rest lightly on the levers. I let the airplane take its own course. I care not whither it goes.

For ten minutes I continue, neither rising nor falling, nor

Louis Blériot poses (after tidying up a bit) with his wife and his airplane after successful Channel-crossing flight on July 25, 1909.

turning. And then, twenty minutes after I have left the French coast, I see the green cliffs of Dover, the castle, and away to the west the spot where I intended to land.

What can I do? It is evident that the wind has taken me out of my course. I am almost at St. Margaret's Bay and going in the direction of the Goodwin Sands.

Now it is time to attend to the steering. I press the lever with my foot and turn easily towards the west, reversing the direction in which I am travelling. Now, indeed, I am in difficulties, for the wind here by the cliffs is much stronger, and my speed is reduced as I fight against it. Yet my beautiful aeroplane responds. Still I fly westwards, hoping to cross the harbor and reach the Shakespeare Cliff. Again the wind blows. I see an opening in the cliff.

Although I am confident that I can continue for an hour and a half, that I might indeed return to Calais, I cannot resist the opportunity to make a landing upon this green spot.

Once more I turn my aeroplane, and, describing a half-circle, I enter the opening and find myself again over dry land. Avoiding the red buildings on my right, I attempt a landing; but the wind catches me and whirls me round two or three times.

At once I stop my motor, and instantly my machine falls straight upon the land from a height of 20 meters (65 ft.). In two or three seconds I am safe.

Soldiers in khaki run up, and a policeman. Two of my compatriots are on the spot. They kiss my cheeks. The conclusion of my flight overwhelms me. I have nothing to say, but accept the congratulations of the representatives of *The Daily Mail* and accompany them to the Lord Warden Hotel.

Thus ended my flight across the Channel. The flight could be easily done again. Shall I do it? I think not. I have promised my wife that after a race for which I have entered I will fly no more.

Latham was shattered. Waking up around 4:30 A.M. to see what the weather was like, Levavasseur had seen Blériot fly over the beach and take his departure for England. He quickly got Latham up, but by the time the Antoinette was ready to go the wind was too strong. The Calais correspondent for the *Daily Mail* describes the scene in the Latham camp:

As I look back upon the crowded hours of the morning, I see against a background of radiant faces and enthusiastic crowds a tall, slim figure with bent head and quivering lips and hands clenched in unavailing regret for lost opportunity. It is the figure of Hubert Latham . . . He looked like a man on the verge of a nervous breakdown. His back was curved almost to a hump. There were deep lines around his mouth. His eyes were narrowed to a slit. More than once he brushed away a tear. The extreme tension of the past fortnight had told upon him severely, and this bitter blow coming at the end of it was having its natural, its inevitable effect.

When Latham learned that Blériot had landed safely in England he cabled him: "Cordial congratulations. Hope to follow you soon." Latham tried again on July 29, got a little farther than the first time, but once again was ignominiously forced down in the water with engine trouble.

Blériot was made a Chevalier of the Legion of Honor for his flight, and the hero's welcome he received on returning to Paris was not equaled until the lifting of the German siege of the French capital in 1918. For a month he was the world's most famous aviator. But then, at the world's first air meet at Reims in August, a dark-horse entry from America defeated Blériot in the speed contest and showed that he was now ready to seriously challenge the Wrights' domination of American aviation. This was Glenn Curtiss.

1909

Glenn Curtiss was several years younger than both the Wright brothers. But he too was swept up in the excitement that followed the introduction of the modern "safety" bicycle. It could go faster than the old-fashioned high-wheeled kind, much faster, and from his boyhood on, Curtiss was fascinated with speed.

He once said that one of his earliest memories was of watching sled races on the snow-covered hills of his home town, Hammondsport, New York. Other early memories were not as pleasant. Curtiss' father died when he was six. By the time he was fifteen he had dropped out of school to help support his family, which had moved to Rochester so that a deaf sister could go to a special school. Characteristically, Curtiss' first job in Rochester was delivering Western Union telegrams by bicycle. When this petered out, he went to work on an assembly line at the Eastman Kodak Company. Times were hard—boys were being hired at four dollars a week to replace men who had been making twelve dollars.

In 1897, Curtiss was back in Hammondsport, living with his grandmother and working in a bicycle repair shop. He soon established a reputation as a bicycle racer, set up his own shop and began making his own brand of bicycle. For a short time, at least, Curtiss and the Wright brothers were in remarkably similar situations. But Curtiss' quest for speed led him into aviation by quite a different route from the Wrights' painstaking theoretical and experimental work in the realm of flight.

From bicycles Curtiss graduated into motorcycles. He soon perfected a family of lightweight one- and two-cylinder gasoline engines which he mounted on beefed-up bicycle frames. On Memorial Day, 1903, he attracted national attention by winning a hill-climbing contest in New York. At Providence, Rhode Island, he set a world record for single-cylinder motorcycle by doing a mile in fifty-six and two-fifths seconds—60.61 miles per hour. Then he headed south with a trim, low-slung two-cylinder racing motorcycle. On January 28, 1904, at Ormond Beach, Florida, near Daytona, he rode 10 miles in eight minutes, fifty-four and two-fifths seconds to set a world record for two-cylinder motorcycles of 89.07 miles per hour that stood for seven years. Three years later he returned to Ormond Beach and set a mark of 136.3 miles per hour with a monster motorcycle that had an eight-cylinder, 40-horsepower engine.

Any engine light enough to fit on a bike frame and powerful enough to set records was also suitable for aeronautics. In 1904 Curtiss built a two-cylinder, 5-horsepower engine for Thomas S. Baldwin. This was used in the *California Arrow*, the small dirigible that made its debut at the St. Louis Fair and was the first in America to maneuver around in a complete circle. Baldwin ordered more and bigger engines from Curtiss and later the two men worked together on a large dirigible for the U. S. Army.

In 1906 Curtiss tried to sell engines to the Wright brothers. He wrote to them in Dayton and even called them by telephone as he passed through Columbus on business in May. Then by chance he met them in person in September. Baldwin had gone to Dayton to fly a dirigible in a local fair but was having engine trouble and asked Curtiss to come down. While Baldwin and Curtiss were there they stopped by the Wright shop and among other things compared notes on propeller performance with the two brothers. Curtiss picked up some new ideas and redesigned the propellers for Baldwin's airships on the basis of what he learned from the Wrights. But he made no engine sales.

With another promising engine customer it was the other way around. Not only did Dr. Alexander Graham Bell have to take the initiative in contacting Curtiss about an engine, but Curtiss

Alexander Graham Bell believed that controllable, powered flight might be possible with a kite composed of thousands of "tetrahedral" cells.

wasn't too interested in supplying it once he found out what it was for.

For years Dr. Bell had been intrigued by the problems of flight. Many times while working on his famous telephone he had talked with his assistant, Thomas A. Watson, about the possibility of making a machine that flew like a bird. In 1891, Bell contributed $5,000 toward Langley's work. Then Bell himself began a series of experiments with kites of every conceivable kind at his summer home on Cape Breton Island, Nova Scotia. He finally developed a design that he liked. It consisted of hundreds—and sometimes thousands—of small triangular cells which could be arranged in any desired size or shape. The triangular-cell kites were unusually stable in heavy winds and the bigger ones could lift a man. The final step, Bell believed, was the addition of an engine powerful enough to convert the kite from a tethered craft to a free-flying machine.

Dr. Bell ordered his first engine from Curtiss in 1906. The engine did not arrive until a year later, and then it was a lemon—underpowered, overweight and unreliable. Bell ordered another engine, taking the precaution to insist that Curtiss deliver it in person and stick around to show Bell and his colleagues how to operate it, for a fee of twenty-five dollars a day. Curtiss appeared with the engine at Bell's summer home, Beinn Bhreagh (Gaelic for "beautiful mountain"), in July, 1907. He got along well with Mrs. Bell, who, like his own sister, had been deaf since childhood. He also met and soon became absorbed in the aeronautical experimental work being planned and carried out by three young men working with Bell: Canadians F. W. "Casey" Baldwin and J. A. D. McCurdy and U. S. Army Lieutenant Thomas E. Selfridge, who had been detailed to duty with Bell as an official observer by President Theodore Roosevelt.

At Mrs. Bell's suggestion an organization known as the Aerial Experiment Association (AEA) was formed and formally chartered on October 1, 1907. It consisted of Bell, Baldwin, McCurdy, Selfridge and Curtiss, who was given the title of "Director of Experiments" and a salary of $5,000 a year. Mrs. Bell financed the organization with a gift of $20,000 from the sale of some inherited real estate. The goal of the group was to build a successful, man-carrying flying machine.

The Wrights, of course, had already accomplished this four years before and had brought their 1905 biplane to a high degree of performance. And in Europe many had either made their first short, tentative hops or were just about to. In spite of the amount of trial and error as well as good experimental work that had been done by this time, the AEA practically began again from scratch.

The group's first project was the completion of a huge man-carrying kite which was 42.5 feet across and almost 10 feet deep. It contained 3,393 triangular cells and was fitted with three floats so that it could be towed behind a motorboat until airborne. The big kite was christened the *Cygnet* and was flown successfully with no one aboard it on December 3. Three days later the *Cygnet* was pulled aloft by the steamboat with Lieutenant Selfridge hanging on. After seven minutes' flight time the wind died down. The speed of the motorboat was not enough to keep the kite up and it fell into the bay and broke up. Selfridge struggled free of the wreckage in the ice-cold water, was rescued by the tow boat and was soon restored to good spirits by a couple of stiff drinks and a brisk rubdown in the motorboat's warm cabin.

Selfridge reported to the group that evening that the kite had been steady while airborne, but seemed sluggish. Though Dr. Bell still felt that the possibilities of the kite approach to a flying machine had not been exhausted, the five men agreed to try a powered biplane as their next major project. To get some actual flying practice before trying out the powered aircraft, they also decided to build a Chanute-type biplane glider in which control was to be maintained by the now obsolete method of shifting the pilot's weight.

With winter approaching, the AEA transferred its operations from Nova Scotia to Hammondsport, where the weather was less severe and the facilities in Curtiss' shop more suitable for their plans. The glider was completed by mid-January and worked well, giving the four younger men a chance to make many short flights in the next two months from the hills around Hammondsport.

Selfridge was elected project director for the AEA's first self-propelled aircraft and was charged with designing it and supervising its construction. One of the first things he did was write a letter to the Wrights to get some information on basic aerodynamics. He also asked them for advice on how to construct ribs in the wings of an aircraft. The Wrights answered the question on aerodynamics and referred Selfridge to some technical papers they had published and to the specifications of one of the patents they had obtained. Curtiss' contribution was a 40-horsepower air-cooled V-8 engine that powered a single pusher propeller.

The wings of the new plane were covered with red silk left over from some of Dr. Bell's kites, and it was thus named *Red*

Wing. The first and only flight with *Red Wing* was made by Casey Baldwin on March 12, 1908. After a run of 100 to 150 feet over the frozen surface of nearby Lake Keuka, Baldwin climbed to a height of about 10 feet and covered a distance of 319 feet before a tail strut buckled and forced him down. But there was an even more serious deficiency in *Red Wing* than just a weak tail strut: with neither wing warping nor ailerons, it lacked any form of lateral control. On its next trial, with Baldwin again aboard, a gust of wind caught the aircraft. It tipped over on its side and crashed during takeoff. Baldwin was uninjured, but *Red Wing* was damaged beyond repair.

The Association's second powered aircraft was begun right away. It used the same engine as *Red Wing*, but was called *White Wing* because Dr. Bell's supply of red silk was now used up and the new plane's wings were covered with lightweight white cotton lingerie fabric. Dr. Bell suggested movable control surfaces at the wing tips as a way to provide lateral control. He was unaware that these forerunners of the modern aileron had already been tried by Blériot and other French pioneers, and he believed for some time that he was the inventor of this device. At any rate, *White Wing* was the first flyable aircraft in the United States to appear with rudimentary ailerons and it marked a turning point in U. S. aircraft design that would ultimately lead to the obsolescence of the Wrights' wing-warping method of lateral control.

Until it crashed, *White Wing* was relatively successful. It first flew for 279 feet with Baldwin at the controls on May 18. The next day Selfridge made two short flights with it. On May 21, Glenn Curtiss made his debut as an aviator with a fine flight of 1,017 feet during which he demonstrated his control of the aircraft by making gentle turns. It was also the first plane that McCurdy flew. But he didn't quite get the feel of the aileron control and when a wing got down after covering some 500 feet he couldn't get it back up. The wing tip struck the ground, then the nose, and the aircraft came to rest upside down. Once again there was no injury, though this had been a close call.

The members of the AEA went to work quickly to build another aircraft. Curtiss was appointed project director for this plane and came up with a design that was similar to *White Wing* and used the same engine again. Slight changes were made in the wing-tip ailerons, the engine and the pilot's seat were moved farther apart for better balance, and the dimensions of the wings, the rudder and the forward elevator were altered slightly. But the machine was basically a rebuilt *White Wing*—in fact, the undamaged cotton fabric from *White Wing* provided most of the covering for this third airplane.

Three attempts were made to fly the new craft on June 20, but it gave no sign of wanting to get off the ground. The experimenters took a closer look at the fabric they had used to cover the wings, decided it was too light and porous, and doped it with paraffin dissolved in gasoline. They also cut down the size of the propeller by three inches in the hope that a smaller and lighter propeller would produce more revolutions per minute.

These changes worked and on June 21 Glenn Curtiss made flights of 456, 417 and 1,266 feet. The new plane reminded Dr. Bell of the way a June bug darted about; so, henceforth, *June*

Glenn Curtiss and the *June Bug* dash down a country road in 1908.

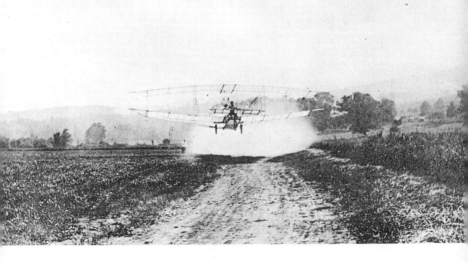

Bug it was called. In the next few flights, trouble with porosity again developed when the paraffin dope began cracking and peeling. A new varnish, pigmented with yellow ochre for picture-taking purposes, was applied and Curtiss now began having difficulty holding the *June Bug* down. Larger control surfaces were installed to keep the plane from zooming up too fast, and on the evening of June 25, Curtiss flew 3,420 feet at 38.9 miles per hour at a height of about 20 feet off the ground. The members of the AEA decided immediately to enter the *June Bug* as a contender for a trophy sponsored by *Scientific American* magazine for the first aircraft to make a public flight of one kilometer (3,281 feet).

Scientific American was in an awkward position. Then, as now, one of the country's leading scientific journals, it had been slow to recognize the work of the Wright brothers. As late as January, 1906, *Scientific American* had been skeptical of reports about the Wrights' long flights in 1905, its editorial board feeling that if the reports were true, then certainly the enterprising American press would have given them great attention. When the reports persisted, the magazine finally obtained confirmation by letter from many reputable people who had witnessed actual flights. On April 7, 1906, *Scientific American* reprinted a letter from one of the witnesses in full and in its December 15 issue the magazine stated its complete acceptance of the facts about the Wright flights, adding: "In all the history of invention, there is probably no parallel to the unostentatious manner in which the Wright brothers of Dayton, Ohio, ushered into the world their epoch-making invention of the first successful aeroplane flying-machine."

From then on *Scientific American* devoted a great deal of space to the rapid progress in aviation and on September 14, 1907, it offered its trophy for the first public flight of one kilometer, fully expecting the Wrights to come forward and win it easily. When they showed no interest by the following summer, the magazine's publisher, Charles A. Munn, wrote on June 4, asking the Wrights to make a bid for the trophy when Orville came to Washington for the Army trials. Shortly thereafter, the Aerial Experiment Association notified the magazine that Curtiss would like to make a try for the trophy at Hammondsport on July 4 with the *June Bug*. Publisher Munn wrote to Orville one more time on June 25, offering to stall Curtiss long enough for Orville to enter a Wright plane in the competition. But this would have meant modifying the aircraft Orville was getting ready for the Army trials so that it did not require the launching rail—*Scientific American* insisted, as one of its conditions for winning the trophy, that the takeoff be completely unassisted—and Orville wrote back that while the Wright planes could easily be fixed to take off on skids or wheels alone, he didn't have time to make the necessary changes before the Army trials. So *Scientific American* now had no alternative but to sanction the Curtiss bid, knowing full well that Curtiss was not the best qualified.

Curtiss seemed to have a flair for publicity and made the most of the opportunity offered by the trophy flight. A large delegation of prominent personalities in the aviation field showed up, including Octave Chanute's assistant A. M. Herring, Langley's intrepid test pilot Charles Manly, and dirigible pilot Thomas Baldwin. Curtiss recalled the big day in a short autobiography a few years later:

When Independence Day finally dawned it did not look auspicious for the first official aeroplane flight for a trophy. Clouds boded rain and there was some wind. This did not deter the entire population of Hammondsport from gathering on the heights around the flying field, under the trees in the valley and, in fact, at every point of vantage. Some were on the scene as early as five o'clock in the morning and many brought along baskets of food and made a picnic of it. The rain came along toward noon, but the crowd hoisted its umbrellas or sought shelter under the trees and stayed on. Late in the afternoon the sky cleared and it began to look as if we were to have the chance to fly after all. The *June Bug* was brought out of its tent and the motor given a try-out. It worked all right. The course was measured and a flag put up to mark the end. Everything was ready and about seven o'clock in the evening the motor was started and I climbed into the seat. When I gave the word to "let go" the *June Bug* skimmed along over the old racetrack for perhaps two hundred feet and then rose gracefully into the air. The crowd set up a hearty cheer, as I was told later—for I could hear nothing but the roar of the motor and I saw nothing except the course and the flag marking a distance of one kilometer. The flat was quickly reached and passed and still I kept the aeroplane up, flying as far as the open fields would permit, and finally coming down safely in a meadow fully a mile from the starting place . . . I might have gone a good deal farther as the motor was working beautifully and I had the machine under perfect control, but to have prolonged the flight would have meant a turn in the air or passing over a number of large trees.

There was no question about it. Curtiss had won the *Scientific American* Trophy. But compared to what the Wrights had done so far, Curtiss was still a long way from catching up. Twice more in July after the trophy flight he tried to make a circular flight in the *June Bug*, but the best he could do was a 180-degree turn.

In the meantime, it was McCurdy's turn to design and build an airplane. While Baldwin and Dr. and Mrs. Bell returned to Nova Scotia, McCurdy remained in Hammondsport with Curtiss. They took turns flying the *June Bug* and working on the Association's fourth airplane. After much tinkering they finally coaxed some circular flights out of *June Bug*. On August 29, McCurdy flew a big, sweeping figure eight, remaining airborne about three minutes. Two days later, Curtiss flew a complete circle in two minutes, twenty-eight seconds.

Selfridge, meanwhile, had received orders to Washington to take part in two important aeronautical trials for the U. S. Army Signal Corps. The first was the acceptance test of Thomas Baldwin's big 88-foot dirigible. It was powered by a 30-horsepower Curtiss engine with a propeller designed by Selfridge. Curtiss also came down for these trials and acted as Baldwin's flight engineer. On August 15, with Baldwin at the helm and Curtiss at the throttle, the dirigible passed all its tests in a two-hour flight over the Virginia suburbs and became *U. S. Signal Corps Dirigible Balloon No. 1*. Selfridge was a member of the aeronautical board that officiated at the trials and he was now frontrunner among a small group of interested young Army officers for whatever plums U. S. military aviation might offer.

The next aeronautical event at Fort Myer was the Army's belated first look at a Wright airplane. With Wilbur in France, this was Orville's show completely, and although these Army trials of 1908 were to end in dusty, bone-shattering tragedy, the publicity surrounding them would mark a turning point in the American public's attitude toward flying.

The plane used was a new one built in Dayton and first tested in a short hop of one minute, eleven seconds on September 3 at Fort Myer. In spite of its short duration, this flight made the front page of the New York *Times* and many other newspapers. From then on Orville was big news. Within a week he consistently circled the field for an hour or more and took up Lieutenant Lahm as his first military passenger. Hundreds then thousands of people flocked to the Fort Myer parade ground to see him fly. There was something about standing there with one's feet planted solidly on the turf while he wheeled overhead that finally convinced the skeptics. "How does it feel to be making history?" Orville was asked by Octave Chanute after a record-breaking seventy-minute flight on September 11. "I'm not interested in making history," said Orville. "I'm a good deal more wrapped up in making speed."

There was good reason for Orville to be concerned. Under the conditions laid down by the Army for the trials, the Wrights would get a bonus of ten percent for each additional mile per hour they clocked above the specified acceptance speed of 40 miles per hour. Conversely, they were to be docked ten percent of the $25,000 price for each mile per hour less than 40. Anything below 36 miles per hour would be considered an outright failure to pass the tests. In Orville's only test hop at Fort Myer in which his speed was clocked, it came to just that—36 miles per hour. It was hard to say which would be a worse fate for Orville: losing $10,000 or failing the tests completely.

To improve the performance of the plane, Orville installed a new set of longer propellers after his thirteenth flight at Fort Myer. On September 17, he invited Lieutenant Selfridge to go up with him while he tried out the new props. They made three circles of the field during which everything was "seemingly working much better and smoother than in any former flight," as

Rescuers at Fort Myer raise the remains of the wrecked airplane to get to Orville Wright, who was trapped in his seat, seriously injured. Men at right cluster around Lieutenant Selfridge, whose skull was crushed as he was thrown clear.

Orville later wrote to Wilbur. But then, as they pointed toward Arlington Cemetery at the beginning of their fourth lap, Orville suddenly had serious trouble on his hands:

I heard (or felt) a light tapping in the rear of the machine. A hurried glance behind revealed nothing wrong, but I decided to shut off the power and descend as soon as the machine could be faced in a direction where a landing could be made. This decision was hardly reached, in fact, I suppose it was not over two or three seconds from the time the first taps were heard, till two big thumps, which gave the machine a terrible shaking, showed that something had broken. At this time I thought only of the transmission. The machine suddenly turned to the right and I immediately shut off the power. I then discovered that the machine would not respond to the steering and lateral balancing levers, which produced a most peculiar feeling of helplessness. Yet I continued to push the levers, when the machine suddenly turned to the left (the right wing was rising high in the air) till it faced directly up the field. I reversed the levers to stop the turning and to bring the wings on a level. Quick as a flash, the machine turned down in front and started straight for the ground. Our course for 50 feet was within a very few degrees of the perpendicular. Lieutenant Selfridge up to this time had not uttered a word, though he took a hasty glance behind when the propeller broke, and turned once or twice to look into my face, evidently to see what I thought of the situation. But when the machine turned headfirst for the ground, he exclaimed "Oh! Oh!" in an almost inaudible voice.

I pulled the front lever to its limit, but there was no response in the course of the machine. Thinking that, maybe, something was caught and that the rudder was not completely turned, I released the lever a little and gave another pull, but there was no change. I then looked at the rudder and saw that it was bent to its limit downward, and that the pressure of air on the under side was bulging cloth up between the ribs. The first 50 ft. of that plunge seemed like half a minute, though I can hardly believe that it was over one second at most. The front rudder in that distance had not changed the course more than five or ten degrees. Suddenly just before reaching the ground, probably 25 feet, something changed—the machine began to right itself rapidly. A few feet more, and we would have landed safely.

Selfridge was found lying unconscious a few feet from the wreck, his skull fractured by something he struck as the impact hurled him clear of the crash. Orville was conscious but trapped within the grotesquely crumpled and twisted wreckage of the airplane with a broken leg, four broken ribs and several fractures of the hip. Selfridge died a few hours later without regaining consciousness. He was the first person to lose his life in an airplane accident.

There was no scorn in the newspapers this time as there had been after Langley's crash less than five years before. The Washington *Evening Star* gave a big play to an interview with Major George O. Squier, the senior officer at the trials, who said, "We deplore the accident, but no one who saw the flights of the last four days at Fort Myer could doubt for an instant that the problem of aerial navigation was solved. . . . If Mr. Wright should never again enter an aeroplane his work last week at Ft. Myer will have secured him a lasting place in history as the man who showed the world that mechanical flight was an assured success." Said the New York *Times*, which had once urged Langley not to waste his time attempting to fly: "The indomitable Mr. Orville Wright, we trust, will recover from his injuries, rebuild his machine, and endeavor to overcome the cause of its first undoing." The *Times* editorial concluded on a sobering note: "It is saddening that Lieut. Selfridge may not be the last martyr to the cause."

Orville asked for some of the parts from the wrecked airplane to be brought to his bedside at the hospital at Fort Myer. He deduced that one of the wooden blades of the pusher-type propeller on the right had split, throwing it out of balance and setting up a strong vibration. As the broken propeller wobbled unevenly at about 400 revolutions per minute it loosened the housing in which the propeller shaft rotated, changed position a few inches and cut the main wire stay that braced the tail control surfaces. The plane then plunged out of control into the ground. Orville was hospitalized almost six weeks after the accident, had to hobble around on crutches for another month after he left the hospital, then used a cane for some time after he was off the crutches.

All the members of the Aerial Experiment Association came to Washington for Selfridge's funeral, which was held with full military honors in Arlington Cemetery two days after the crash. A few days later the members of the Association met to decide whether or not to continue their work. With the loss of their colleague and the convincing show put on by Orville Wright, there didn't seem to be much point in continuing the Association's work. However, the remaining members agreed to carry on for six months more in order to give McCurdy a chance to complete and fly his plane. It was already pretty far along and had been christened *Silver Dart* because its wings were covered with balloon cloth that had a shiny silver finish on one side.

The *Silver Dart* was very close in design to its predecessors *Red Wing, White Wing* and *June Bug*. However, its wings were a bit longer and narrower, giving it a slightly more graceful appearance, and its Curtiss-built V-8 water-cooled engine was a bit more powerful, developing 50 horsepower at 1,600 r.p.m. The new plane made its first short test hops, with McCurdy at the controls, at Hammondsport on December 6, 1908. After some more short and generally inconclusive trials, *Silver Dart* was crated and sent off to Nova Scotia, which had once again been designated as the Association's headquarters. On February 23, *Silver Dart*, with McCurdy at the controls, became the first airplane to make a flight in Canada. Arising from the ice of Baddeck Bay after a short run, it flew about half a mile, then landed easily, to the delight of more than a hundred people whose names were recorded as witnesses. The next day McCurdy made a fine flight of four and a half miles, which was the best that any of the Association's four planes had ever done. This made *Silver Dart* a contender, the group felt, for the next leg of the *Scientific American* Trophy, which now called for a flight of 25 kilometers (15.5 miles). A few days later Curtiss went down to New York to formally enter *Silver Dart* in the trophy competition and to go over the rules with officials of the recently organized Aero Club of America, which was to conduct the trials on behalf of *Scientific American*. But he soon stumbled onto something even more intriguing.

In November, 1908, an enthusiastic but inexperienced aviation club known as the Aeronautic Society of New York had staged what they called the world's first "public exhibition of flying machines." The show was also unique for another reason—it was the world's only exhibition of flying machines in which none of them were able to fly. In fact, the Aeronautic Society's show was an unparalleled fiasco from beginning to end.

There were three principal attractions. One was a helicopter with twenty electric-fan blades in what looked like a huge set of box springs. A second flying machine—built by a Langley disciple who apparently felt that the old scientist had been on the right track but just hadn't gone far enough—had four sets of wings in tandem, all of them so flimsy that the merest breeze fluttered and wrinkled their covering. Finally there was an immense, bulky biplane that stood 10 or 12 feet tall and looked as if it might have gotten off the ground if 500-horsepower engines had been available in those days.

These three machines were excused from flying on the grounds that they weren't completed yet. That left a special collection of kites that the Society had assembled for the exhibition. But the wind was never strong enough to try them out. And then the hydrogen-generating apparatus for the balloons broke down and none of these could be launched. Finally a manned kite was pulled aloft behind an automobile with a teen-aged boy in it, but it crashed, putting the boy in the hospital with a broken ankle. On the plus side, a Harvard professor demonstrated a man-sized tricycle propelled by a fan, someone made one ascension in a Montgolfier-type hot-air balloon and there were motorcycle races.

Oddly enough, the exhibition was a financial success, drawing some twenty thousand people to the old race track at Morris Park where it was held. If the Society could do this well without actually flying, the members reasoned, it might stir up even more interest if it had an airplane that could make some real flights. The Society contacted Curtiss in January, 1909, about building a plane, and when he visited New York to discuss the entry of the *Silver Dart* in the *Scientific American* Trophy competition, he firmed up a deal with the Aeronautic Society in which he agreed to build an airplane for the organization for $5,000. He promised that it would be ready in May.

The news of this transaction came as a disappointment to Dr. Bell and the remaining members of the Aerial Experiment Association, for it meant that Curtiss had lost interest in the Association's work and was charting a new and independent course for himself. It also meant the end of the Association's hopes of capturing the *Scientific American* Trophy with *Silver Dart*. Since its first successes the plane had developed engine trouble and without Curtiss there was little chance of clearing it up. The *Silver Dart* was withdrawn from the competition in the middle of March, and on March 31 the Aerial Experiment Association quietly came to an end at a nostalgic evening at Dr. Bell's Nova Scotia home which Curtiss did not attend.

With the order for his first plane in his pocket, Curtiss joined forces with Octave Chanute's protégé A. M. Herring, who was instrumental in attracting some $300,000 capital from New York financial interests. They founded a new firm, the Herring-Curtiss Company, and made their headquarters at Curtiss' shop in Hammondsport. By early June, Curtiss had completed and was test-flying the airplane destined for the Aeronautic Society of New York.

The new plane differed in two important details from its AEA predecessors. Its biplane wings were trussed and braced to make them stronger and to eliminate the less efficient bowed wings which were characteristic of all the earlier AEA planes. Then, instead of hinged control surfaces at the wing tips, Curtiss introduced small ailerons placed between the top and bottom wings out toward each wing tip. These movable control surfaces were not only much easier to manipulate than the Wright wing-warping system, but they also permitted a stronger, more rigid wing construction. This latter characteristic would make it possible, in a short time, for Curtiss planes to catch up with and surpass the performance of Wright-built planes. For without the need to warp the wings of his planes, Curtiss could pick a fast, efficient airfoil shape and make his wing so sturdy that it would hold its shape. On the other hand, the warped wing of the Wrights, while perfectly adapted for slow speeds, could not be built strong enough to hold its shape at higher speeds and still be flexible enough to provide control through warping.

While a substantial improvement over the others Curtiss had worked on, the new plane for the Aeronautic Society was, as yet, no threat to the Wrights. After testing it at Hammondsport, Curtiss brought it to New York and made several more test hops on the straightway at the Morris Park race track. Curtiss is generally credited with making the first airplane flight in New York City on June 26, when he succeeded in making a turn around the race track at an Aeronautic Society exhibition. After this flight, the Society was ready and eager to buy the plane from Curtiss, but he stalled, for he now had something else in mind.

Unknown to the public, Curtiss had been building a second airplane at Hammondsport which he wanted to enter in the Gordon Bennett speed races to be held at Reims, France, in August:

I began . . . to build an eight-cylinder, V-shaped, fifty-horse-power motor [Curtiss recalled later]. This was practically double the horsepower I had been using. Work on the motor was pushed day and night at Hammondsport, as I had not an hour to spare. I had kept pretty close watch on everything that had been printed about the preparations for the Gordon Bennett race and although it was reported that Blériot, in his own monoplane, and Hubert Latham, in an Antoinette monoplane, had flown as fast as 60 miles an hour, I still felt confident. The speed of aeroplanes is so often exaggerated in press accounts that I did not believe all I read about Blériot's and Latham's trial flights.

To win the Gordon Bennett, Curtiss not only needed a fast plane, but also had to know how to fly it. Prior to coming to New York with the new plane for the Aeronautic Society, Curtiss' total flight time was just a few seconds more than fifteen minutes, almost all of this in the *June Bug*. And so, while the finishing touches were being put on the second plane at Hammondsport, Curtiss decided to get as much practice as he could get away with in the Aeronautic Society's plane. He also picked up some more prizes and got some good publicity. On July 17, just a little more than a year after the *Scientific American* Trophy flight of the *June Bug*, Curtiss won the trophy a second time at Mineola, Long Island. The conditions for winning the trophy became stiffer each year; in 1909, it was to be presented for the longest officially observed flight over 25 kilometers (15.5 miles). Curtiss covered almost 25 miles in nineteen circuits of a 1.3-mile triangu-

The crowd that turned out for the Reims Meet dressed as elegantly as for a day at the races.

lar course. His average speed was a little less than 30 miles per hour. In a much shorter flight earlier in the day he won a $250 prize offered to the first four pilots who could fly one kilometer. He made many other practice flights at Mineola besides these two for the prizes and also gave Aeronautic Society members Charles F. Willard and Alexander Williams some lessons in how to fly. Just before he sailed for France, Curtiss formally turned over the plane to the Aeronautic Society. This was the first sale of an airplane in the United States.

Coming shortly after Blériot's sensational Channel flight, the Reims meet absorbed the attention of Europe during the last two weeks of August, almost to the exclusion of everything else happening at the time. The "Grande Semaine d'Aviation de la Champagne," as the air meet was called in honor of the champagne industry, which sponsored it, attracted huge crowds to the race track at Béthney plains near Reims. There were some 200,000 paid admissions to the fairgrounds during the week of aviation events and it was estimated that 100,000 more watched the flights from nearby hills. Though Curtiss was the only American aviator on hand, virtually everyone else in the European aeronautical world showed up either to watch or to fly. It was also an excellent opportunity for political leaders to observe and evaluate the progress of the new science. Among those who came for a look was Britain's Chancellor of the Exchequer, David Lloyd George, who was accompanied by the President of the Board of Trade, a young man named Winston Churchill. Said Lloyd George: "I felt rather ashamed that the English are so hopelessly behind." But he reassured Britons: "As to the use of the aeroplane in warfare it appears too frail and flimsy to be taken seriously and I apprehend no danger of any airship invasion."

In those days the general public's interest in aviation was simple and unsophisticated. People wanted to know how fast a plane could go, how high it could climb, how long it could stay up and whether the pilot would get killed. The sponsors of the Reims meet thus offered substantial prizes for speed, altitude and endurance, and the French press encouraged the aviators to be daring. This was hardly necessary with such men as Blériot, Latham, Farman and Curtiss, who emerged as the principal contenders among some twenty-five entrants.

Curtiss arrived with an airplane that had never been flown and an engine that had not been installed and tried out in the plane, though it had been run on a test stand. The speed competition appealed to him most, and, though sorely tempted, he decided to forgo any attempts to win the altitude and endurance prizes and to concentrate instead on speed. "I had just one aeroplane and one motor," he said. "If I smashed either of these it would be all over with America's chances in the first International Cup Race. I had not the reserve equipment to bring out a new machine as fast as one was smashed, as Blériot and other Frenchmen had. Incidentally, there were many smashed during the big meet on the plains of Bétheny. At one time, while flying, I saw as many as twelve machines strewn about the field, some wrecked and some disabled and being hauled slowly back to the hangars, by hand or by horses."

Louis Blériot was flying a souped-up monoplane with a tremendous eight-cylinder, 80-horsepower rotary engine. "When I learned this, I believed my chances were very slim indeed, if in fact they had not entirely disappeared," said Curtiss. Hubert Latham, another French favorite, also made a serious bid for the speed prize in an Antoinette, but from the start of the meet it was obvious to Glenn Curtiss that the fight would be between him and Blériot:

In the try-outs it became evident to the Frenchman that my aeroplane was very fast and it was conceded that the race for the Gordon Bennett Cup would lie between Blériot and myself, barring accidents. After a carefully timed trial circuit of the course, which, much to my surprise, I made in a few seconds less than M. Blériot's time, and that too with my motor throttled down slightly, I gained more confidence. I removed the large gasoline tank from my machine and put on a smaller one in order to lessen the weight and the head-resistance. I then selected the best of my three propellers, which, by the way, were objects of curiosity to the French aviators, who were familiar only with the metal blades used on the Antoinette machine, and the Chauvière, which was being used by M. Blériot. M. Chauvière was kind enough to make a propeller especially fitted to my aeroplane, notwithstanding the fact that a better propeller on my machine would lessen the chances of the French flyers for the cup. However, I decided later to use my own propeller, and did use it—and won.

August 28 dawned hot and clear. It was agreed at a meeting of the Committee, at which all the contestants were present, that each contestant should be allowed to make one trial flight over the course and that he might choose his own time for making it, between the hours of ten o'clock in the morning and six o'clock in the evening. The other starters were Blériot, Lefebvre, and Latham for France, and Cockburn for England. As I have already stated, Blériot was the favorite because of his trip across

Serious and unsmiling, Glenn Curtiss raced to an upset victory at Reims.

the English Channel and because of his records made in flights at various places prior to the Reims meet.

As conditions were apparently good, I decided to make my trial flight shortly after ten o'clock. The machine was brought out, the engine given a preliminary run, and at half past ten I was in the air. Everything had looked good from the ground, but after the first turn of the course I began to pitch violently. This was caused by the heat waves rising and falling as the cooler air rushed in. The up and down motion was not at all pleasant and I confess that I eased off on the throttle several times on the first circuit. I had not then become accustomed to the feeling an aviator gets when the machine takes a sudden drop. On the second round I got my nerve back and pulled the throttle wide open and kept it open. This accounts for the fact that the second lap was made in faster time than the first. The two circuits were made safely, and I crossed the finish line in seven minutes, 55 seconds, a new record for the course.

Now was my chance! I felt that the time to make the start for the cup was then, in spite of the boiling air conditions, which I had found existed all over the course and made flying difficult if not actually dangerous. We hurriedly refilled the gasoline tank, sent official notice to the judges, carefully tested the wiring of the machine by lifting it at the corners, spun the propeller, and the official trial was on. I climbed as high as I thought I might without protest, before crossing the starting line—probably five hundred feet—so that I might take advantage of a gradual descent throughout the race and thus gain additional speed. The sun was hot and the air rough, but I had resolved to keep the throttle wide open. I cut the corner as close as I dared and banked the machine high on the turns. I remember I caused great commotion among a big flock of birds which did not seem to be able to get out of the wash of my propeller. In front of the tribunes the machine flew steadily, but when I got around on the back stretch, as we would call it, I found remarkable air conditions. There was no wind, but the air seemed fairly to boil. The machine pitched considerably, and when I passed above the "graveyard," where so many machines had gone down and were smashed during the previous days of the meet, the air seemed literally to drop from under me. It was so bad at one point that I made up my mind that if I got over it safely I would avoid that particular spot thereafter.

Finally, however, I finished the 20 kilometers in safety and crossed the line in 15 minutes, 50 seconds, having averaged 46½ miles an hour. When the time was announced there was great enthusiasm among the Americans present, and everyone rushed over to offer congratulations. Some of them thought that I would surely be the winner, but of this I was by no means certain. I had great respect for Blériot's ability, and besides, Latham and his Antoinette might be able to make better speed than they had thus far shown. In a contest of this sort it is never safe to cheer until all the returns are in. I confess that I felt a good deal like a prisoner awaiting the decision of a jury. I had done my best, and had got the limit of speed out of the machine; still I felt that if I could do it all over again, I would be able to improve on the time. Meantime, Cockburn, for England, had made a start but had come down and run into a haystack. He was only able to finish the course in 20 minutes, 47⅗ seconds. This put him out of the contest.

Latham made his trial during the afternoon but his speed was five or six miles an hour slower than my record. The other contestants were flying about 35 miles an hour and were, therefore, not really serious factors in the race.

It was all up to M. Blériot. All day long he tinkered and tested, first with one machine and then another; trying different propellers and making changes here and there. It was not until late in the afternoon that he brought out his big machine, Number 22, equipped with an eight-cylinder water-cooled motor, mounted beneath the planes (wings), and driving by chain a four-bladed propeller, geared to run at a speed somewhat less than that of the engine. He started off at what seemed to be a terrific burst of speed. It looked to me as if he must be going twice as fast as my machine had flown; but it must be remembered that I was very anxious to have him go slow. The fear that he was beating me was father to the belief.

As soon as Blériot was off, Mr. Cortlandt Field Bishop and Mr. David Wolfe Bishop, his brother, took me in their automobile over to the judges' stand. Blériot made the first lap in faster time than I had made it, and our hearts sank. Then and there I resolved that if we lost the cup I would build a faster aeroplane and come back next year to win it.

Again Blériot dashed past the stand and it seemed to me that he was going even faster than the first time. Great was my surprise, therefore, when, as he landed, there was no outburst of cheers from the great crowd. I had expected a scene of wild enthusiasm, but there was nothing of the sort. I sat in Mr. Bishop's automobile a short distance from the judges' stand, wondering why there was no shouting, when I was startled by a shout of joy from my friend, Mr. Bishop, who had gone over to the judges' stand.

"You win! You win!" he cried, all excitement as he ran toward the automobile. "Blériot is beaten by six seconds!"

A few moments later, just at half past five o'clock, the Stars and Stripes were slowly hoisted to the top of the flagpole and we stood uncovered while the flag went up. There was scarcely a response from the crowded grand stands; no true Frenchman had the heart to cheer.

As if to rub it in, Curtiss won a second speed prize the following day, the last of the Meet, by flying three laps around the race

On the final day of the Reims Meet, Louis Blériot's plane crashed and burned spectacularly, but he escaped with minor injuries.

track in twenty-five minutes, forty-nine and two-fifths seconds. This win was due as much to Blériot's bad luck as anything else. On the first lap, the Frenchman's rudder failed to respond. Said one eyewitness: "His monoplane turned completely over three times, landed with such force that the petrol tank burst and, catching fire from the hot motor, enveloped the machine and pilot in flames. Before Blériot could extricate himself, he was burned about the face and hands but fortunately not seriously."

All in all, the Reims Meet had been quite a show.

1910: i

In the midst of all the excitement stirred up by Blériot's Channel crossing, the Reims Meet and other public flights of 1909, another development was taking place, almost unnoticed, that would have a profound effect on the course of aviation. This was the emergence of airplanes that could carry two or more people. With them, one man could teach another to fly much more easily. And when this happened, it was almost inevitable that a new crowd would come along and eclipse the glamour of the world's first generation of fliers.

The first two-seat airplanes were those demonstrated by the Wrights in 1908 at Fort Myer and in France. Orville carried passengers several times at Fort Myer prior to the crash that killed Lieutenant Selfridge, but it was Wilbur, riding on the crest of the great French ground swell of interest in aviation, who really stirred up a rage to fly. People came from Paris to Le Mans in such great numbers to see Wilbur in action that a grateful local bus company was moved to suggest a banquet in his honor because of the extra business he had created. He carried many notables up for rides in the fall of 1908, including his first woman passenger, Mrs. Hart O. Berg, the wife of the Wrights' business representative in Europe. In the fashion of the day, she wore a long, ankle-length skirt, which her husband gathered and tied with a rope to keep it from billowing immodestly in the wind. Wilbur also took up the first Englishman to fly, Griffith Brewer, on October 8, an interesting indication of just how far England trailed the United States and France in the development of the airplane.

Wilbur's first student pilots were three Frenchmen whom he contracted to teach under the terms of the agreement with the French syndicate. These men were Count Charles de Lambert, Paul Tissandier and Captain Paul-Nicolas Girardville. They all got their first rides in the fall, but Wilbur was so busy making demonstration flights and taking other eager passengers up that he was unable to devote much time to his students until he moved his headquarters to Pau in early 1909.

Altogether, Wilbur made fifty flights at Pau. He was the pilot on forty of these and was the passenger of one or the other of his students on the other ten. By the end of March his three students had all soloed. Count de Lambert later put in an appearance at the Channel-crossing competition in July, 1909, and subsequently made a famous flight over the city of Paris. But aside from this Paris flight, Wilbur's first three pupils turned out to be cautious men who stirred aviation circles very little. Both de Lambert and Tissandier raced in Wright planes at the Reims Meet but turned in lackluster performances and were outclassed by Curtiss, Blériot, Latham and Farman. Girardville dropped out of sight soon after his training with Wilbur Wright.

Before returning home to Dayton in May, 1909, Wilbur Wright taught one more pilot to fly in Europe, a lieutenant in the Italian Navy named Mario Calderara. Wilbur gave him twenty-three training flights, but never felt quite right about him—for reasons that had nothing to do with his flying ability. Said Wilbur: "I left him with greater misgivings than my other pupils because he was a cigarette fiend." It came as no surprise to Wilbur to learn later that Calderara had had an accident, though it had nothing whatsoever to do with his smoking.

In his last weeks in Europe, Wilbur was joined by Orville, still hobbling about on a cane, and their sister Katharine. They returned to a staggering welcome in the United States after their conquest of the Continent. The brothers were awarded medals by President William Howard Taft in Washington and were feted in New York. Dayton declared June 17 and 18 holidays in their honor. The celebration featured bands, parades, fireworks, and a very moving moment when Bishop Milton Wright, then eighty years old, gave the invocation at ceremonies at which his two sons received a special medal from the United States Congress, another from the Ohio legislature and still a third from the city of Dayton.

But there was much to be done, and the day after the celebration ended the brothers caught the overnight train to Washington, where a new airplane awaited them for another go at the Army contract.

The new plane, the only one of its kind that the Wrights made, was slightly smaller and lighter than the model flown in France and at Fort Myer the previous year. It was balky at first—on one flight the engine quit and the machine sailed into a dead tree, ripping the covering off the bottom wing and breaking seven ribs. But soon the brothers had the bugs worked out of their plane. On Tuesday, July 27—just two days after Blériot crossed the English Channel—Orville satisfied the Army's endurance requirement by flying around the Fort Myer parade ground for one hour, twelve minutes, thirty-seven and four-fifths seconds with Lieutenant Frank Lahm as his passenger. This was also a new world endurance record for a flight with a passenger. All that now remained was to meet the speed requirement, which was the same as in the previous year—an average of 40 miles per hour over a 10-mile course. The penalties and incentives which worried Orville so much in 1908 also remained the same: a loss of ten percent of the purchase price of $25,000 for every mile per hour less than 40, a bonus of ten percent for every mile per hour over.

This time Orville had every reason to be much more confident. He knew his new plane was faster than the old, and after breezing through the endurance test he felt that it was reliable. The Army surveyed a course of five miles out and back from Fort Myer and marked the turning point with a tethered balloon. This was located at Shuter's Hill in Alexandria, Virginia, where an imposing Masonic temple now stands. The man selected as Orville's passenger was Lieutenant Benjamin D. Foulois, a young Signal Corps officer who had observed some of Orville's flights at Fort Myer the previous summer and who also piloted *Dirigible No. 1* many times after Thomas Baldwin sold it to the Army.

The qualifying trip was rather routine. But it was Foulois' first airplane ride and a vivid experience in a remarkable career that carried him to the top as Chief of the Army Air Corps and into the space age as a writer and lecturer until just a few weeks before his death in April, 1967. Here is the way he remembered it:

The 30th of July started off with rain which continued on and off until mid-afternoon when the weather cleared up, and the Wright Brothers informed the Aeronautical Board that they were ready. After the engine had been warmed up, Orville motioned me to take my seat and, after he had comfortably settled in the pilot's seat, he turned to me again with his nice little smile and told me, in effect, that in the event of engine failure he would pick out the thickest clump of trees he could reach and land in them!

We got off at approximately 6:45 P.M. and fortunately for my peace of mind, I was kept so fully occupied with my jobs as Observer and Navigator on the outbound flight that I had not time to worry about a tree-top landing. However, upon reaching the turning point (a captive balloon) at Shuter's Hill, Orville, presumably for the benefit of the ground observers at that point, came in low and rounded the turning point in a steep banking left turn, just missing a small group of trees, and then squared away on the home-bound trip. A fine demonstration of his piloting skill but, as I told him later, a bit too close to the tree tops to suit me. On the home-bound flight, however, we ran into a down trend of air which dropped the airplane to about 25 feet from the tree tops and I began to wonder which clump of trees Orville would pick out for his landing place. The little engine, however, continued to behave and, with the best pilot in the world at the controls, we climbed back to our normal altitude—thence over Arlington Cemetery and in to a perfect landing at Fort Myer, where we were happily greeted by Wilbur Wright who I later learned had experienced a few unhappy moments when the down trend dropped us out of sight on the home-bound flight. I also learned later that, as the airplane arrived over the edge of Arlington Cemetery adjacent to the Fort Myer parade ground, some of the spectators numbering approximately 6 to 8 thousand had voiced their enthusiasm in connection with our safe return.

Judging, however, from my personal experience with the normal crowd of spectators which had thronged about the Fort Myer parade ground during all of the prior test flights, I had no doubt that there were also many bloodthirsty individuals present who returned to their homes sorely disappointed because we failed to land in Arlington Cemetery and thus provide them with a real old fashioned "Roman Holiday" with all its bloody trimmings.

On the trip to Alexandria and back, Wright and Foulois averaged 42.58 miles per hour. This earned the Wrights a bonus of $5,000, bringing the purchase price paid by the Army up to a total of $30,000. The Wright plane was formally accepted by the Army on August 2 and Lahm and Foulois were designated as the first two pilots to receive flight training from Wilbur Wright. To Foulois' great disgust, however, he was soon given orders to go to Europe to observe an international aviation convention, and many weeks passed before he could get into a plane again. Second Lieutenant Frederic E. Humphreys was picked as Foulois' replacement for flight training.

Before the Wrights could go to work with Lahm and Humphreys, they had two more dates to fill. Right after the Army acceptance trials, Orville left again for Europe, where he spent several weeks demonstrating a plane in Germany as part of a business deal to set up a German Wright company similar to the one already established in France. Again, part of the deal included the training of two pilots, German Army Captain Paul Engelhardt and a civilian, Fridolin Keidel. While Orville was in Germany he also took the Crown Prince up for a ride and set a new world altitude record of 1,637 feet.

Meanwhile, Wilbur was booked at a staggering fee to make flights up the Hudson River during New York City's gala Hudson-Fulton Celebration. This event commemorated the three-hundredth anniversary of the discovery of the Hudson River by Henry Hudson in 1609 and the one-hundredth anniversary of the first trips Robert Fulton's steamboat *Clermont* made up the river in 1807. And what if the dates didn't coincide exactly? New Yorkers have never needed much excuse for a wingding, and 1909 was no exception. The celebration began officially on Sep-

As hundreds of thousands of New Yorkers watched, Wilbur Wright flew up the Hudson River from Governor's Island with a canoe strapped beneath his plane in case he was forced down in the water.

tember 25 with a naval parade up the Hudson of forty of the proudest warships from the fleets of the United States, Britain, France, Germany, Mexico, Italy and the Netherlands. This imposing display was followed during the next two weeks by four big parades up Fifth Avenue.

The takeoff spot selected for Wilbur's flights was Governor's Island. Located right off the lower tip of Manhattan, it possessed the dual advantages of being flat and far enough from the jagged rooftops of the city to permit safe takeoffs and landings. Wilbur arrived at Governor's Island on August 20. The next day Glenn Curtiss showed up, fresh from his triumph at Reims. He had also been booked for exhibition flights during the celebration and, since Wilbur had filed an injunction just a month earlier to stop Curtiss from flying because of patent infringement, the confrontation promised to spice up the proceedings at the celebration. Much to the disappointment of all the gathered newspapermen, Wilbur Wright's first meeting with Curtiss was cordial. Since the injunction had not yet been granted, Curtiss was still legally free to fly as he wished and the newspapers speculated hopefully that an exciting aerial competition might still develop between the two men.

But the weather turned bad and, after making short test hops, both men were kept on the ground by high winds. Finally, on the morning of October 4, Wilbur took off with a canoe strapped between his landing skids just in case he landed in the river and wanted to paddle home. He flew 20 miles up the Hudson, turned around the British warship *Drake* which was anchored off Grant's Tomb, and returned to Governor's Island. The flight lasted a little over half an hour and was witnessed by thousands of spectators along the Battery and up the West Side of Manhattan. Wilbur attempted a second flight that afternoon, but his engine exploded while warming up and he called it quits. For the one flight he was paid $15,000. Curtis, despite the damage to his prestige, was reluctant to take a chance in the still strong winds and did not fly at all during the remaining days of the celebration. The Wrights were still the world's leading aviators, and though he had never won any races or competitive prizes, Wilbur reigned over New York, at least, as "King of the Air."

By October 8, Wilbur was back in Washington. He began giving flight instruction to Lahm and Humphreys at a field in College Park, Maryland, and had them both ready for their solos by October 26. During the training flights, Wilbur also experimented with the design of the control surfaces of the 1909 Army flyer. He removed one of the two movable forward "rudders" (elevators) and attached one of them in a fixed position on the tail of the airplane. This seemed to give the plane added stability, and in the next year the forward "rudder" was dispensed with altogether—a transition by which the shaky tail-forward airplane that rose from the sands of Kitty Hawk in 1903 completed its basic evolution to something more closely related to the modern tail-aft configuration.

One late afternoon, while Wilbur was flying with Humphreys,

he stayed up past sunset and thus became the first pilot techni-cally to make a night flight. However, a lingering sunset and a three-quarter moon gave him excellent visibility when he landed, and the question of whether or not an airplane could be landed in darkness remained for someone else to try to answer.

As 1909 drew to a close, there were perhaps three dozen men, mostly French, who had learned to fly an airplane. Orville's altitude record of 1,637 feet still held and the world speed record was still Blériot's fastest lap at Reims, 47.75 miles per hour. This is neither very high nor very fast. (For a good feeling of what it was like to fly an early airplane at these speeds, slow your car to 45 miles per hour on an expressway or other smooth road and look out the side windows.) But the interest in the new sport or science—no one was really sure just what it was—was enormous, and was still growing rapidly.

At this point there was big money to be made in two distinct areas of aviation: in the building and selling of airplanes, and in the fees and prizes from exhibitions, meets and contests. At the Reims Meet alone, fifty-two orders for new airplanes were taken by various manufacturers. In France, Gabriel Voisin, Henri Far-man and Louis Blériot were beginning to turn out standard models to meet this demand, while the recently organized Wright companies in France and Germany were taking orders for foreign-built Wright biplanes. In the United States, Curtiss was now organized for commercial sales, and in November, 1909, "The Wright Company" was formed to build and sell Wright airplanes domestically. Backed by such prominent figures as Cornelius Vanderbilt, August Belmont, Robert J. Collier, Howard Gould and several others, the firm was incorporated with a capital of $200,000. The brothers turned over their patent rights to the new firm and, in exchange, received 40 percent of the stock and a royalty on each new airplane sold. They were expected to con-tinue their experimental work and to exercise general supervision of the company. However, the corporation would take over the responsibility of prosecuting patent infringement cases, and a general manager was to be hired to look out for the day-to-day details of running the company.

After Wilbur's experience at Governor's Island in making

$15,000 for a half-hour flight, it seemed to the brothers that there might be more money, at least in the beginning, in making similar exhibition flights in other parts of the country. Consequently, they decided to concentrate their efforts on exhibition flying rather than manufacturing. The first step they took was to hire Roy Knabenshue as the business manager for their exhibitions. Knabenshue had considerable experience barnstorming with balloons and dirigibles and had attracted the Wrights' attention at the St. Louis Fair of 1904, where his flights in Baldwin's dirigible stamped him "a man possessing qualities placing him in the first rank," in Wilbur's estimation.

The Wrights' next move was to develop a capable group of pilots who could go on tour with several machines and not tie up either brother in what, for them, was essentially unproductive work. The first person hired for this was a twenty-one-year-old Dayton man named Walter Brookins who had hung around the Wright shop as a boy and who had studied under Katharine Wright in public school.

By this time it was midwinter and the weather was too bad around Dayton for the intensive kind of work the Wrights liked to do in training their pilots. So Orville headed south looking for a good place to establish a flying school. On Thursday, March 24, he arrived in Montgomery, Alabama, where, he noted with some satisfaction in his diary, the winds were "not over 4–5 miles at any time." In two days he was up in the air, and before a week had passed, Orville had begun teaching Brookins how to fly from a field where present-day Maxwell Air Force Base is located.

Brookins was trained as a "left-hand pilot." This referred to the arm that operated the all-important wing-warping lever. In the current configuration for the Wright biplane, there were two seats side by side. The right seat (which was actually on the center line of the aircraft in order to balance the weight of the off-center engine and was often called the "center" seat) was intended for the passenger. The left seat was for the pilot. Between the two seats was the wing-warping and rudder-control lever, which the pilot operated with his right arm, thus making most fliers "right-hand pilots." Dual elevator-control levers, working in unison, were located on the outboard sides of both seats.

Orville figured that if he could break Brookins in as a "left-hand" pilot, Brookins could then go on to teach other members of the group to fly in the conventional "right-hand" way. Brookins caught on quickly after his first flight on March 28 and soloed after a total of two and a half hours of instructional flying. Orville returned to Dayton on May 8, leaving Brookins in Alabama with one aircraft and two new students: Arch Hoxsey, an auto-racing friend of Knabenshue's from California, and a Dayton auto driver named Spencer C. Crane, who soon dropped out of the flying lessons.

The flying in Montgomery was good and Brookins and Hoxsey, both of whom were soon to become almost legendary exhibition figures, were natural pilots. They were young, their plane was one of the best in the world at that time and they were on their own with nothing to do but get as much flight time as possible.

As better weather came to Dayton, the flying school was moved back north and established at Huffman Prairie, the same field where the Wrights conducted their great flights of 1904–5. Orville trained a second pilot, A. L. Welsh, a Washingtonian who had become interested in flying when he saw Orville fly at Fort Myer, as another "left-hand" instructor pilot. He also gave some lessons to Duval La Chapelle, a French mechanic who had worked with Wilbur in France in 1908. When Brookins arrived from Alabama, he taught two more men to fly: Frank Coffyn, a young New Yorker whose father was a banker with connections among the stockholders of the Wright Company, and Ralph Johnstone, a trick bicycle rider and circus clown who had attracted Knabenshue's attention on the carnival circuit out West.

Under the Wrights' personal tutelage, it didn't take long to shape this interesting group of men into the exhibition team they wanted. The Wrights were effective instructors as well as first-rate pilots and they took great pains to make sure that no one was allowed to fly who was not fully qualified and able to meet their high standards. They even built a fairly sophisticated flight simulator so that students could practice safely on the ground in between flights with their instructor pilots. This device left a strong impression on one later student, Grover Cleveland Bergdoll (who was to achieve considerable notoriety as a draft

Early students at the Wright flying school and their teacher: (from left) Duval La Chapelle, A. L. Welsh, Orville Wright, Walter Brookins, Ralph Johnstone, Frank Coffyn.

dodger in World War I). He once described his experience with the simulator to aviation writer Alexander McSurely:

I went to Dayton early in 1912 and told Orville I wanted to learn to fly the Wright biplane. He put me on the practice plane, inside the factory building, which was supported on a trestle so that it could tip over to right and left, but could be righted and kept horizontally level if the unnatural method of using the warping lever was correctly applied. I had read of this and was already prepared for this, so I had little trouble in getting used to it. Orville used to come up unexpectedly from behind and suddenly pull down one wing to see if I would react promptly and bring it to the level in the correct manner.

The practice plane was really a Wright biplane which had thousands of flights behind it. It was probably taken out of commission due to its age and need of general overhauling. The motor was taken out, but the propellers were still in place. It was mounted on a kind of wooden trestle which permitted it to tip over from side to side, and would not remain in a horizontal position if left to itself. At the left wingtip there was attached a board about four feet long which pivoted at its center, the plane of the board parallel to [the] plane of the wings. To this were attached the cables from the warping lever. On the floor was a three H. P. electric motor pulling a round belt (on a large pulley) which went over a corresponding pulley, mounted on the rafters of the low roof. The one side of the belt went up and the other side downward, just beside the pivoted board. The motor ran steadily during practice period. When the warping lever was operated the edge of one (or other) end of the board rubbed against the round belt and was lifted or depressed according to whichever way the lever was pulled. This lifted or lowered the left wingtip and so balance could be maintained. It was an improvised affair but did its work very well for years.

In this connection I might mention that there was a student named Southard (from Youngstown, O.) who used to sit in this trainer for days and days at a time and practiced so long that he could finally read a newspaper and keep the wings level without any thought of same. But every time he was up in the air with instructor Al Welsh he invariably pushed or pulled the warping lever in the wrong direction. When they would come down Welsh used to lecture Southard on his mistakes. Southard, on one occasion, replied to Welsh: "Oh, I just wanted to see if you would notice it.

Welsh answered: "*You* sure will notice it when you get up there alone, sometime!"

Southard had more time in the air than any student ever before had and he still could not learn to balance. Finally Welsh told Orville that Southard was a hopeless case and he would waste no more time on him. Then Southard bought a plane from the Wrights; but Orville told him he would not be allowed to fly it until after Orville had given him still more lessons and had okayed him. But one day, when Orville could not be at the field, Southard went out with a friend, broke the lock off the hangar, rolled his new plane out and took off alone. He got no more than 50 feet up when the plane rolled over on one side and skidded to

Frank Coffyn

the ground a total wreck and Southard killed. Evidently he
pulled the warping lever in the wrong direction for the last time.
This student, by the way, had more confidence in his own ability
to fly, yet he could not learn.

While the Wrights were training their exhibition team at Huffman's field in the spring of 1909, they also got in some memorable flights themselves. On Wednesday, May 25, Orville and Wilbur went up together, with Orville piloting. It was the first and only time the two men, who had worked so closely all their lives, ever made a flight in the same airplane. Then Orville took their eighty-one-year-old father up for his first ride. Bishop Wright's only comment while up in the air was, "Higher, Orville, higher!" They flew around at 350 feet for six minutes, fifty-five seconds, according to the old man's diary. A few days earlier Wilbur made an insignificant hop of one minute, twenty-nine seconds, his first since the Governor's Island jaunt. It was also the last in which he was ever to pilot an airplane, for he died of typhoid fever a little over two years later at the age of forty-five without having flown again.

When it came time for the Wright flyers to make their debut as an exhibition team, all were ready except Frank Coffyn, who had not soloed. Knabenshue had booked the team into Indianapolis for a six-day show from June 13 to 18, and that was where Coffyn got his solo—before a crowd of 120,000 spectators. In a remarkable tape-recorded interview for the Columbia Oral History Collection shortly before he died, Coffyn recalled his solo flight and gave a vivid flashback of what it was like to be a member of the Wright exhibition team:

My father was vice-president of the Phoenix National Bank, and they were doing some financing for the first Wright companies. I had seen a person by the name of Louis Paulhan fly at the Jamaica race track in the fall of 1909. He made just a short hop in the infield of the Jamaica race track. I thought, after seeing this man fly that far, that if I could get hold of an airplane I could do much better myself. So I told my father about it, and he said, "Well, you come down to the office and I'll introduce you to Mr. Wilbur Wright. He's going to be there soon to see about the financing of their company."

I was delighted. In a couple of days he let me know that Wilbur Wright was going to be there that afternoon, and told me to come down to his office. I talked with Mr. Wright, who was a very charming character, and told him all about why I wanted to fly—and, I imagine, bored him to death about it. But he finally said, "Well, Frank, you come out to Dayton in about a month and we'll see how we like each other."

And that's how I happened to go to the Wright Company in Dayton.

Though I met Wilbur first, Orville was the one who first showed me how to fly. I sat in the seat next to the engine, and he was in the other seat, near the left wing. He gave me about an hour and a half of instruction, and then wanted me to be able to fly this plane from the seat that he was sitting in. So he got Walter Brookins (who was the first man he taught to fly, of the five of us) to give me about two hours of instruction, so I could fly from that other seat on the left side away from the engine.

They had what they called an aviation meet at Indianapolis in the infield of the Indianapolis Motor Speedway, which had just been built. We used that infield to do our flying from. I was scared to death. But anyway, Wilbur Wright, who was a very thoughtful and wonderful character, held on to the right wing. In those days, we had to put the plane on a starting rail, with a cross-piece on a skid, and the only control we had of the engine was the advancing and retarding of the magneto, which was a German Mayer, a very fine magneto, with a long range to advance and retard.

Wilbur ran along, holding the wing, so I could get up enough speed to get off the starting rail. In my excitement, I'd forgotten to advance the spark on the magneto, and I just plunked on the ground, much to my embarrassment. But later on that afternoon, I tried it again. I remembered that I had to advance the magneto spark, and was able to get off.

I planned in my mind to follow the contour of the Motor Speedway track. Suddenly, I realized that there wasn't any track below me. It had disappeared. I had forgotten to bank the plane and was just slung out sideways. But I corrected that and came back and landed the plane way out on the end of the infield of the track. That was the only way I could get down without smashing up. All of my teammates were furious with me because I'd landed it so far away. We had to truck the plane back to the starting rail.

The Indianapolis Meet also produced a memorable flight for Walter Brookins. On the last day of the exhibition, he decided to try again to set a world's altitude record. He had attempted to do this ever since the meet began, but one thing after another went wrong and he hadn't gotten up very high so far. Later he recalled the flight:

I took off, with flying conditions about perfect, and started to climb. By the way, I climbed at the rate of about 70 feet a minute as compared to 700 for a good ship today. More or less to my surprise everything went well. I struck no strong winds and the air was pretty firm.

I intended to keep on going up until I reached the climbing limit of the motor. And then it happened. At first, from the noise, I thought the motor was tearing itself loose from the ship. As a matter of fact, a valve had broken, shifted out over the top of its piston, and on the next upstroke pushed the whole top of the cylinder off. There I was, up 4,200 feet with a dead motor. I had broken the altitude record, and if my luck held, I'd break the gliding record too. If it didn't, I'd probably break my neck. It held. I came down in a very wide spiral, nosed into the field and landed without the least trouble.

Indianapolis was also the airplane-flying debut of another famous pilot, Lincoln Beachey. But it was an inauspicious beginning, to say the least, and on the basis of what happened it did not appear that Beachey had much of a future as an exhibition pilot.

In the publicity surrounding the meet Beachey was listed as an "amateur" although he had done quite a bit of balloon and dirigible flying and had built a monoplane of his own, vaguely along the lines of a Blériot, that looked as though it should fly. But Beachey was in no class with the Wright team. The first time he took his monoplane out he revved up the engine, went bounding over the infield turf, hit a hole and broke his rudder before he could get airborne. Two days later he managed to get a few feet off the ground, but lost a wheel as he touched down, careened to one side and splintered his propeller. That ended Beachey's first public appearance as an airplane driver, but marked the beginning of a fabulous career in stunt flying.

Apart from giving the citizens of Indianapolis a good look at the Wright airplanes and the men who flew them, the six-day meet failed to produce the thrills and daring feats the crowd was hoping for. Except for Brookins' altitude attempts, most of the flying consisted of laps around the Speedway. The Indianapolis *News* complained of the sameness of the events day after day and quoted the president of the Speedway as saying, "The age is one of speed and competition, and I want to see a flock of airships fighting for first place under the wire." But there was an indication of where some of the missing excitement might come from: during the Indianapolis Meet, a Curtiss-trained pilot had stolen the headlines in the nation's leading papers by flying from New York to Philadelphia and back in the same day.

In direct competition with the Wrights Curtiss was still no match, as the Governor's Island meeting had proven. Curtiss' planes were lighter and smaller than those of the Wrights. He had no two-seaters yet, and with their bamboo construction the early Curtiss planes had a somewhat rickety appearance compared to the stolid, spruce-framed Wright planes.

But Curtiss understood publicity and the value of a good press. Thus the shows he put on tended more and more as time passed to capture the public's imagination. Coupled with this was a vague feeling of resentment among the general public over the Wrights' patent infringement suit against Curtiss, which was now toiling its way through the courts. Aviation was obviously a big enough field to accommodate everyone, and it seemed to many that the Wrights were simply being greedy in their insistence that no plane with movable lateral control surfaces could fly without a license from them under the patents they had obtained.

After the abortive—from Curtiss' point of view—Governor's Island show, he headed west. He flew his plane at St. Louis in October at an exhibition which also featured flights by Thomas Baldwin, Lincoln Beachey and Roy Knabenshue in dirigibles. Curtiss' unerring instinct for publicity led him next, in January, 1910, to Dominguez Field near Los Angeles, where America's first really big air show was shaping up.

The flying at Dominguez Field centered around an elliptical

In 1910 airships could still race airplanes without looking ridiculous. Here Louis Paulhan beats out an airship piloted by Lincoln Beachey at Dominguez Field, California.

race track that measured about a mile and a half in circumference. There were two dirigibles at the meet piloted by Lincoln Beachey and Roy Knabenshue, and this was just about the last time that dirigibles and airplanes could perform together without looking ridiculous. It took the dirigibles about five minutes to lumber around a lap of the race track, and some of the airplanes took as long as three and a half minutes to make the same trip.

Curtiss brought a new airplane with him and picked up $6,500 in prize money for speed, endurance and quick starting. However, his performance was overshadowed by Frenchman Louis Paulhan, who set an altitude record, won an endurance prize and won $10,000 for making a forty-five-mile cross-country flight to the Santa Anita race track and back. This gave him a grand total of $19,000—not bad for a man whose flying career had begun when he unexpectedly won a Voisin in a contest in Paris just a year before. Paulhan flew his Voisin at the Reims Meet, but the big flying-box-kite design was outclassed by the new types and he soon switched to a Farman, which he flew in America. Paulhan was a superb pilot. When a court injunction by the Wrights prohibited him from using wing warping on a Blériot that he had also brought to California, he proceeded to fly it anyway *without* the crucial control that banked the wings. There wasn't much in the way of stunting that he could do with a Blériot crippled in this fashion, but the fact that he was able to take off and get down again without killing himself attests to considerable skill.

In the meantime, a $10,000 prize offered by the New York *World* at the time of the Hudson-Fulton Celebration was still open to the first person to fly all the length of the Hudson River from Albany to New York. After the Dominguez Field Meet, Curtiss packed up his plane and returned to Hammondsport, where he supervised the building of a new plane during the spring of 1910. The Hudson River flight was an ambitious undertaking and Curtiss considered it more difficult than Blériot's Channel crossing or a recently proposed London-to-Manchester cross-country flight for which a prize of $50,000 had been offered in England. The total distance down the Hudson River from Albany is 152 miles, much farther than the distance across the Channel and about the same as the mileage from London to Manchester. However, for much of its length the Hudson flows between high hills and cliffs which not only offer few places for a safe emergency landing but—and this was of even greater concern to Curtiss in his light airplane—create erratic wind currents and eddies along the way. He therefore took great pains to go over his route very carefully before setting out on what proved to be one of the great flights of early American aviation:

While awaiting the completion of the new machine, I took a trip up the Hudson from New York to Albany to look over the course and to select a place about half way between the two cities where a landing for gasoline and oil might be made, should it become necessary.

There are very few places for an aeroplane to land with safety around New York City. The official final landing place, stipulated in the conditions drawn up by the New York *World,* was to be Governor's Island, but I wanted to know of another place on the upper edge of the city where I might come down if it should prove necessary. I looked all over the upper end of Manhattan Island, and at last found a little meadow on a side hill just at the junction of the Hudson and Harlem rivers, at a place called Inwood. It was small and sloping, but had the advantage of being within the limits of New York City. It proved fortunate for me that I had selected this place, for it later served to a mighty good advantage.

There was quite a party of us aboard the Hudson river boat leaving New York City one day in May for the trip to Albany. As an illustration of the skepticism among the steamboat men, I remember that I approached an officer and asked several questions about the weather conditions on the river, and particularly as to the prevailing winds at that period of the year. Incidentally, I remarked that I was contemplating a trip up the river from New York to Albany in an aeroplane and wanted to collect all the reliable data possible on atmospheric conditions. This officer, who I afterward learned was the first mate, answered all my questions courteously, but it was evident to all of us that he believed I was crazy. He took me to the captain of the big river boat and introduced me, saying: "Captain, this is Mr. Curtiss, the flying machine man; that's all I know," in a tone that clearly indicated that he disclaimed all responsibility as to anything I might do or say.

The captain was very kind and courteous, asking us to remain in the pilot house, where we might get a better view of the country along the way, and displaying the keenest interest in the project. He answered all questions about the winds along the Hudson and seemed to enter heartily in the spirit of the thing until we approached the great bridge at Poughkeepsie and I began to deliberate whether it would be better to pass over or beneath it in the aeroplane. Then it seemed really to dawn upon the captain for the first time that I was actually going to fly down the river in an aeroplane. He apparently failed to grasp the situa-

tion, and thereafter his answers were vague and given without
interest. It was "Oh, yes, I guess so," and similar doubtful expres-
sions, but when we finally left the boat at Albany he very kindly
wished me a safe trip and promised to blow the whistle if I
should pass his boat.

On our way up to Albany we stopped at Poughkeepsie, in
order to select a landing place, as at least one stop was deemed
necessary to take on gasoline and to look over the motor. We
visited the State Hospital for the Insane, which stands on the hill
just above Poughkeepsie, and which seemed to be a good place
to land. Dr. Taylor, the superintendent, showed us about the
grounds, and when told that I intended stopping there on my
way down the river in a flying machine, said with much cordial-
ity: "Why, certainly, Mr. Curtiss, come right in here; here's where
all the flying machine inventors land."

Notwithstanding the Doctor's cordial invitation to "drop in on
him," we went to the other side of Poughkeepsie, and there found
a fine open field at a place called Camelot. I looked over the
ground carefully, locating the ditches and furrows, and selected
the very best place to make a safe landing. Arrangements were
made for a supply of gasoline, water, and oil to be brought to the
field and held in readiness. It was fortunate that I looked over
the Camelot field, for a few days later I landed within a few feet
of the place I had selected as the most favoured spot near
Poughkeepsie. This is but one thing that illustrates how the
whole trip was outlined before the start was made, and how this
plan was followed out according to arrangement.

My machine was brought over from Hammondsport. The
newspapers of New York City sent a horde of reporters. A special
train was engaged to start from Albany as soon as I got under-
way, carrying newspapermen and Aero Club representatives, as
well as several invited guests. It was the purpose to have this
train keep even with me along the entire trip of one hundred and
fifty-two miles, but as it turned out, it had some trouble in living
up to the schedule.

The aeroplane, christened the *Hudson Flier*, was set upon
Rensselaer Island. It was now up to the weather man to furnish
conditions I considered suitable. This proved a hard task, and for
three days I got up at daybreak, when there is normally the least
wind, ready to make an early start. On these days the news-

papermen and officials, not to mention crowds of curious spectators, rubbed the sleep out of their eyes before the sun got up and went out to Rensselaer Island. But the wind was there ahead of us and it blew all day long. The weather bureau promised repeatedly, "fair weather, with light winds," but couldn't live up to promises. I put in some of the time in going over every nut, bolt and turnbuckle on the machine with shellac. Nothing was overlooked; everything was made secure. I had confidence in the machine. I knew I could land on the water if it became necessary, as I had affixed two light pontoons to the lower plane, one on either end, and a hydro-surface under the front wheel of the landing-gear. This would keep me afloat some time should I come down in the river.

We bothered the life out of the weather observer at Albany, but he was always very kind and took pains to get weather reports from every point along the river. But the newspapermen lost faith; they were tired of the delay. I have always observed that newspapermen, who work at a high tension, cannot endure delay when there is a good piece of news in prospect. One of those at Albany during the wait, offered to lay odds with the others that I would not make a start. One of the Poughkeepsie papers printed an editorial about this time, in which it said: "Curtiss gives us a pain in the neck. All those who are waiting to see him go down the river are wasting their time." This was a fair sample of the lack of faith in the undertaking.

The machine was the center of interest at Albany during the wait. It seemed to hold a fascination for the crowds that came over to the island. One young fellow gazed at it so long and so intently that he finally fell over backwards insensible and it was some time before he was restored to consciousness. Then one of the newspapermen dashed a pail of water over him and at once sent his paper a column about it. They had to find something to write about and the countryman, the flying machine, and the fit made a combination good enough for almost any newspaperman to weave an interesting yarn about.

Our period of waiting almost ended on Saturday morning, May 30th. The *Hudson Flier* was brought out of its tent, groomed and fit; the special train stood ready, with steam up and the engineer holding a right-of-way order through to New York. The newspapermen, always on the job, and the guests were

Professor J. S. Zerbe dashes furiously across the turf at Dominguez Field, but fails to fly.

watching eagerly for the aeroplane to start and set out on its long and hazardous flight.

Then something happened—the wind came up. At first it did not seem to be more than a breeze, but it grew stronger and reports from down the river told of a strong wind blowing up the river. This would have meant a head gale all the way to New York, should I make a start then. Everything was called off for the day and we all went over and visited the State Capitol. The newspapermen swallowed their disappointment and hoped for better things on the morrow.

Sunday proved to be the day. The delay had got somewhat on my nerves and I determined to make a start if there was half a chance. The morning was calm and bright—a perfect summer day. News from down the river was all favourable. I determined it was now or never. I sent Mrs. Curtiss to the special train and informed the *World* representative and the Aero Club officials that I was ready to go. Shortly after eight o'clock the motor was turned over and I was off!

It was plain sailing after I got up and away from Rensselaer Island. The air was calm and I felt an immense sense of relief. The motor sounded like music and the machine handled perfectly. I was soon over the river and when I looked down I could see deep down beneath the surface. This is one of the peculiar things about flying over the water. When high up a person is able to see farther beneath the surface.

I kept a close lookout for the special train, which could not get under way as quickly as I had, and pretty soon I caught sight of it whirling along on the tracks next to the river bank. I veered over toward the train and flew along even with the locomotive for miles. I could see the people with their heads out the windows, some of them waving their hats or hands, while the ladies shook their handkerchiefs or veils frantically. It was no effort at all to keep up with the train, which was making fifty miles an hour. It was like a real race and I enjoyed the contest more than anything else during the flight. At times I would gain as the train swung around a short curve and thus lost ground, while I continued on in an air line.

All along the river, wherever there was a village or town, and even along the roads and in boats on the river, I caught glimpses of crowds or groups of people with their faces turned skyward, their attitudes betokening the amazement which could not be read in their faces at that distance. Boatmen on the river swung thin caps in mute greeting, while now and then a river tug with a long line of scows in tow, sent greetings in a blast of white steam, indicating there was the sound of a whistle behind. But I heard nothing but the steady, even roar of the motor in perfect rhythm, and the whirr of the propeller. Not even the noise of the speeding special train only a few hundred feet below reached me, although I could see every turn of the great drive-wheels on the engine.

On we sped, the train and the aeroplane, representing a century of the history of transportation, keeping abreast until Hudson had been passed. Here the aeroplane began to gain, and as the train took a wide sweeping curve away from the bank of the river, I increased the lead perceptibly, and soon lost sight of the special.

It seemed but a few minutes until the great bridge spanning the Hudson at Poughkeepsie came into view. It was a welcome landmark, for I knew that I had covered more than half the journey from Albany to New York, and that I must stop to replenish the gasoline. I might have gone on and taken a chance on having enough fuel, but this was not the time for taking chances. There was too much at stake.

I steered straight for the center of the Poughkeepsie bridge, and passed a hundred and fifty feet above it. The entire population of Poughkeepsie had turned out, apparently, and resembled swarms of busy ants, running here and there, waving their hats and hands. I kept close watch for the place where I had planned to turn off the river course and make a landing. A small pier jutting out into the river was the mark I had chosen beforehand and it soon came into view. I made a wide circle and turned inland, over a clump of trees, and landed on the spot I had chosen on my way up to Albany. But the gasoline and oil which I had expected to find waiting for me, were not there. I saw no one for a time, but soon a number of men came running across the fields and a number of automobiles turned off the road and raced toward the aeroplane. I asked for some gasoline and an automobile hurried away to bring it.

I could scarcely hear and there was a continual ringing in my ears. This was the effect of the roaring motor, and strange to say, this did not cease until the motor was started again. From that time on there was no disagreeable sensation. The special train reached the Camelot field shortly after I landed and soon the newspapermen, the Aero Club officials, and the guests came climbing up the hill from the river, all eager to extend their congratulations. Henry Kleckler, acting as my mechanic, who had come along on the special train, looked over the machine carefully, testing every wire, testing the motor out, and taking every precaution to make the remainder of the journey as successful as the first half. The gasoline having arrived, and the tank being refilled, the special train got under way; once more I rose into the air, and the final lap of the journey was on.

Out over the trees to the river I set my course, and when I was about midstream, turned south. At the start I climbed high above the river, and then dropped down close to the water. I wanted to feel out the air currents, believing that I would be more likely to find steady air conditions near the water. I was mistaken in this, however, and soon got up several hundred feet and maintained about an even altitude of from five hundred to seven hundred feet. Everything went along smoothly until I came within sight of West Point. Here the wind was nasty and shook me up considerably. Gusts shot out from the rifts between the mountains and made extremely rough riding. The worst spot was encountered between Storm King and Dunderberg, where the river is narrow and the mountains rise abruptly from the water's edge to more than a thousand feet on either side. Here I ran into a downward suction that dropped me in what seemed an interminable fall straight down, but which as a matter of fact was not more than a hundred feet or perhaps less. The atmosphere seemed to tumble about like water rushing through a narrow gorge. At another point, a little farther along, and after I had dropped down close to the water, one blast tipped a wing dangerously high, and I almost touched the water. I thought for an instant that my trip was about to end, and made a quick mental calculation as to the length of time it would take a boat to reach me after I should drop into the water.

The danger passed as quickly as it had come, however, and the machine righted itself and kept on. Down by the Palisades we soared, rising above the steep cliffs that wall the stream on the west side. Whenever I could give my attention to things other than the machine, I kept watch for the special train. Now and then I caught glimpses of it whirling along the bank of the river, but for the greater part of the way I outdistanced it.

Soon I caught sight of some of the sky-scrapers that make the sky-line of New York City the most wonderful in the world. First I saw the tall frame of the Metropolitan Tower, and then the lofty Singer building. These landmarks looked mighty good to me, for I knew that, given a few more minutes' time, I would finish the flight. Approaching Spuyten Duyvil, just above the Harlem river, I looked at my oil gauge and discovered that the supply was almost exhausted. I dared not risk going on to Governor's Island, some fifteen miles farther, for once past the Harlem river, there would be no place to land short of the island. So I took a wide sweep across to the Jersey side of the river, circled around toward the New York side, and put in over the Harlem river, looking for the little meadow at Inwood which I had picked out as a possible landing place some two weeks before.

There I landed on the sloping hillside, and went immediately to a telephone to call up the New York *World*. I told them I had landed within the city limits and was coming down the river to Governor's Island soon.

I got more oil, some one among the crowd, that gathered as if by magic, turned my propeller, and I got away safely on the last leg of the flight. While I had complied with the conditions governing the flight by landing in the city limits, I wanted to go on to Governor's Island and give the people the chance to see the machine in flight.

From the extreme northern limits of New York to Governor's Island, at the southern limits, was the most inspiring part of the trip. News of the approach of the aeroplane had spread throughout the city, and I could see crowds everywhere. New York can turn out a million people probably quicker than any other place on earth, and it certainly looked as though half of the population was along Riverside Drive or on top of the thousands of apartment houses that stretch for miles along the river. Every craft on the river turned on its siren and faint sounds of the clamor reached me even above the roar of my motor. It seemed but a moment until the Statue of Liberty came into view. I turned westward, circled the Lady with the Torch and alighted safely on the parade ground on Governor's Island.

Aside from aviation events, 1910 was a quiet year and American newspapers didn't have very much to write about. Consequently, the amount of space devoted to Curtiss' trip was staggering. The New York *Times* alone gave thirty-one and a half columns—four and one half pages—to Curtiss in the edition that came out after the flight. In other newspapers, such as the *World* and the New York *American,* the coverage of Curtiss' flight practically drove everything else out of the issue.

Curtiss' actual flying time from Albany to New York was two hours and fifty-one minutes over a distance of 152 miles. This gave him an average speed of 52 miles per hour, a substantial improvement over the speed records set at Reims the previous year. In addition to winning the *World's* $10,000 prize, Curtiss also walked off with the *Scientific American* Trophy for the third time for his 87-mile nonstop flight from Albany to Poughkeepsie. The rules for the trophy specified that anyone who won it three times in a row could keep it, so the trophy now became Curtiss' personal property. The competition was never revived.

Not to be outdone by the *World*, the *Times* and the Philadelphia *Public Ledger* quickly offered a $10,000 prize for the first flight from New York to Philadelphia and return. The *Times* put up $25,000 for the first flight between New York and Chicago. William Randolph Hearst then upped the ante even further by offering a $50,000 prize for the first transcontinental flight from New York to California in thirty days or less.

The longer New York–Chicago and New York–California flights were considerably beyond the capability of any pilot or airplane flying in 1910. But the New York–Philadelphia round-trip prize was quickly pocketed by Charles K. Hamilton in a Curtiss airplane. The trip itself was routine, almost effortless. Hamilton left Governor's Island at 7:43 A.M. on June 13, flew to Philadelphia nonstop and landed at a field at Front Street and Erie Avenue at 9:25 A.M. He stayed for lunch, then headed back, stopping once at South Amboy, New Jersey, to change some spark plugs. He reached his starting point at Governor's Island at 6:40 P.M.

The man who made the trip was anything but ordinary, however. Small and wiry, Hamilton had red hair and oversize ears and went through life with an aura of alcohol generally surrounding him. He began his flying career by jumping out the window of a school in his home town, New Britain, Connecticut, with an umbrella. When he was eighteen he left home and took up hot-air-balloon flying and parachute jumping at exhibitions and circuses throughout the country. He was one of the most daring parachutists of the era and perfected a stunt of leaping from a balloon with a parachute and cutting loose from it, then opening and discarding another and another and another until he reached the ground with his fifth and last chute.

Hamilton switched to dirigibles in 1906, teamed up with Roy Knabenshue for a while and in early 1909 took a dirigible on a wild tour of Japan, in which he was mobbed by Shinto fanatics who considered his ascents toward heaven as somehow irreligious. He became interested in airplanes after Blériot's Channel crossing and the Reims Meet and went to Hammondsport in October to see if Curtiss would teach him to fly. But Curtiss had not yet set up a flying school and told Hamilton he couldn't take him on as a student. Hamilton hung around anyway, and when Curtiss left town one day on business he climbed aboard a new plane while no one was looking and made several short flights without ever having had any instruction at all. He tried this again the next day, but Curtiss returned and caught him at it. Curtiss was furious at the way Hamilton had risked a brand-new $5,000 airplane, but was so impressed at Hamilton's demonstration of his natural ability that he agreed to give him some lessons. In November Curtiss hired Hamilton as an exhibition pilot for Curtiss airplanes.

Hamilton's days as a pilot were numbered, for he suffered from tuberculosis. Thus he went about his flying with a daring sort of fatalism that awed his fellow pilots and led to more than the usual number of bad crashes. Someone once figured that he had broken both legs, smashed his collarbone twice, fractured two ribs, dislocated an arm, broken an ankle and been badly scalded by the hot water from his engine's radiator in various airplane accidents. "There is little left of the original Hamilton," Lincoln Beachey remarked at one point. Yet it was not an airplane that killed Hamilton in the end. On January 22, 1914, he died of a lung hemorrhage at the age of twenty-nine.

By July, 1910, Curtiss felt confident enough to challenge the Wrights once again in a direct competition. This time he took on Walter Brookins at an exhibition at Atlantic City from July 6 through 13. There were two main prizes of $5,000 each. One was for altitude, the other for flying 50 miles out over the ocean. Curtiss was the first on the scene and intrigued reporters by rigging his airplane with inflated bicycle tubes to keep it afloat if he should come down at sea while trying for the prize. He also wore a life jacket of sorts consisting of another inflated bicycle tube under his arms. Curtiss had bad luck in the opening days of

Charles K. Hamilton

the meet, damaging his propeller while trying to take off from the beach, but managed to fly enough to become quite popular with the thousands of people who watched from the boardwalk.

Then Brookins took to the air and for a few days Curtiss was outclassed once again. On July 10, before a tremendous crowd of

Glenn Curtiss is put out of action temporarily by a damaged propeller at Atlantic City.

150,000, Brookins set a new altitude record of 6,175 feet. In his flying nearer the ground, he awed the spectators—and Curtiss—with steep, almost vertical turns. The general consensus, as the exhibition moved into its last week, was that Curtiss and his plane were faster, while Brookins' Wright plane was steadier and easier to handle, especially in strong or gusty winds.

The closing days of the meet belonged once again to Curtiss. On July 10 he took off and headed out to sea to make a bid for the $5,000 prize for overwater flight. For over an hour and a half he flew back and forth in front of the piers, the hot-dog stands and the bathers at the resort, remaining far enough offshore most of the time that it was obvious to everyone that any trouble would force him down in the ocean before he could make it back to the beach. This performance won him the prize he was seeking, and on the last day he added a final piece of showmanship to the whole affair by dropping oranges on a lifeboat crew in a demonstration of "aerial bombing."

In between flying dates, Curtiss had finally found time to organize a flying school and was teaching others the fine art at his headquarters at Hammondsport. Lacking a two-seat aircraft, flight instruction under Curtiss was rudimentary, but it seemed to work. The student pilot was first given ten days or so of fairly intensive work on the ground so that he learned to make the right movements with the controls and became familiar with every detail of the airplane.

The Curtiss control system was quite different from that of the Wrights, and not nearly as awkward. The pilot perched directly in front of the engine on a small, hard seat without armrests or safety belt. Between his legs was a tall lever with a wheel on top. Pushing the wheel forward tilted the nose and the tail elevator surfaces so that the plane nosed over. Pulling the control wheel back brought the nose up. Turning the wheel right or left turned the plane's vertical rudder to the right or left. To make the plane bank in a turn, the pilot leaned in the direction he wished to bank while turning the rudder wheel. As he did so, he moved a yoke around his shoulders which in turn moved the small ailerons located between the biplane wings. The virtue of this system was that the movements were natural. To go down, one pushed forward; to go up, one pulled back. To make a smooth turn, the pilot turned his wheel the same way as in an automobile and simultaneously leaned in the direction of the turn. One disadvantage was that with the yoke around his shoulders, it was difficult for the pilot to look back and see what was happening to his engine without throwing the plane into a violent bank. But with practice even this problem could be overcome.

When Curtiss felt that a student pilot had learned his ground-school lessons well enough, he allowed the student to make straight runs over a half-mile course in an airplane with its throttle wired back so that it couldn't possibly take off. After a few days of this "grass cutting," as it was called, a different propeller was put on the practice plane. While the engine could be turned up to full power with this propeller and the plane raced across the ground, the propeller did not have enough thrust to lift the aircraft off the ground. In this way the pupils learned how to handle the aircraft on the ground without running the risk of actually taking off.

After this phase was mastered, still another practice propeller was put on. This one permitted the student to make hops of 20 to 50 feet at a height of a few feet at the most. These jumps gave the pilots their first taste of flight and developed their ability to control the aircraft without getting so high that a bad landing could lead to a serious smashup. In the final phase of his training, the student pilot was given a plane with a regular propeller, in which he could take off and remain airborne. He then worked his way up higher and higher, practicing turns, glides and dives in succeeding flights until Curtiss felt the student was ready to leave the Hammondsport nest on his own.

Curtiss gave this course to many pilots in 1910, and as the summer wore on he too was able to organize an exhibition team. In addition to Hamilton, Curtiss trained and fielded such outstanding pilots in 1910 as Lincoln Beachey, Eugene B. Ely and Beckwith Havens, as well as a score of others of lesser fame; and by August Curtiss was able to manage the unique stunt of getting five Curtiss planes in the air at the same time at Sheepshead Bay, Long Island.

Meanwhile, the Wright team was busy, too, putting on shows at Montreal, Toronto, Detroit, Asbury Park, Boston, Chicago, St. Louis, and Washington, Pennsylvania. With this stepped-up tempo in the aviation world came a great surge of interest in the rivalry between the Wright and Curtiss teams and between individual team members, particularly Wright pilots Arch Hoxsey and Ralph Johnstone. Newspapers began sending their more talented reporters to cover air shows. Some of the finest and most vivid writing about aviation ever done lies tucked away in the yellowing pages of 1910–11 newspapers across the land.

Here, for example, is the way that a nameless reporter for the New York *American* captured the flavor of the Asbury Park, New Jersey, air show in August, 1910:

The rivalry existing between Archie Hoxsey and Ralph Johnstone, two of the Wright aviators, manifested itself today in a thrilling aerial duel with their biplanes. Undaunted by the accident to young Brookins yesterday, they went through a series of hair-raising evolutions which made today's exhibition one of the greatest demonstrations of eccentric aeroplane riding ever seen in America. They twisted, spiraled and steeplechased over the course while the 10,000 spectators wildly applauded. . . .

Johnstone's machine bounded into the air like a rubber ball, darting towards the end of the field at an altitude of 50 feet. He carefully steered away from the grand stand to avoid another catastrophe in case he fell. The wind was blowing 25 miles per hour through the trees, but the sky was cloudless and the biplane tossed and tumbled on the turns like a leaf in a wind eddy.

Curving at the corners with the sharp perpendicular turns which brought Brookins to grief yesterday, Johnstone caused many spectators concern, but after five minutes he came down and was congratulated by Wilbur Wright (who came from New York to see Brookins) for the judgment displayed in selecting his landing place.

Then Hoxsey went up. Like a rocket he shot to a height of 200 feet. After a few gently careening circuits of the field, he began the exhibition which made Johnstone frantic to take to the air. Not content with sidewise slanting turns, he soared higher and set out to cut figure eights.

Much like a skillful skater he moved in the graceful craft through the air above the aviation field. Then he commenced a series of wild dips, toboggan slides and curves that distinguished him even from Hamilton. With unerring judgment, the young man coasted from a height of 600 feet at an angle of 55 degrees, his motor running full power. As the crowd stood on its toes to see what seemed like an inevitable crash, he daintily raised the front planes and bounded cleanly and beautifully over the invisible hurdle on the ground. But he had scarcely switchbacked 25 feet in the air when he put his craft over another of those imaginary hurdles. The aerial steeplechase continued almost around the entire field.

As he repeatedly dipped up and down, at times seeming to glide on the turf itself, pandemonium broke loose. Women cried their approval, while men yelled themselves hoarse to outdo the shrieking automobiles. After he had almost clipped chips out of telegraph poles, and seemingly grazed the top of the dirigible tent, he came safely to the earth after being eleven minutes in the air. The tremendous ovation that greeted him as he tried to steal away caused Johnstone to walk impatiently back and forth in front of his machine. He wanted to be up and away but it was not his turn. . . .

Johnstone had already taken his seat in the machine. He announced he would fly to an altitude of 1,500 feet. For this purpose he used an untried aeroplane, stripped of its upper front control plane. He believed he could make the machine respond more quickly by omitting this detail. Without much ado he swung the biplane into the air and it rose rapidly, pushing upward in a wide circle.

On the second lap around the course Johnstone was 700 feet up. On the next circle he was 900 feet high and the last time he drove around he was at an estimated altitude of 1,200 feet.

Then he came coasting down. Plunging from this height to a scant 25 feet above the ground, he began a series of evolutions that for daring have scarcely been equalled in the air. Skipping, sliding, twisting, turning, dipping twice, thrice and even four times in succession, he plunged over the field in a manner that plainly indicated he wished to do everything that Hoxsey had done.

He played leapfrog and he coasted at angles that seemed but a hair line removed from a complete somersault. In one wild, final bacchanalian swoop he dropped his goggles and finally finished his orgy of flying with a wild flourish of corkscrew spirals around the field.

This put Hoxsey on his mettle. He was soon in the air and boring upward to a height of at least 2,000 feet. Then he came

An uncomfortable-looking Theodore Roosevelt gets ready for a hop with an equally nervous-looking Wright pilot, Arch Hoxsey, at St. Louis.

coasting down in a long, curving sweep and repeated his earlier performance of steeplechasing with new embellishments. At one time the machine whizzed through the grass scarcely 8 inches off the ground. He finished his startling performance by landing in the center of a marked square 190 feet wide.

The Brookins accident mentioned in the New York *American* article was one of two that marred the show. It was a serious one that came awfully close to killing Brookins and it demonstrated the ancient truth of the aviator's proverb, "Flying is inherently safe, but it is mercilessly unforgiving of human error." Said Brookins later:

I was scheduled to take the Wright ship up for the first flight on opening day. A crowd of 50,000 was there to see the show.

They had stands on four sides of the field. There were about 50 press photographers on the field. And to the last man they insisted in standing in front of my ship to get a picture as I was taking off. I had to stop the motor three times to keep from running over them.

Finally after warning them to keep the field clear when I landed, I managed to take off. I flew for about 20 minutes and then started down.

Of course I had to land into the wind which was blowing diagonally across the field. This brought me in over one of the stands and the hospital tent. And then, right where I intended to land, were the 50 photographers. My motor was off so I couldn't fly over them. I did the only other thing possible—nosed down from an elevation of 50 feet and tried to land in front of them.

Well, all they had to do was raise the flap of the hospital tent and drag me in. I had a broken nose, a broken ankle and several teeth knocked out. And the ship was a complete wreck.

As I said, that was the first day of the meet. They sent another ship by express from Dayton and on the sixth day they carried me out of the hospital, sat me in the new ship and I flew every day for the rest of the meet.

Brookins wasn't the only casualty in this accident. Seven spectators were hurt and a boy, George Burnett, was pinned under the motor in the wreckage of Brookins' plane and badly injured. The other accident took place a few days later and was not nearly so serious.

Ever since the 1904 flights at Huffman Prairie, the Wrights had been using a starting rail to help get their skid-equipped airplanes off the ground. Despite the obvious advantages of using wheels in their undercarriage as all other airplane builders now did, the Wrights stubbornly refused to make this improvement in their design for many years. Finally they decided to make the change and try it out at Asbury Park. As Frank Coffyn once recalled:

I remember that very well, because it just happened that when Orville made any changes in the plane he always seemed to want me to test them in my public flights. At Asbury Park they had just put wheels on the skids. I made the first flight in public with that Wright plane with the wheels. At the same meet, Ralph Johnstone made his first flight with wheels on the skids. He didn't gauge his landing speed well enough and cracked into a lot of automobiles. He broke the plane up considerably and smashed the headlights on the automobiles. We all laughed at him.

But the Wright pilots soon learned to cope with their faster rolling speed across the ground, and the wheels were adopted as a standard feature on Wright planes from then on.

1910: ii

The Wright and Curtiss teams had aviation in America pretty much to themselves throughout the spring and summer of 1910. Some fine new airplanes and first-rate pilots were now coming along in France and England but, with the one exception of Louis Paulhan, they had virtually no impact on the American scene. An invasion was imminent, however. Because Curtiss, an American, had won the Gordon Bennett speed trophy at Reims in 1909, the 1910 Gordon Bennett speed competition would be held in the United States. A date was set in October for the prestigious event, and the Aero Club of America, under whose jurisdiction the official contests would be held, arranged for the use of the race track at Long Island's Belmont Park.

The British contingent was the first to arrive. Although Britain still lagged far behind the United States and France in aircraft design—the only new aircraft to emerge in Britain up to now were a big biplane designed by American expatriate S. F. Cody and a triplane designed by the rising young engineer A. V. Roe—a number of first-rate British pilots had been trained on the Continent and were beginning to attract considerable attention with their skill.

Foremost of these was Claude Grahame-White, a good-looking young sportsman who had learned to fly at the Blériot school in late 1909. Grahame-White came from a well-to-do country family and had the charm and the manners to make his way easily in England's most sophisticated circles. But he was much more than a playboy. When he was sixteen he set an independent course and apprenticed himself to an engineering company rather than go on from grammar school to something more appropriate to an Edwardian gentleman.

From here on, Grahame-White's career is like something out of *The Wind in the Willows*. He began with bicycles and became a champion racer. Then he saw his first automobile, had to have one of his own and was so enthusiastic that he helped found the Automobile Club of Great Britain. By 1905 Grahame-White was in business in London selling foreign cars not far from the showrooms of his good friend Charley Rolls, another well-to-do young blueblood, who had recently teamed up with Manchester manufacturer Henry Royce to build England's first fine car, the Rolls-Royce.

Next Grahame-White turned to ballooning. He made several ascents with a medium-sized sport balloon. Then this proved too tame, for Grahame-White saw Wilbur Wright fly in France and was awestruck. He returned to his motorcar business and tried, with no success, to develop aircraft designs of his own. When the Reims Meet opened on August 22, 1909, Grahame-White was there. His colleagues at the motorcar company saw little of him after this.

During the next four months he reversed the usual procedure by first making a solo in a Blériot and then settling down to a full, formal course of flight instruction from Louis Blériot himself at Pau, which had become the winter headquarters for aviation on the Continent because of its good weather. Aviation was growing up rapidly in France; now one needed a license to give public demonstrations and take part in competitions sanctioned by the Fédération Aéronautique Internationale (FAI), the official body that to this day functions to validate flying records. The requirements for an FAI *brevet de pilote-aviateur* in the spring of 1910 in France give an interesting indication of what the experts felt a qualified aviator should be able to do: three figure eights, then a climb to 500 feet, followed by a descent and landing with touchdown no more than 10 feet off a specified mark on the ground. For a talented pilot like Grahame-White this was a breeze, and he qualified easily on December 16, 1909. But there were many who didn't make it.

Grahame-White was the thirtieth aviator and the first Englishman to win the internationally recognized FAI *brevet*. He set out with messianic fervor to stir slumbering England's interest in the great possibilities of aviation. It was an uphill fight. For several years Lord Northcliffe, owner of the influential London *Daily Mail*, had been trying to do the same thing, but with little success. After Santos-Dumont's flight in *No. 14-bis* in October, 1906, the *Daily Mail* was the only English paper to sense the more profound implications of aviation. "England is no longer an island," the paper editorialized. "There will be no more sleeping safely behind the wooden walls of old England with the Channel our safety moat. It means the aerial chariots of a foe descending on British soil if war comes."

Shortly after this, the *Daily Mail* offered a £10,000 prize to the first man to fly from London to Manchester, a distance of 185 miles, within one 24-hour period. Now, after the prize had gone begging for three and a half years, Grahame-White stepped forward to make a bid for it. On his way back to England in the spring of 1910, Grahame-White bought a new Farman biplane with a Gnome rotary engine for $1,500. This was the type of plane with which Farman had won the distance prize at Reims. Grahame-White felt it would be more suitable for a long cross-country flight than the Blériot XI that he was used to.

The *Daily Mail* gave Grahame-White a tremendous publicity buildup. Overnight the handsome young man who was as much at home in the drawing rooms of high society as on the flying fields of England and France became the great romantic hero of the day. Telegrams, letters and lucky charms deluged him. Among the messages he saved up until his death in 1959 were these: "Should all love you to win from girls number eleven dressing-room Merry Monarch Company Savoy Theatre." "Goodluck, Grahame-White. England forever." "Two thousand Southamptonians assembled at the Palace Theatre wish you every success in your plucky effort."

Grahame-White made his first attempt for the prize early on the morning of April 23. He got as far as the town of Lichfield, only 68 miles from Manchester, when he was forced down by engine trouble. Before his plane was ready to go again, a windstorm came up and blew the Farman over on its back, damaging it so badly that it had to be dismantled and carted ignominiously back to London for a major overhaul and a fresh start.

The same day Louis Paulhan arrived in London to try for the *Daily Mail* prize. He also flew a Farman biplane and, with a full year's flying experience behind him, including the Reims and Dominguez Field meets, he was formidable competition for the newly fledged Grahame-White. After their planes were made ready the two men met cordially in London while waiting for the weather to clear up enough for their cross-country dash. They agreed that neither would start without notifying the other, in order to make a more dramatic race.

In the late afternoon of Wednesday, April 27, the weather began to improve and Paulhan got ready to take off from the airfield at Hendon. He sent the agreed message to Grahame-White, who was worn out by round-the-clock work to get his plane rebuilt and was napping at a hotel near his headquarters at Wormwood Scrubs. For some reason—no one was ever able to figure out why—Paulhan's takeoff message was never delivered, and while Grahame-White slept on, Paulhan got off to a good start. He was seventy-one minutes ahead by the time Grahame-White could get airborne.

By starting late in the day the two pilots were soon up against one of the great terrors of aviation in 1910—darkness. Paulhan avoided the problem by landing shortly after 8 P.M. near Lichfield while there was still enough light to see in the dusk. He had covered 117 of the 185 miles to Manchester by this time. It was a good day's work and Paulhan now retired for the evening at a nearby hotel.

Grahame-White was also forced down by the gathering gloom, at about the same time as Paulhan. He had closed the gap some, but was still 57 miles behind the Frenchman, and the honor of England was at stake. To his startled retinue of friends, helpers and newspapermen, he announced calmly that he intended to push on through the night to catch up with Paulhan.

There is an old aviator's saying that flying at night is no

Crowds gather around Claude Grahame-White's plane as word spreads that he will attempt to fly cross-country at night, something no aviator had ever done before.

different from flying in the daytime except that you can't see. Nowadays in England, Western Europe and most parts of the United States the old saw is no longer valid, because of the tremendous energy radiated upward every night when the lights go on in thousands of cities and towns, in millions of homes, streets, cars, factories and office buildings. The light from the larger American cities on a clear night is so intense and dazzling that colors are distinguishable, even though the human eye normally needs daylight in order to see color. But in Grahame-White's time the night sky was not lit with such displays. Rural electrification hadn't yet come to the English countryside, and there were few automobiles to light up the roads with their acetylene headlights.

Grahame-White was counting on the moon to help him once he got airborne. At 2:30 A.M. he rallied all the motorcycle and auto drivers in the area around his Farman and had them turn on their lights. Their illumination of the plane and the short patch of field ahead was just enough to encourage him to risk a takeoff. He revved up his engine and began to roll. In a few seconds he was off the ground—and in serious trouble. Just as he cleared an embankment at the end of the field and passed out of range of the automobile headlights, a heavy cloud passed in front of the moon. Now without any visual reference at all, Grahame-White was plunged into dizzying total blackness. There was no reassuring red glow from an instrument panel to dispel the void as there is in a modern airplane. In fact, there were no instruments on the plane whatsoever, no cockpit even. Just a chilling black wind. At this point Grahame-White's engine quit. He clutched desperately at his engine controls and in a moment it coughed to life again. In the confusion after takeoff the sleeve of his coat had snagged the ignition switch and turned it off. All he had to do was switch the ignition back on and the engine ran normally.

Somehow Grahame-White managed to maintain his altitude in the darkness and pick up the route to Manchester. But as the first gray light of dawn appeared, the wind began to rise and the Farman bounced around viciously. Numb with cold and fatigue, Grahame-White decided to land until he could better cope with the turbulence. He touched down at 4:13 A.M., still trailing Paulhan. Meanwhile Paulhan had been warned of Grahame-White's approach and had taken off at 4:09 A.M. The more experienced Paulhan was able to handle the wind and he pushed on through to Manchester, landing there at 5:30 A.M., cold and badly shaken. "I would not do it again for ten times ten thousand pounds," he said. Grahame-White took the news in the best tradition of British sportsmanship. He wired Paulhan: "I offer you my heartiest congratulations on your splendid performance. The better man has won."

The surge of interest following Grahame-White's daring gamble was tremendous and he took full advantage of it to press his crusade to make England more air conscious. Throughout the

Claude Grahame-White

rest of the spring of 1910 and on into the summer, Grahame-White flew in dozens of meets and exhibitions, logging 773 cross-country miles and thrilling hundreds of thousands of Englishmen in the process.

With the Belmont Meet in the offing, Grahame-White sailed for America in late August, docking at Boston with both his Farman and Blériot airplanes on September 1, just in time to enter the Boston-Harvard Meet at Squantum Field. America had never seen as dashing an aviator as this; next to Grahame-White, sober, silent Wilbur Wright and dour Glenn Curtiss, both of whom were also at the Boston Meet with their exhibition teams, were as awkward as country cousins. With his manners and looks, Grahame-White was a great hit with the ladies, and he took up several reigning beauties of Boston and New York society for their first flights. President William Howard Taft brought his family out to the field to see what all the fuss was about and was gallantly invited for a ride by the English aviator. The portly President declined, fortunately, for with his three hundred pounds aboard, Grahame-White's Farman could never have gotten off the ground. Instead, Grahame-White took up Boston Mayor John F. "Honey Fitz" Fitzgerald, grandfather of John F. Kennedy, for three laps around the field. This was Mayor Fitzgerald's first flight.

Not only did Grahame-White outshine the American aviators socially at Boston, but he also outflew them. He was the only aviator to get airborne every day of the meet, he won the meet's top $10,000 prize for the fastest time twice around a course from Squantum to Boston Light, his Blériot easily defeated Curtiss for the speed prize, and he was the winner of the bombing, landing-accuracy and shortest-takeoff events. Ralph Johnstone salvaged something by flying farther and longer than anyone else, and Walter Brookins set the meet's altitude mark with an unimpressive 4,732 feet, but that was all the American pilots could claim.

Before heading to New York for the Belmont Meet, Grahame-White picked up a whopping $50,000 purse for flying at a fair at Brockton, Massachusetts. Then he put in an appearance in Washington, where among other things he swooped down among some giant elm trees and landed on the street between the White House and the Executive Office Building.

Other aviators, meanwhile, were beginning to show up in New York for the big event. In a bold bid to reassert their formerly unchallenged mastery of the skies, the Wright brothers checked in with their exhibition team and three new machines, one of them a trim, small racing biplane that had never been seen before. It was rumored to have a top speed of 70 miles per hour. Glenn Curtiss also fielded three airplanes, including his first monoplane, but his team was pretty shaky. His star pilot, Charles K. Hamilton, was in no shape to break any records. He arrived "limping, scarred and speaking with an impediment on account of an injury to his jaw in his accident in Sacramento last month," according to a New York newspaper. The only other Curtiss team pilots on hand were Eugene Ely and J. C. "Bud" Mars, both of whom were still relatively inexperienced. Two other aviators at the meet flew Curtiss planes, though. They were Charles Willard, Curtiss' first student, and Canada's J. A. D. McCurdy.

From France came Hubert Latham and his graceful, crowd-pleasing Antoinette; a three-man Blériot team composed of Émile Aubrun, Alfred Le Blanc, and Count Jacques de Lesseps; and the Blériot-trained pilot Roland Garros, who brought over a tiny Santos-Dumont Demoiselle. There was another Demoiselle at Belmont; it was flown by a Swiss pilot, Émile Audemars. The British entered Alec Ogilvie in an English-built Wright and James Radley in a Blériot, in addition to Grahame-White.

Finally there were some interesting new faces among the American entries. Clifford Harmon was there, the only American regularly flying an imported Farman biplane. From Philadelphia came J. Armstrong Drexel, a millionaire playboy whom Grahame-White had taught to fly in a Blériot in England. A new Wright pilot named Phil O. Parmelee hoped to make his debut at Belmont, and John B. Moisant, an American who had never flown in the United States, was entered as an alternate on the American team defending the Gordon Bennett cup, largely on the strength of a fine flight he had made in August in a Blériot from Paris to London with one passenger and a three-week-old kitten. Of all the Americans entered at Belmont, Moisant was the only one who could offer Grahame-White any competition in the way of glamour. Tanned, handsome and still a bachelor, Moisant was from a family that had become fabulously wealthy through banking, shrewd speculation in sugar plantations in Central America, and a thriving New York import-export business. Tales of Latin American intrigue and revolutionary activity in San

John B. Moisant

Salvador swirled about him, and he never denied any of them.

One of the people recruited to handle arrangements at Belmont was Ross Browne, who had left the Blériot flying school in the spring of 1910 to come back home and see what was going on. In the interview he tape-recorded for the Columbia Oral History Collection, he gives us a rich, insider's account from behind the scenes at the Belmont Meet and describes what it looked like to an experienced pilot:

We decided on the meet in the latter part of June or the first part of July and there was not much time. I can remember staying up till about two o'clock in the morning at the Aero Club, drafting plans. I was to be in charge of rounding up the aviators.

The next morning, Allan Ryan, the general manager of the meet, called me up and said he'd got Belmont Park. He asked me to meet him that afternoon, take a run out in his car, and see where we would place the hangars.

We went out there and I suggested that we have the hangars between the back stretch of the race track and the Long Island Railroad tracks, which were probably a hundred or a hundred fifty feet away from the back stretch. Lo and behold, two days later I went out there and there were the excavators and contractors marking out the place and up went the hangars. Ryan asked me about pylons. I suggested probably seven or eight would be enough. He said, "No, put a dozen in!" So they put in twelve thirty-foot pylons, painted red and white, in different parts of the outfield. So I was busy, going back and forth to Belmont, sending cablegrams to France and England trying to get these aviators signed up and so forth.

Unfortunately, Ryan, or somebody connected with him, got hold of a few circus men and they wanted to make the place a circus. Well, it was pretty muddled up. I tried to tell Mr. Ryan. He said, "Well, you can't do everything. We'll go ahead as we can. The main thing is to get the fliers in the air and it's up to you to keep them in the air."

"I'll do that," I said, "but it isn't coordinated. This is the first time we've had an international meet in this country, and probably ninety percent of these people have never seen a machine in the air. We have to educate them."

"I have a publicity man who'll take care of it. Forget about it," he said.

When we started out, unfortunately—this was October 22, 1910—it rained the first two days. But the crowds were terrific anyway.

I was stopped every two feet. "Tell me, what kind of a machine is that?" "What is that kind of a machine?" "What is this machine?" "What is that machine?" And out of all of them, there was only one machine that was distinctive, that people really knew what it was: it was the Antoinette, flown by Hubert Latham, the French airman. It was much more birdlike than any other machine. But outside of the Antoinette, they didn't know a Curtiss or a Blériot or a Wright. They were just planes. That's what I explained to Mr. Ryan. I said, "It's a shame. These people don't know what they're seeing."

So anyway, as bad as the weather was, the meet went on. In those days, the machines didn't have any protection for the motors and the ignition and so forth. At least a dozen aviators tried to get off the ground and couldn't even get their motors started. Some of them, when they did, would conk out. Grahame-White, for instance, with his Blériot, had even put a blanket over his motor and a heater underneath it, like a little salamander, to dry it out, and at last it did.

Grahame-White, the great showman that he was, was always in the air. He got his Blériot off. When it came down—he had a little trouble with it—he borrowed a Farman from Clifford B. Harmon and went back up. Then Johnny Moisant was up. Most of them just circled around. They didn't dare leave the place, because if you did you didn't know whether you'd ever get back, and there weren't too many landing places near there. But we managed to keep three or four machines going most of the time. Arch Hoxsey and Ralph Johnstone, for instance, were supposed to have a schedule for duration, for altitude, for speed, and for landing. We just forgot about that. We said to get a machine in the air was the main point, and the people seemed to be satisfied.

After two or three days, the rain stopped, and naturally it was much better.

The Michelin tire people, Champion Spark Plugs, the Curtiss Motor Company, the Hall-Scott Motor Company and other people gave different prizes. For instance, there was a prize of $10,000 for a flight around the Statue of Liberty.

Numerous individuals gave prizes. You see, the people interested in this, along with Mr. Ryan, were the Belmonts—Mrs. August Belmont was there the first day, for instance—the Vanderbilts, and all sorts of wealthy people, and they contributed to the various prizes.

The flights went along very well. The Statue of Liberty flight was the big thing of the week. The Wrights wouldn't allow any of their men to enter. They said it was too dangerous, flying over those towns on the way to Brooklyn. But that wasn't the problem. I'll tell you frankly what it was: they didn't have a chance to win it, because the Wright was the slowest machine in the field. It was nip and tuck with Grahame-White and Johnny Moisant, both of them flying Blériots, and it wasn't determined positively until the next day that Johnny Moisant had won.

Getting back to the fact that no one seemed to know one

machine from another, most of the aviators used to use the Astor Hotel as their gathering point in the evening, and they all said the same thing: "These people haven't the knowledge of airplanes and no one knows what is what."

So lo and behold, the following evening I was over at the Waldorf-Astoria and met Kid McCoy, the old-time prize fighter, who at that time had the Breslin Hotel on Broadway. He was quite a flamboyant chap. He'd been down at Belmont all day, and I saw him there. So he came up to me in the hotel and said, "Why in hell don't they put names on these machines to tell what they are? I'm going to do something about it." So the next day in the Breslin Hotel Bar they had photographs of every machine with the names of the aviators and everything else. He was a character, that Kid McCoy.

That was just one of the things we were learning. Some people wanted to put the meet on a circus basis, and it wasn't really. It was an exhibition, not a circus, and it was a darn dangerous thing, because every time a man went up in the air in those days, he was taking his life in his hands. They had no parachutes. There was nothing. If your motor conked out, well, you just looked for a flat spot to land—a cornfield or anything else. You couldn't just let the machine go and drop in a parachute, like you can do today.

About the third day, the weather broke and it was very nice. We decided we'd have the competition for altitude and for duration. Arch Hoxsey, Glenn Curtiss and Clifford B. Harmon went up for altitude. Arch Hoxsey went up in the air until you couldn't see him. He was up there about an hour, and if I remember correctly, it was just under ten thousand feet, which was a record at that time.

Two or three others went up, but never attained that height. But there was always one thing that I kept on insisting on, to all the boys—"Keep up in the air." There were always three or four machines up in the air circling around, to keep the people's attention. Then, of course, we'd announce, and the announcements were very bad. The third day, I told Mr. Ryan, "Oh, my God, you can't hear that announcer across the track!" I told him that someone had told me about a chap I could get in New York, a fellow named Harry Lebrecque. He was quite a character. He had a voice like a foghorn, and he used two big, enormous megaphones. The next day, when he came out, we hired him for the balance of the week. You could hear him in any part of the track and the grandstands. It was a marvelous thing.

Incidentally, this Harry Lebrecque had made quite a name for himself in the windows of Macy's, Gimbel's, and Wanamaker's in Philadelphia. He used to stand for hours at a time and never close his eyes or flash or move, and people used to think he was a dummy. It was quite an advertising thing at the time. He used to get good money for it. He told me that he used belladonna to keep his eyes from flickering. He said the longest he stayed still was an hour and a half. They usually had a real dummy standing there with him and people used to bet on which was the dummy and which was the man. Once in a while they would fix the dummy so that its hands would move and people would bet on the wrong one.

Then we had competitions for such things as landings. Well, that was a natural for Charlie Hamilton, C. K. Hamilton. He had a peculiar way of landing. He'd be up about two hundred feet and point his nose straight down, just like a power dive, and at about five feet from the ground he'd straighten up, and he'd stop right on the line in front of the grandstand. People used to think it was wonderful. Le Blanc, the Frenchman, would try the same thing with his Blériot. But the Blériot wasn't as quick to act as the Curtiss that Hamilton flew. However, Le Blanc would fly around the opposite side of the field, over the hangars, go up to about two hundred feet, then dip down to about three or four feet, on the infield. It would look as if he was going to crash right into the grandstand. At the last minute he would pull up and go over the grandstand.

There wasn't too much stunting except for Hoxsey and Johnstone. They had a new Wright machine called the Baby Grand. It was much smaller than the regulation Wright, only made for one person, and it was speedier. Arch Hoxsey would go down the track and follow it right around, not over two or three feet from the ground. It was very exciting. But of course, these were the early days of aviation. It wasn't like today.

The crowds were exceptional. It was crowded practically every day. Fortunately there were no serious accidents. We had a few little minor crack-ups, but no one was killed and it left a very nice taste in everyone's mouth, as far as aeronautics was concerned.

One who was quite a hit also was little Émile Audemars, and

Wright hopes at Belmont Meet lay in the compact, speedy Baby Grand warming up here with Orville at the controls.

his Demoiselle. The Demoiselle was a little machine with only seventeen-foot wingspread, made by the Brazilian flier, Santos-Dumont. Garros could fly it also, but Audemars—he only weighed about a hundred twenty-five or a hundred thirty pounds —would fly around most of the time and I'll swear he looked like a butterfly. It was a tricky little machine to fly, but he used to get a big hand every time he took it up.

Successful as the Belmont Meet was for the crowds that flocked to it, it was frustrating for the aviators at first. As Ross Browne pointed out, it rained for the first two days. But despite this, several pilots got airborne on the first day, Saturday, October 22. Some didn't last very long. Curtiss pilot Eugene Ely lost his goggles on his first lap around the course and had to land because the rain was blinding him. An obscure American pilot named Tod Shriver crashed on the first turn in a homemade plane, and Drexel and de Lesseps both made short hops. Grahame-White carried the day by flying twenty laps in fifty-eight minutes, while Moisant made a 20-mile round trip to Hicksville, Long Island, in the fog, steering with a compass that he had learned how to use on his Paris–London flight.

The second day was even worse. Grahame-White and Moisant were the only two who tried to take off, but both failed, banging up their planes considerably in the process. Then a rebellion flared up. "The international course as it has been laid out by the Aero Club of America is a death trap," complained Alfred Le Blanc, the leader of the French team. "It goes over houses, trees, telegraph wires and railroad tracks with scarcely a patch three hundred feet wide at any place where an aeroplane may land." When nothing was done about his complaint, Le Blanc and the other French Blériot pilots boycotted the Meet and would not fly.

When the weather finally cleared, the flying was superb. On the third day of the meet, the crowd was treated to the spectacle of ten planes airborne simultaneously. Two days later, the aviators topped this by getting twelve planes up at the same time. An exciting contest developed for the altitude record, and the pilots pushed each other higher and higher. First de Lesseps reached 5,615 feet. He was beaten on the same day by "Chips" Drexel, who got up to 7,105 feet. Then Johnstone took over, raising the mark ultimately to 9,714 feet, a new world record. Just how far aviation had advanced in one year can be seen by comparing Johnstone's record with the best altitude at the Reims Meet—508 feet.

The weather kicked up one more time. On Friday, October 28—the day before the Gordon Bennett race—a 45-mile-an-hour gale roared in from the west. This is enough to keep most present-day airplanes and all but the hardiest pilots on the ground. But Hoxsey and Johnstone, in an unusual demonstration of flying skill, both took off in the face of this high wind and got safely airborne. Getting down safely was another matter. The higher they went, the fiercer the wind they encountered—one unofficial estimate was 80 miles per hour. At speeds like this the wind was blowing faster than a Wright biplane could fly and soon, to the astonishment of the crowd in the Belmont grandstands, the two planes began to drift backward. Neither could get back to the field; Hoxsey landed some 35 miles northeast of Belmont, near the town of Brentwood, while Johnstone was blown all the way to Middle River, a distance of 55 miles, before he came down.

The day of the Gordon Bennett international speed competition was cold, clear and calm once again, at least in the morning. The excitement was terrific, for this was the day on which the world's most advanced aircraft would be driven to their limits to win the Gordon Bennett Trophy and a $5,000 purse that went with it. It was also the day on which the public would at last get a good look at three sensational airplanes that had been kept pretty much under wraps so far.

The three planes were Le Blanc's high-performance Blériot, which had not been flown because of the Frenchman's protest over the course, a new Blériot for Grahame-White that had arrived in New York just thirty-six hours before the race was due to start, and the specially designed Wright Baby Grand racing plane. The two Blériots had huge, beautifully machined fourteen-cylinder, 100-horsepower Gnome rotary engines. These were the largest engines of this type seen up to now, and the engineering talent involved in producing a design so complex in 1910 was almost incredible. The Wright Baby Grand also boasted a big engine, a V-8 of 60 horsepower (the standard Wright engine at that time was a four-cylinder vertical that produced 30 to 40 horsepower), and with its clipped 21-foot wings and scaled-down proportions it looked like speed personified. In a brief flight prior to the Gordon Bennett, Orville Wright, dressed in an unusually natty new leather jacket, had put the Baby Grand through its paces and had hit a top speed of 72 miles per hour. Walter Brookins was assigned to fly it in the race and checked out in it in a three-minute flight on the morning of the big day. "There's nothing she can't do," he reported exuberantly after he landed. "The Blériots aren't in it with her."

On his way to an easy victory at Belmont, Alfred Le Blanc's engine suddenly spluttered to a stop and he sailed into a telephone pole.

A few minutes after the official start of the race at 8:30 A.M., Grahame-White became the first contestant airborne. He was in his eighth lap when Le Blanc got off and slowly began to creep up on the British champion. By the time Grahame-White had completed the required twenty laps, the Frenchman was four and a half minutes ahead on time. Grahame-White had clocked a respectable 61.5 miles per hour, but it looked as though nothing could stop Le Blanc. Then suddenly his engine went dead and he crashed.

Brookins was getting the Baby Grand ready for its twenty laps when he saw Le Blanc go in:

He was on his last lap, flying low for greater speed. Something went wrong and he swooped down and hit a telephone pole. He hit it so hard that he took an eight-foot section out of the middle of the pole, leaving the upper part still suspended from the wires.

The accident occurred at the far side of the field, so I decided to fly over and see what had happened.

I took off into a 30-mile wind, rose to about 100 feet and then turned around and started with the wind. Just as I had straightened away, a connecting rod broke.

Well, of course, the motor stopped, and there I was at a low altitude with a dead motor, and my own speed and the wind carrying me at 100 miles an hour. I tried to set her down as lightly as possible, but the light landing gear wouldn't stand the terrific speed. The first three or four somersaults were enough for me. I got off then, and what was left of the ship turned a dozen or so more. . . . As for me, I had started out to see what had happened to Le Blanc. And when they brought him into the hospital tent, there I was lying on the operating table waiting for him.

Le Blanc's engine stopped because someone had neglected to fill his fuel tanks completely and he had run out of gas. He and Brookins both came through their mishaps with minor injuries, but meanwhile, back at the race, the other contestants were having a hard time, too. After seven laps, the rising wind proved too much for Chips Drexel and his 50-horsepower Blériot and he gave up. Because of engine trouble, neither Charles K. Hamilton nor Bud Mars got his Curtiss biplane to the starting line, a discouraging blow to the man who had won the Gordon Bennett just a year ago. Ironically, the meet's two slowest planes, Hubert Latham's Antoinette and a standard Wright biplane piloted by Englishman Alec Ogilvie, did get off and began grinding their way through the required twenty laps.

Brookins and Hamilton had been chosen as the principal U. S. contenders when the American team was picked, and Bud Mars and John Moisant as first and second alternates. With Brookins, Hamilton and Mars all out of the race now, America's last hope lay with Moisant. Never dreaming that he would have to race, Moisant was taking it easy in his hangar, eating a piece of pie, when he got the word. He dashed to his plane and took off with a minimum of warm-up. With only a 50-horsepower engine in his Blériot, Moisant had no chance of bettering the speed of

Grahame-White, who had double the power, so he concentrated on beating Ogilvie and Latham for second place. As it turned out, however, this was settled on the ground, not in the air. All three—Moisant, Ogilvie and Latham—were forced down temporarily during the course of the twenty laps, and this down time was counted into the elapsed time around the course. Moisant was able to get back in the air much quicker than his competitors and thus beat them out for second place with a shorter elapsed time. Ogilvie was third and Latham fourth.

For the people of New York the final event of the meet, the race from Belmont around the Statue of Liberty and back, was anticipated with greater excitement than anything else so far, including the Gordon Bennett competition. For the route from Belmont to the Statue of Liberty lay directly over teeming Brooklyn and close enough to the tip of Manhattan Island for tens of thousands to be able to watch from the Battery if it was a nice day. And there would be tens of thousands free to watch, since the race was on a Sunday, the big day off in that bygone time of the six-day work week.

But for a while it seemed that the crowds that gathered along the Battery and on the Brooklyn rooftops were in for a disappointment. As the Sunday afternoon starting time approached, there simply weren't enough contestants left to make a race. Grahame-White refused to fly, because the race committee had changed the rules on him. Originally the committee had said that only those who had made at least one flight of an hour or more during the meet could enter the 35-mile Statue of Liberty dash, a sensible restriction in view of the heavily populated route and the unreliability of the 1910 planes and pilots. But then, when it became apparent that Grahame-White would be the only one to log an hour-long flight, the committee changed its mind and ruled that any aviator could enter. Grahame-White lodged a strong protest and, when the committee ignored his protest, withdrew from the race.

The Wright planes were all grounded because of the brothers' strict observance of the Fourth Commandment—perhaps fortunately, as Ross Browne noted, since the Baby Grand was still wrecked and the two standard models were too slow to show up well. The Curtiss crowd had done so poorly—the new monoplane was never even tested—that no Curtiss pilots came forward for the tempting $10,000 prize and the substantial publicity that surrounded the event. Le Blanc was still out of action, his 100-horsepower Blériot racer hopelessly smashed.

On the morning of the race Grahame-White relented and, encouraged perhaps by the thought that his 100-horsepower Blériot was by far the fastest plane still left flying, agreed to fly. Rather than see France outclassed by default, Jacques de Lesseps entered with his 50-horsepower Blériot, even though it was no match for Grahame-White's plane. John Moisant was the only American entry, and as he taxied out for a short pre-race test flight he slammed into a parked Farman and damaged his Blériot so badly that it couldn't fly.

That left only two contestants. De Lesseps was off first. Grahame-White followed a few minutes later and caught up with and passed the Frenchman before he reached the Statue. It was an easy victory for Grahame-White, or so it seemed as he relaxed back at Belmont after the race. The official cutoff time for further entries was 4 P.M. The hour arrived and passed with no more action.

Then suddenly, at six minutes after four, an announcement was made that John Moisant was about to take off in the Statue of Liberty race. After Moisant's accident his older brother Alfred had rushed out onto the field and offered to buy him any plane he could locate, regardless of the cost. "You find the airplane; I have a checkbook and a fountain pen," he told John, and together they hastily arranged a deal with Alfred Le Blanc to buy the third of the three Blériot-team airplanes, a 50-horsepower model, for $10,000. The race committee obligingly altered the rules once again to permit the American entry a late takeoff, and by taking a more direct route Moisant made the flight in an elapsed time that was a shade under a minute less than Grahame-White's.

The ensuing flap was terrific. The press was deliriously happy over the fact that an American had "won" the Statue of Liberty race. "Moisant's flight was the most superb thing the world has ever seen in an aeroplane," said the New York *Herald*. Grahame-White protested, asked for another flight, was refused, then challenged Moisant to a rematch. Moisant declined, saying, "I don't care a farthing for the ten thousand dollars, but I do care for the honor of America."

Not all the Americans were on Moisant's side. Chips Drexel was outraged. At a special press conference he stated, "I am an American myself, but I cannot allow such startling unfairness to pass without a protest. As a result it will be freely said in Europe that the Statue of Liberty prize was juggled into an American's hands. My disgust at this betrayal is more than I can express. It is my intention to resign immediately from the Aero Club, and I hope all American sportsmen will follow my example." He organized a boycott of the Aero Club dinner at the end of the meet and attracted about half the aviators, including Grahame-White, to a monumental dinner and drinking party. Grahame-White left the rebel party early, though, for he felt duty bound to appear at the official Aero Club banquet and pick up his Gordon Bennett Trophy and prize money that totaled $13,600.

Two years later, after much debate and investigation, the internationally governing FAI ruled that Grahame-White had won the Statue of Liberty race and he was awarded the $10,000 prize, plus five percent interest. But this was really *ex post facto* quibbling. As far as the American press and public were concerned, a new hero had been crowned: the handsome, enigmatic John Moisant.

1910: iii

The Moisants—aviator John and financier Alfred—moved quickly to capitalize on the favorable publicity the younger brother had received at Belmont. With several other Belmont pilots they formed a new aerial exhibition team and got booked into towns which hadn't seen a Wright or Curtiss team so far. In virgin territory where people had never seen an airplane fly, it didn't take much of a show to turn out a crowd, and as long as Moisant and the Wright and Curtiss pilots performed in places where the airplane was an unfamiliar sight, they were safe. They didn't have to push their planes or themselves too hard. The main thing, as Ross Browne sensed at Belmont, was to keep somebody up in the air as long as there were paying customers in the grandstands. It was a nice setup, but it couldn't last. More and more men were learning to fly and more and more airplanes were being built.

Elsewhere in America other men were becoming active who founded firms that would carry their names proudly into the space age. Kansas-born Clyde Cessna was one of these. He built his first plane in the winter of 1910 and tested it on some salt flats near Cherokee, Oklahoma. It wasn't altogether successful, as he once related in *Chirp*, the journal of the Early Birds, a society of aviators who soloed before World War I:

I had many trials and heartbreaking experiences and as many wrecks, for a wreck was as sure to occur as was the trial. One trial, one wreck was about the proportion, for in those days there was no such thing as aircraft information available or any aircraft magazines. In fact, I approached this subject with no more knowledge of the problem than a nursing babe. My experiences there on those salt plains in rebuilding and attempting to fly with an Elbridge two-cycle engine, which would overheat in about ten minutes of operation, was one that I shall never forget. Many a time I found it necessary to spend what little money I had for repairs instead of for something to eat. It was a common occurrence at our camp, which consisted of my brother and myself, to salt our flapjacks with the crude salt from the surface of the plains.

But this got him started and today there are more Cessna private planes flying throughout the world than any other type.

Another big name today in American aviation is Lockheed—which once was spelled "Loughead." Allan Loughead made his

Clyde Cessna's 1911 airplane crashed regularly, but he finally mastered it and went on to found the world's largest light-plane manufacturing company.

first flight in Chicago in 1910 in a Curtiss biplane. He flew exhibitions for a while, then returned to his native California, where he teamed up with his brother Malcolm to design and build a new kind of floatplane capable of carrying a passenger. They chris-

Telephone lines were one of the greatest natural hazards to early pilots. This one brought down Allan Loughead's first airplane.

tened it their "Model G" to create the impression that they had built several prior successful types. The company that Allan and Malcolm Loughead started had many financial setbacks over the years, but under aggressive new management in the 1930's the Lockheed Aircraft Corporation emerged as one of the leaders of America's aviation industry.

During this early period Glenn L. Martin, founder of the Martin Marietta Corporation, also got his start in aviation. He built his first airplane in 1907. It was a primitive monoplane which was smashed beyond repair after a wild and fruitless dash across a pasture near Santa Ana, California, the first time he tried to fly it. This was before the Wrights convinced the skeptics with their performances in France and at Fort Myer; thus Martin's first attempt was greeted with the same kind of ridicule that had been directed at Langley, though in a smaller dose since Martin was not a well-known scientist but a somewhat obscure automobile dealer and mechanic. He built his next aircraft secretly in an abandoned church with his mother as his only helper. He rolled it out in the summer of 1909, a large biplane with a decided resemblance to the standard Curtiss machine. On August 1 he made his first successful flight, a hop of 100 feet. He continued to improve the plane and put in an appearance with it at a second meet at Dominguez Field, in December, 1910, making two short, undistinguished flights.

Martin felt that the future of aviation lay in building aircraft, so he hit the exhibition trail with an improved airplane to earn enough capital to put himself in business. A shy, introverted man with a sober expression and steel-rimmed glasses, he operated alone instead of with a team. Shrewdly sensing the value of ballyhoo, he billed himself as "the Flying Dude" and wore a black leather jacket, black trousers, black puttees and a black helmet with goggles whenever he put on a show. Though there wasn't much of a market for airplanes when Martin incorporated his company in 1912, he made enough money from his exhibition flying to keep things going and ultimately to prosper.

The ripples made by the careers of Martin and the Lougheads have indeed washed some distant shores. One of the first men hired by the fledgling Loughead Aircraft Manufacturing Company was the visionary airplane designer John K. Northrop, who later founded his own company. Martin sold a Seattle engineer named William E. Boeing his first airplane, thus launching him on a distinguished aviation career, and hired Donald Douglas, Sr., Lawrence D. Bell and J. A. "Dutch" Kindelberger as designers and engineers. Douglas and Bell founded famous firms of their own—today they are the Douglas Aircraft Corporation and the Bell Aerosystems Company—while Kindelberger became president of North American Aviation in 1934, a few years after it was formed as a holding company, and was instrumental in building it into one of the nation's largest corporations.

There were many others drawn into aviation in the early days besides those who rose to the top, and as the field became more crowded the competitive pressure began to build up among the established aviators. By September, 1910, Wilbur Wright felt it

Glenn L. Martin's first successful airplane was built in 1910.

necessary to lay down the law to Hoxsey and Johnstone about dangerous flying. "I am very much in earnest when I say that I want no stunts and spectacular flights," he wrote to Arch Hoxsey before a meet in Detroit. "If each of you can make a plain flight of ten to fifteen minutes each day keeping always within the inner fence well away from the grandstand and never more than three hundred feet high it will be just what we want. Under no circumstances make more than one flight each day apiece. Anything beyond plain flying will be chalked up as a fault and not as a credit. Please let Mr. Johnstone see this letter so that both may have the same instructions."

Despite the Wright debacle at Belmont, Hoxsey and Johnstone were still billed as the world's greatest aviators—"the Star Dust Twins," people called them. It was ridiculous to order them to take it easy and still expect them to put on the kind of show that would draw the crowds and make lots of money. And so when they resumed their exhibition flying after Belmont, they also resumed their now famous rivalry.

Mid-November found them both performing in Denver, a city that presented some difficulty in putting on a good show because of its altitude. It is about 5,000 feet above sea level, which was not far from the altitude record at that time. Takeoffs in the thin air required a longer run, it took more time to get up to a safe altitude for stunts, and it was harder for the pilots to hold this altitude once they were there. Johnstone analyzed the problem for a reporter: "If there should be an accident and the machine falls, it will come down straight as a rocket. The heavier air in the East acts as a cushion. This air a mile above sea level is too rarefied. It has no body."

Hoxsey and Johnstone started out cautiously in Denver, first getting the feel of the unfamiliar environment with leisurely flights in front of the grandstand at Overland Park. The first day's flying was marred by an accident which damaged the wing of one aircraft. On the second day, the pilots grew bolder. Hoxsey thrilled the crowd with a spectacular dash over the nearby foothills of the Rockies. When it was Johnstone's turn, he did the usual dips and glides in front of the grandstand, then climbed to

800 feet and began a "spiral glide," a maneuver for which the Wright pilots were famous. This was not a difficult stunt, being nothing more than a descending spiral with the engine throttled back. But Johnstone liked to add some special touches of his own, such as wrapping his plane up in a steep bank in the turns and pulling out at the last possible moment.

No one is quite certain what went wrong this time. One eyewitness thought he saw a strut snap and the tip of Johnstone's left wing fold up during the second turn of the spiral. To Walter Brookins, who was also performing at Denver, it seemed as though Johnstone fell out of his seat in a tight turn and threw the plane violently out of control as he clutched for the control levers in a vain attempt to save himself. (No safety belts were used in those days, the dubious theory being that it was better to be thrown clear of a crash than trapped inside the wreckage by seat belts and shoulder harnesses.) The plane dove into the ground out of control from an altitude of about 500 feet. Johnstone was dead when the first rescuers reached the crash, his back, neck and both legs broken.

After Johnstone's accident, the Wright pilots continued on their exhibition tour and ended the year on the West Coast with a flying date at Dominguez Field near Los Angeles, the site of Curtiss' and Louis Paulhan's flights in January. As the end of the year approached, a contest began to shape up for a prize of 20,000 francs, or $4,000, offered by the French tire manufacturer André Michelin for the longest sustained flight of the year. Wilbur Wright had won it in France in 1908 with his December 31 flight of 124 kilometers in two hours and twenty minutes. In 1909, Henri Farman was awarded the prize for a flight of 234 kilometers.

While the Wright team was in California, word came from New Orleans that John Moisant would make an officially sanctioned bid for the prize while his International Aviators were in that city for a year-end show. Then, on December 30, Maurice Tabuteau, a newcomer on the French aviation scene, logged an impressive 362.66 miles in seven hours and forty-five minutes. This would be hard to beat, but nevertheless Arch Hoxsey decided to try for a new record on December 31.

A stunned crowd gathers around the wreckage of the Wright airplane in which Arch Hoxsey died in Los Angeles in 1910.

It wasn't a very promising day. The weather in Los Angeles was stormy and cold and the gusts of wind were troublesome. Hoxsey took off, flew for an hour and a half and got up to 7,000 feet in an attempt to beat the new world altitude record of 11,474 feet which he himself had set only ten days earlier. But the weather was too bad to continue the flight—or did something go wrong with his plane? No one ever found out for sure. A reporter covering the exhibition for the New York *American* gave this eyewitness account:

He started down in a spiral descent. As the little speck gradually grew larger, it could be seen that the daredevil birdman was rushing earthward with one perpendicular swirl after another. At times it seemed as if the craft almost stood on beam end. Even those who had watched him day after day grew afraid. The cheering subsided to a silent prayer for the man in the frail thing of cloth and sticks.

Suddenly, after he had made a waltzing turn around the purlieus of the field, 500 feet up in the air, he attempted another hair-raising bank. But as the craft almost stood on its end, an unexpected puff of gusty wind blew full blast in its rear. Instantly the craft turned over. . . . The cracking of the spars and ripping of the cloth could be heard as the machine, a shapeless mass, came hurtling to the ground in a series of somersaults.

When the attendants rushed to the tangled mass of wreckage they found the body crushed out of all semblance to a human being. The crowd waited until the announcer megaphoned the fatal news and then turned homeward. All flying was over for the day.

First Johnstone, then Hoxsey. The Wright team was crushed. But just a few hours before Hoxsey's death, the uncertain science of aviation had claimed the life of another great pilot, John Moisant, who, flying in New Orleans, had also set out to win the Michelin Prize on December 31.

Ross Browne was there at the end:

He started in the morning, quite early, about seven o'clock. He loaded up his plane with gas and took off. I think he had flown about two and a half or three hours—I'm not quite positive—but, anyway, he'd been past us a couple of times, going from City Park to Hallahan and back. He was long overdue on one lap and Roland Garros and Maurice, one of the French mechanics, and I were standing there saying, "What happened? He must have come down somewhere. He was due here at least two or three minutes ago."

We were in the middle of the field, or near the middle, and looked over to the grandstand. A fellow was waving a flag at us. He yelled, "You're wanted on the telephone," so we went over there. Whoever it was that phoned said, "He's down, but we haven't got to the machine yet."

I said, "Get to the machine as quick as you can. See what's happening and let us know."

We kept the line open, and about ten or fifteen minutes later the man came back. He said, "Well, he's killed."

I said, "Oh, my God!"

Garros immediately got in his machine and flew up there, but he had to come back. He said, "No use flying up there—you can't land."

We all got in a car and went to see what happened. Johnny was killed instantly. His neck must have been broken. But he wasn't bruised much. We looked at the machine. His gas was only about half gone. But Maurice, Garros and myself were absolutely sure what had happened was that he had some ignition trouble, and had come down for a landing. In coming down, coming down quick, all of that gas flew to the front of the tank and kept his center of gravity too low, so that he couldn't pull back quick enough. We could tell that he crash-landed, because the wheels were bent right back, and ordinarily he would never have landed that way. But it's the only thing we could lay it to. We're not positive, but it's the only thing we could figure out.

That put a damper on our New Orleans thing, and here is the ironic part of it. The day before this, Garros and I had been taken out and shown the Métairie Cemetery, which is quite a showplace in New Orleans. Everybody is buried aboveground there, because everywhere there is water just below the surface. They've got ornate tombs all over that cost thousands and thousands of dollars. Here we were there for a visit and two days later Johnny's there for good.

The deaths of Johnstone and Hoxsey confirmed what had been hinted at Belmont—that high noon had come and gone in the careers of the Wright brothers. Much substantial flying still lay ahead for Wright pilots and airplanes, but the great moments were almost over. The French and German Wright companies were in trouble by the end of 1910 because of poor supervision. At home the brothers were embroiled in patent infringement suits with Glenn Curtiss and others. These took time and energy and slowed down the work of the two men in the design and production of new airplanes. The infringement cases had the further effect of committing the Wrights almost irrevocably to their basic wing-warping biplane design. After their dogged defense of the principles behind this design in the patent cases, they could not then discard them very easily and adopt some of the newer ideas.

As long as the exhibition flying lasted, the Wrights were able to make considerable money at it. According to Frank Coffyn, they charged a fee of $1,000 per day for each one of their pilots who flew in an exhibition. They paid the pilots only $20 per week plus $50 for every day they flew. Thus, in a six-day week of flying (they never permitted any of their pilots to fly on Sunday) the Wrights collected $6,000 per pilot and paid him only $320. This wasn't bad money for the pilots in those days, but the Curtiss crowd was getting fifty percent of the take and as time went by most of the better pilots gravitated toward work with Curtiss airplanes.

But the Wright pilots were proud men. Frank Coffyn put it this way in his interview for the Columbia Oral History project:

We were taught by the Wrights that the Curtiss crowd was just no good at all. We turned up our noses at them. But we found out later on, by flying at the same meets, that they were a pretty nice bunch of fellows.

One of them was Eugene Ely, who became a great friend of mine later on after I got to know him better. Down at the Army maneuvers at Fort Sam Houston I took him up for a flight in my plane, and then he said, "I think you ought to have a flight with me."

I said, "I don't know. I don't much care about flying in that Curtiss plane." The Wrights had always hinted that they didn't think the Curtiss planes were any good and that they were dangerous to fly. But I went ahead anyway with Ely. I sat on a strip of canvas right back of him with my legs around him and he took me up. He just scared the devil out of me!"

The lure of easy money in exhibition flying seems to have further dimmed the Wrights' vision of new directions in the field which they had founded. "The strange part of it was that they never thought there was any future for aviation except for exhibition flights," said Frank Coffyn. "They never visualized anything else for it. They saw no potential for commercial or passenger flights. At least they never mentioned it if they had any ideas of this kind, and I was pretty close to them during those years I worked for them."

But others were looking ahead. In 1910, Glenn Curtiss hired his first salesman, a young automobile dealer named Beckwith Havens. All the leads to prospective buyers of Curtiss airplanes were turned over to him. But he was at a great disadvantage, for he had never been up in an airplane, much less flown one, and the first question his prospects always asked was, "What is it like up there?" So Havens went to Hammondsport to see if Curtiss would teach him to fly. Thus began one of the most unusual flying careers in the history of aviation. He died in May, 1969, the last of the aviators from the early exhibition teams that Curtiss and the Wrights fielded, and he had a valid pilot's license until the end. When he used to talk about how he learned to fly and what it was like on the exhibition trail, the exciting, carnival world of the exhibition pilot came to life again as though it were yesterday:

When I went to Hammondsport, Curtiss was still kind of a little country boy. He told me that he was going to start a school to teach people to fly.

"It'll be five hundred dollars," he said. "If you have five hundred dollars, we'll teach you to fly. School hasn't opened yet."

I said, "Mr. Curtiss, I'm already working for you, I'm on the payroll and have been for some time. So I think you ought to teach me how to fly for nothing."

"No, I can't do that, I've got to charge you."

I was furious, and I went tearing back to New York and our business manager, Jerome Fanciulli, just laughed. "Just sign a note for the five hundred dollars," he said, "and I'll endorse it for you. I'm just inundated with telegrams and letters from all over the world. They want to see exhibition fliers, because people don't believe an airplane can fly. I'll put you right on, flying, and the first couple of days, you'll make the five hundred dollars."

That was all right with me, so back to Hammondsport I went, to school. Curtiss himself had just taught Spuds Ellyson, the first Navy flier. The Wrights, you see, had gone to the Army and gotten started with them, two years before that, and Curtiss wanted to get in on this military business. So he wrote a letter to the Navy Department and told them that if they'd detail three officers to him, he'd teach them to fly at no cost to the government. So the first one they sent him to teach to fly was Spuds Ellyson. Spuds and I got a room together in a boardinghouse there at Hammondsport, and Curtiss began teaching us how to fly.

We started out in a little plane with the throttle wired back so it wouldn't take off. Well, there was such a demand for fliers that it wasn't long before Curtiss came down to the field one day and set up a new machine that was supposed to be a little faster than the old one. He said, "Let me see if you can fly that thing," and I said, "Sure." So I made a hop—there wasn't much room to fly there at Hammondsport anyhow—and he sent me out on the road with it right away. It wasn't any good. I had a terrible time getting out of those fields where we flew. Of course, I was green as grass anyhow. The first date I flew was with Lincoln Beachey, the great exhibition flier, at Erie, New York. Then I went to Maine and filled some other dates, but I was having trouble getting this thing up in the air, so I wired Curtiss and said, "I will not be responsible for any damage done to this machine. It will not fly."

So Curtiss wired me to stop off at Squantum and pick up another airplane and send it to my next date, which was Lewiston. So I did, and oh, my gracious, it was like being on a skyrocket to take off with that thing. It was then that I finally found out how they were doing this wonderful flying.

We were so busy that year that before the season was out, I had flown exhibitions all over thirteen states and Cuba. I'd be on a sleeper every night, catching up with the boys and the ships. I'd make the flight, then back on the train to make the next town. But we were killing them off so fast that I was beginning to fill everybody else's dates, you see. They started us out with a machine and two mechanics. Most of the others had managers with them to do the collecting and arranging, but they sent me alone. I ended up with three machines and three sets of mechanics.

You know, people always ask, "How could you fly those awful crates?" but they weren't awful crates. We thought they were the finest flying machines in the world—and they were, then, and very modern, right up to the minute. But the worst problems we had were the fields. Fanciulli would book a date wherever he could get it, see, and he'd say, "You got a place to fly from?"

Beckwith Havens

They'd always answer, "Oh, yes." Well, they always seemed to assume that an airplane went up like a balloon.

This was a standard procedure: I'd go out to the field with Lou Krantz—I had a wonderful head mechanic, Lou Krantz, a Hammondsport boy—and Lou would say, "Can't fly here, don't you try to fly out of here." I'd say, "Let's see, let's look it over a little bit. Maybe if they took those wires down, maybe if they took a couple of those trees out." We'd talk to the fair manager and they'd usually do what we wanted, so we could get out.

The infield would be a half-mile track—that's what they considered a place where you could get out. Sometimes it was a ball field. Gosh, the worst place I ever got out of was Charlottesville, Virginia. They had me booked there to fly at an old low stadium, a natural stadium, just a little bowl, a horseshoe place, and they had the seats up on these banks. The curve of the horseshoe faced down into a valley and was fenced in, of course. So I had them take down that fence and away I went. The trouble was that the wind was from the other direction, and when I started down that valley, I couldn't get enough altitude to turn. I was flying five or six feet off the ground, missing trees and barns and haystacks. I was wondering how I'd get down that valley without hitting anything. Then I shot up in the air, on a puff of wind— and a good thing I did, too, because up the valley was a railroad trestle. But all of a sudden I shot up and I was looking down at it. I thought, "If I ever get down on the ground now, I'll sure get out of this place." That's the way it was.

The contracts all called for three ten-minute flights, or two fifteens. We would usually fly between two and four o'clock in the afternoon. The people who came to watch thought we were fakes. There weren't many yet who believed an airplane would really fly. In fact, they'd give odds. But when you flew, oh my, they'd carry you off the field. . . .

We had trouble, sometimes. I had a date, a single-plane date, in Chippewa Falls, Wisconsin, two days, and it was a terrible place to get out of. They had to take some wires down. They had a tent to put the airplane in, and charged admission to the tent. The two dates were so successful that they asked us to stay another day and made me a very generous proposition to stay over. It was a mistake, for the next day the weather was awful, the wind was howling, and we had to put a lot of extra guys on the tent to hold it down. I stalled off the flight as long as I could, hoping this wind would go down, and finally took off, and I was fighting this awful wind. I was thin in those days, only weighed about a hundred thirty pounds, and was having a terrible time trying to control the plane. I thought, "I'm going to have to come down in the street, nobody lands in the street," and then I landed and smashed everything up. I hit some wires that were across the street, but they hadn't turned on the power. I wasn't hurt.

To make a long story short, I had no airplane but I did have a date to fly in Chanute, Kansas. I wired ahead to Curtiss and a new plane arrived on the day we were supposed to fly, just before two o'clock. So we trucked it out to the field—horse trucks in those days—and opened the crates. The plane had never been set up. The bolt holes weren't even drilled. So we went to work and started to put it together and the crowd got out of hand. They started roughing us up. We had police protection, but you know, in case of trouble like that, the police were always with the townies. So they just disappeared.

We put a rope around the plane to keep the crowd back while

we were working. They tore that down. Then they started pushing the machine around, pushing us around, and we got in a couple of fights. They were saying, "Fake! Fake! Fake! You know that thing can't fly!"

We finally got it set up, and the boys and I pushed it out on the field. I hadn't even run the engine yet. The crowd was still all milling around it. I was furious. I finally stood up on the seat and yelled at them, "This thing doesn't go up like a balloon the way you think it does. I have to go over the ground at sixty miles an hour before I get any lift, and if I hit anybody, he's going to get killed. But I'm starting now!"

I started the engine—I've often thought since, it would have been awful if it hadn't started, but the engine started and of course they made a terrific noise in those days. It seemed to be going all right, so I gunned it, and the crowd fell back, and I didn't hurt anyone. But then they all milled back on the field again. It was late in the evening and the lights were beginning to come on. "I've got to land while I can see a little bit," I thought. The crowd was all over the field, but the boys had armed themselves with wooden struts, and that way they cleared some room for me.

We were there, of course, to show the public we could fly—but those crowds! They didn't believe the plane would fly!

One time I was flying in Ashland, Wisconsin, on Lake Superior, and the infield of the race track was so full of rocks that I was taking off on the straightaway. But I had to land in the infield. The minute I'd land on the ground, I'd jump out and hold on the seat and drag. One of the mechanics would take one wing and the other the other wing, and we'd all drag and stop the plane before we hit the fence. Here everybody was getting bruised up with all these rocks and everything. So I decided I'd try a trick with a rope. We got a long rope and I had the boys, just the two of them, hold it so it would be just high enough in the center, at the lowest point, to snag the front wheel. Then I said, "Now, I'll go right into that, and you fellows just hold on."

Well, it worked like a charm. Before the Navy thought up their arresting gear for aircraft carriers, I was using this.

When I was flying a date at Springfield, Illinois, the next spring, and I didn't have my own machine and boys with me, just a couple from the factory, it was a two-plane deal. Charlie Moss was there with me. We had a long narrow field with a great big red barn at one end of it, and we had to go out and come in the same way, no matter where the wind was. So Charlie went out first, and his engine quit right off the bat and he crashed. So I told these men from the factory how to handle this rope. "I'm going to fly right up to that barn," I said. "I'll hit the ground here, and you check me there, and hold the rope loose."

They didn't understand how two men could stop me with a loose rope. So they got all the help they could get to hold it. They pulled the rope as tight as they could get it and it was like an iron bar. It went right through the plane and caught me in the legs and the rope just cut right to the bone. It stopped the airplane but it almost cut my leg off.

We shipped the planes by express everywhere because they were only good for short flights. The tank only held five gallons of gas. Those engines wouldn't run very long anyhow. The early Curtiss planes had that long boom sticking out in front with a sort of box kite on the end that was supposed to be a forward control surface. Lincoln Beachey was flying one day and hit a fence and broke his front controls. Well, there was a lot of money riding on this date and Beachey was out after it. So even though he didn't have any front control he flew anyway. He did some wonderful flying! So I thought, "There's something about this— he couldn't fly that much better than anyone else. I'll take my front control off, too." So I said to my head mechanic, "Lou, here's a chance to take my front control off." But he didn't want to do it. "Not unless Curtiss tells me to," he said. So I kept after him for a couple of days.

Finally he gave in. "All right, I'll do it on one condition, and that is I'll set the thing up the day before, and you come out and fly it before the crowd is here."

So I did, and it was just like you'd been shackled all your life and you suddenly tore off your shackles. Oh, it could fly! It was a mistake having those two controls, one in front and one in back, because the two controls were just fighting each other.

The first year I was on the road was 1911. In the winter of 1911–1912 I was putting on an air show in Havana, Cuba, with Beachey and two other pilots, Charley Watts and Gene Goday. It was at Camp Columbia, which was way out in the country. We had to chase cows off the field before we could take off. And Gene Goday cracked up—poor fellow, he always did. Then they wanted us to fly over the city. Well, it's quite a flight from Camp Columbia to the city, and there was no place to land anywhere around there. We didn't want to do it. They went ahead and said in the paper we were going to do it. This boxed us in. If we had backed out, it would have looked terrible. So Beachey said all right, he'd do it. I said, "All right, I'll do it." So Charley Watts said he'd do it. He had his wife with him—his wife and children traveled with him—and she took a pair of pliers and stood right ahead of the machine and said, "Charley, if you take off I'll throw these pliers right through your prop!" So he didn't take off.

So Beachey and I had to do it. We flew across the town, around Morro Castle—me thinking all the time about all those sharks that are off Morro Castle—and out to the field. Oh, we got a terrific hand. It was the first flight over Havana.

Of course, it was crowd-pleasing like this that killed a lot of pilots. With no inherent stability, it was very hard to handle turbulent air. When it was blowing hard, nobody wanted to fly if they could help it, but the crowds would demand that you go up. The program said you were going to fly at two-thirty. Well, maybe the wind was blowing pretty hard. You were always watching the wind, you know—watching smoke, watching flags, laundry on the line and everything. I still do it. I always watch to see what the wind is like, whether it's rough or strong and so forth. I think with the crowds yelling at them and everything, some pilots would take off when they shouldn't.

I can tell a lot of anecdotes to back up that thesis about the wind and the crowds. I remember I once had a one-day date at Enid, Oklahoma, on a Sunday. The flight was put on by the newspaper there. The editor met me at the train and took me up to his house for Sunday lunch. While we were having lunch he told me that they had had John Curry there the year before but due to the high winds he hadn't been able to fly. Then he said, "You know, our people just don't believe it's possible to fly."

With that, a gust of wind slammed the front door and blew a picture off the wall. I thought, "Oh, boy, am I going to have trouble here!"

We went out to the field, where they had set up a kind of

bleachers or grandstand right out there on the prairie. A big crowd began to gather. As usual they were kind of skeptical, and there was booing and so on going on. The wind was pretty high, and I thought, "This is going to be rugged." In that kind of situation we used to try to stall, because usually the wind would go down towards sundown. The first flight was usually scheduled for two o'clock, and that would be about the worst time because of the sun's effect upon the ground. To kill time, and also to see if there were any gopher holes that might trip me up, I started walking away from the grandstands. Also I wanted to get away from them because all those people hooting at me and so on were making me nervous. I started to walk across the prairie looking for gopher holes, got out a ways and heard a horse galloping after me. It was the sheriff in a buckboard behind a calico pony. He was in a buckboard because he only had one leg—he'd had a leg shot off in a gunfight. He pulled his pony back so that he slid up alongside me, looked down at me and said, "Son, are you going to fly?"

I said, "Yes."

"Git in here!" I got in with him, he pulled the pony around, back we went at a gallop and pulled up in a sliding stop in front of the grandstand. He got up on his one good leg, hitched his gun belt up, held up one arm for quiet, and when the crowd had quieted down a bit he yelled at the top of his lungs so that everybody heard him, "Folks, give this boy a chance! This is the last ride he takes before he rides with the undertaker."

With that everybody laughed. That broke the tension. I took off, and everything was all right, so I was a big hero—but that's the way it was. We were out there convincing the skeptics that it was possible to fly heavier-than-air. That was in 1911. That was the great year of exhibition flying.

I was with Curtiss four years altogether—as a salesman in 1910, then three years of exhibition flying from then to 1913. The great year of exhibition flying was 1911. We took our planes around in 1912 too. In 1913 I don't suppose I flew half a dozen dates, and one of the reasons was that Curtiss had gotten into flying boats and it was some time before I got to fly one.

The seaplane and its natural habitat offered the early pilots a tantalizing vision of no rocks, no potholes, no power lines, and no crowds swarming about the plane before it started or, worse, milling around the field where they were trying to land. There were still only half a dozen or so facilities in the world that could be recognized as airfields as we think of them today; thus the world's vast stretches of coastal waters, rivers, lakes and bays began to look awfully inviting.

But operating from water is not a simple matter. In addition to the obvious problems of waves, spray and leaking floats, there is the phenomenon of surface tension. The same force that keeps a glass of water from overflowing when it has been filled above its rim also makes floating objects act as though they are stuck to the surface. Considerably more force is needed to lift something off water than off land.

Glenn Curtiss was the first American pilot to grapple with these problems. In November, 1908, he mounted two pontoons on his pioneering airplane, the *June Bug*, rechristened her the *Loon*, and made several attempts to take off from Lake Keuka near Hammondsport. It was difficult enough getting the underpowered *June Bug* to rise off land; the extra effort to unstick the *Loon* from the surface of Lake Keuka was too much for her, and after taxiing around the lake for a while Curtiss gave up, unable to coax the *Loon* to rise from water.

However, his interest in water operations continued and, stimulated by the work the Wrights were doing for the U. S. Army, Curtiss set out to get some business from the U. S. Navy. The Navy was surprisingly receptive and interested, not only in seaplanes but also in the possibilities of taking off and landing aboard ship, and made the cruiser *Birmingham* available to Curtiss for trials in the fall of 1910. It was fitted out with a wooden platform, and while it was at anchor in Hampton Roads, Virginia, Eugene Ely came down from Baltimore, where he had been flying in a meet, and loaded his plane aboard. On November 14, he started up his motor, raced down the platform and disappeared over the bow. Seconds later, up he came again, still flying. His wheels had touched the water, but nevertheless he had made the first takeoff from a ship. He flew straight to shore and landed without further incident.

Curtiss pilot Eugene Ely makes a perfect approach to the U.S.S. *Pennsylvania* for the world's first shipboard landing.

That winter Curtiss transferred some of his flying operations to California, where the weather was better, and resumed his work with the Navy. This led to a fantastic piece of airmanship in January, 1911, which he later wrote about with considerable pride:

It began to look, even to the doubters, as if an aeroplane could be made adaptable to the uses of the Navy, as the aeronautic enthusiasts of the service had claimed. The experiment begun would have to be completed, however, by flying from shore to the vessel, and for this opportunity we were eager. The chance came when we were all at San Francisco and the big armored cruiser *Pennsylvania* was in the bay. Rear Admiral Thomas, and Captain Pond, in command of the *Pennsylvania*, readily consented to assist in these further experiments. The *Pennsylvania* went to Mare Island to be outfitted, Ely and I going there to tell the Navy officials at the station just what would be required for such a hazardous test.

The platform was like that built on the *Birmingham,* but in case of a flight to, instead of from, a ship the serious problem is to land the aeroplane on the deck and stop it quickly before it runs into the masts of the ship or other obstructions. The platform was built over the quarterdeck, about one hundred and twenty-five feet long and twenty-five feet wide, with a slope toward the stern of some twelve feet. Across this runway we stretched ropes every few feet so they could catch in grap-hooks which we placed under the main centerpiece of the aeroplane, so that catching in the ropes the heavy sand bags attached would drag until they brought the machine to a stop.

To protect the aviator and to catch him in case he should be pitched out of his seat in landing, heavy awnings were stretched on either side of the runway and at the upper end of it.

When all the arrangements had been completed, and only favourable weather was needed to carry out the experiment, I was obliged to leave for San Diego, and, therefore, was unable to witness the flight. I regarded the thing as most difficult of accomplishment. Of course, I had every faith in Ely as an aviator, and knew that he would arrive at the ship without trouble, but I must confess that I had misgivings about his being able to come down on a platform but four feet wider than the width of the planes of the aeroplane, and to bring it to a stop within the hundred feet available for the run.

Ely rose from the Presidio parade grounds, flew out over the bay, hovered above the ship for an instant, and then swooped down, cutting off his power and running lightly up the platform, when the drag of the sand bags brought him to a stop exactly in the center, probably one of the greatest feats in accurate landing ever performed by an aviator. As I have said, the platform was only four feet wider than the planes of the Curtiss biplane that Ely used, yet the photograph taken from the fighting top of the ship shows the machine touching the platform squarely in the center. When one stops to think that the aeroplane was traveling about forty miles an hour when it touched the deck and was brought to a stop within a hundred feet, the remarkable precision of the aviator will be appreciated.

Not only was there not the least mishap to himself or to the machine in landing, but as soon as he had received a few of the many excited congratulations awaiting him, he started off again and flew back the ten miles to the camp of the 30th Infantry on the Aviation Field, where wild cheers greeted the man and the machine.

So, at a surprisingly early date, there were all the basic ingredients for the aircraft carrier: the large naval vessel, the flight deck with lines stretched across it for arresting gear, and an airplane that could use it. All that was lacking was vision; eleven years were to pass before the second landing and takeoff were made from a U. S. Navy ship, the *Langley*, in 1922. In the meantime, the British Navy independently developed the aircraft carrier and had several operating by the end of World War I. Attack planes from one of them, H. M. S. *Furious*, even conducted a successful bombing raid on German North Sea zeppelin sheds in July, 1918, and destroyed two of the immense airships that were being readied for raids on London.

But the U. S. Navy was still interested in doing business with Curtiss. "When you show me that it is feasible for an aeroplane to alight on the water alongside a battleship and be hoisted aboard it without any false deck to receive it," said Secretary of the Navy Meyer in a letter to Curtiss, "I shall believe the aircraft to be of practical benefit to the Navy." Curtiss wasted no time responding to Secretary Meyer's challenge and in early January, 1911, established a base at North Island in San Diego Bay. Here he began experimenting once again with seaplanes. He also finished teaching the Navy's first pilot, Lieutenant Theodore G. Ellyson, how to fly.

According to legend, Curtiss came up with a successful float design for his pusher biplane while attending the theater with Mrs. Curtiss in New York just before moving to California. As the first act moved toward its high point, he turned to his wife and said, "I've got it!" and showed her a design he had sketched on the theater program. Or so the story goes.

Unfortunately, the seaplane that Curtiss shipped to California from his Hammondsport factory was not a great success at first.

Curtiss "hydro-aeroplane" is hauled out for a test flight from North Island in San Diego Bay.

"Instead of the usual three-wheeled landing gear, there was a short, wide pontoon under the wings, where the rear wheels had been, and a very small pontoon where the front wheel had been," recalls George E. A. Hallett, chairman of the historical committee of the San Diego Aerospace Museum, whom Curtiss hired to help out temporarily with the new plane. Says Hallett:

When this rig was put in the water, it needed flotation on the wing tips to keep the plane from tipping over in the wind, so we added inflated motorcycle tubes to the ash "shingles" which acted as planing surfaces on the wing tips while the craft was taxiing on the water.

When we started the engine the thrust of the propeller, which was about four feet above the water, pushed the nose down under the water. We then added a wood planing surface at the nose. With this combination, Curtiss could taxi slowly, but water boiled over the top of the rear pontoon and the plane could not get up any speed.

After some more trial-and-error engineering, Curtiss finally coaxed his seaplane into the air on January 26, 1911. He made several short hops that day of a half mile or less at a few feet above the water. The honor of making the first takeoff from water does not go to Curtiss, however, but to a Frenchman, Henri Fabre, who managed to get an awkward-looking *canard* monoplane to rise from the Bay of Martigues, near Marseille, twice in the spring of 1910, but never again. Curtiss continued to make flights throughout January, 1911, and finally settled on a very successful, stable design which consisted of a single, scow-shaped wooden float that was 12 feet long and 2 feet wide. It was placed under the airplane so that the weight of the aircraft was slightly to the rear of the center of the float, causing the float to slant upward slightly. This tilt provided the angle needed for the float to plane over the surface of the water and free itself from the suction of the surface tension. On February 17, Curtiss took off from water in San Diego harbor, flew out to the U.S.S. *Pennsylvania* (the same ship Ely had landed on in San Francisco Bay) and alighted near it. The seaplane was hoisted aboard for ten minutes, then lowered into the water again, and Curtiss flew back to North Island, landing in the water a few feet from the beach. It was a disarmingly simple performance, as Ely's carrier landing had been, and it meant that the seaplane was now a practical reality for the U. S. Navy.

1911: i

E arly in 1911, the word got around among reporters covering aviation in the New York area that something unusual was going on at an airfield near Mineola, Long Island. But it wasn't until June 28 that an anonymous journalist from the New York *Herald* nailed it down. "For the first time since the sport of aviation was started in this country," he wrote, "two women were in flying machines at the same field and time yesterday." His story was flashed to newspapers across the country, and the two ladies, Blanche Scott and Harriet Quimby, were overnight sensations.

It is difficult for us to comprehend now just how much the news of America's first women pilots must have meant to a generation of women trapped in the hopelessness of sweatshops and menial labor or suffocated by the respectability of a middle-class life that permitted no step—not even a glance—beyond certain narrow, circumscribed patterns of life. In 1911, women were not able to vote—that issue was not laid to rest until the Nineteenth Amendment was ratified in 1920. They could not serve on juries or hold public office in most states; they found such professions as medicine and law closed to them more often than not; they were discriminated against in laws relating to ownership of property; and whenever they tried to do something about their situation, they were branded as wantons or worse.

Blanche Scott was the first American woman to break into aviation and was still living when this was written (she died in January, 1970). She came from Rochester, New York, originally and started out, as did so many early pilots, as an automobile driver. In 1910 she made a daring cross-country trip in an Overland car from New York to San Francisco, the first woman to accomplish this grueling feat.

She became interested in flying shortly after this and got Glenn Curtiss to teach her to fly. He trained her in Hammondsport as a member of his exhibition team, but backed out of the deal after she made her first public flight—in Fort Wayne, Indiana, in the fall of 1910. Miss Scott then went to Dayton and was promptly turned down by the sober, conservative Wrights, who wanted no part in the emancipation of women. Meanwhile, a Frenchwoman, Hélène Dutrieu, learned to fly a Santos-Dumont Demoiselle and got a head start on the American girls and with a lot less difficulty.

Blanche Scott

But some Americans were sympathetic to the idea of teaching women to fly. Alfred Moisant was one. In the six months following John Moisant's death near New Orleans, older brother Alfred had presided over the disbanding of the touring International Aviators team and had set up a flying school at Hempstead Plains, Long Island, near Mineola. From France he imported several Blériot machines and a pilot named André Houpert as his chief instructor. And he kept a promise that John had made to Harriet Quimby before he died.

"I think she was the prettiest girl I've ever seen," the Moisants' sister Matilde recalled many years later. "She was a California girl, born in San José. She had the most beautiful green eyes—oh, what eyes she had! And she was tall and willowy."

And glamorous. She was only twenty-seven years old, but was already the drama critic for *Leslie's Weekly* in New York City. This was the gay, golden era of Laurette Taylor, Billie Burke, the Barrymores—Ethel and John—and the great team of Weber and Fields. *Leslie's Weekly* catered to a fashionable and sophisticated New York crowd, and Harriet Quimby was an opening-night part of the scene. She had other strings to her bow and departed from time to time from her Broadway beat with such articles as "Saving One Thousand Babies' Lives," a report on infant mortality, and "The Girls Who Do NOT Go Wrong," an exposé of white slavery from the point of view of those who escaped its iniquitous clutches.

Her world touched John Moisant's on the night after he had made his triumphant Statue of Liberty flight at the Belmont Meet. He was celebrating his victory at a dinner party at the old Astor Hotel. Harriet Quimby met him as she was making her rounds with the theater crowd. "Will you teach me to fly?" she asked. "Any time you want," said Moisant. It was just casual chitchat on a splendid evening, but it gave Harriet Quimby an idea that would not leave her alone.

The Moisant flying school was set up in April, 1911. Harriet Quimby was first spotted taking lessons at the field by newspaper reporters in May, but she kept her identity a secret and was called "the woman aviator in trousers" until her story broke,

Harriet Quimby

along with that of Blanche Scott, a month later. The latter had
come to New York to see if she could work with veteran flier
Captain Thomas Baldwin. After his pioneering work with dirigibles, Baldwin was having difficulty making a place for himself in
the rapidly expanding airplane business. But by 1911 he had
built a biplane of his own design which seemed to fly pretty well,

and he too was sympathetic to the idea of women learning to fly.

Matilde Moisant was at the field the day when Blanche Scott signed up with Thomas Baldwin, and was standing with her brother when Baldwin came over to see if there was any objection to his giving Blanche Scott lessons.

"There's a young lady here who wants me to teach her to fly," Baldwin said. "The Wright brothers wouldn't do it. Their sister wouldn't let them teach a girl. I see that you have Miss Quimby and your sister out here, and I thought if you thought it was safe for them it might be all right for her."

Alfred Moisant agreed and soon Miss Scott was making hops in Baldwin's biplane, she in one seat and Baldwin in the other. It was almost inevitable that Matilde Moisant would also be bitten by the flying bug, with these two girls now going through the greatest adventure of their lives at her brother's field.

In a long and vivid tape-recorded interview for the Columbia Oral History Project, Miss Moisant relived these moments one last time before she died in 1964 at the age of seventy-six:

When my brother started this school on Long Island, Harriet Quimby asked him if he would take her as his student. She had a mother and father to take care of and she wanted to fly. So my brother said it would be all right, and that he would be glad to teach her gratis. So he did, and she said to me one day, "Kim, why don't you come and learn to fly? You've got just as much sense as I have."

My brother John had been killed just six months before that. "I don't know whether my family will let me do it or not," I said, "but I'll ask my oldest brother." He'd been like a father to me ever since Father died when I was a little girl. So I went to his office in New York and I said, "Fred, I want to fly."

Alfred looked at me very seriously. If he had said, "You can't," that would have ended it, but he looked at me and said, "What do you want to fly for?"

"Just for fun," I said.

He said, "Well, if you promise me you will not fly commercially, I'll let you do it."

So he got me some rooms and I started on the first of July. It was thirteen days before I could even sit in the machine. If there was more than a five-mile wind, they wouldn't let us sit in the machine. So from the first to the thirteenth I'd been going there every morning and every evening, and on the morning of the thirteenth, Mr. Houpert, the instructor my brother had brought from France, said to me, "Hurry up, Miss Moisant, the wind is four miles an hour, but if we can keep it at that, you'll have time to make a run on the ground."

We were all taught to fly the same way. We just had little single-seat machines. The first step was in a heavy machine not designed to leave the ground. That was *Saint Geneviève*. I remember her. She was the patron saint of the fliers in France. So we all started on *Saint Geneviève*.

When it came my turn, Mr. Houpert said, "Now, you see that clump of bushes way over there? Well, you're going to aim for that, but your first time, you're not going to reach there, because the machine has a tendency, when it starts to run on the ground, to swing to the right. You just cut off your motor as quick as you can and we'll come and get you and we'll start over again."

I said to myself, "If I make a turn this first time I'll never sit in the machine again." That was going to end flying for me.

The boy who used to wait at the other end to turn us around was going to stay behind to see the fun, because some students didn't cut off their motors in time and then the tail would go up. I said to the boy, "Quick, Henry, you go as fast as you can to that clump of bushes over there. The fun isn't going to be here, but over there. You can come right back as soon as you turn me around. I won't even cut off my motor, I'll just play with it, and you just spin the tail, and hang on to it if you want, but turn me on my track." So he did, and I followed my tracks right back to the starting place. "Did you like my circle?" I said. Mr. Houpert looked at me and said, "Well, you'll cut one next time." I said, "All right, I'll cut one every time you want me to, but not the first time."

Then he told my brother, "You know, your sister is what I call a natural-born flier."

The first stage of teaching was on the ground because they say the hardest thing is to guide a machine on the ground, not in the air. This was to teach you to keep it straight. Yes, quite a few people had trouble with that.

Then, your next machine was the *Grasshopper*. We could run a little bit, take her up five or six or eight feet, then come down. That was to get the feeling of being in the air. We were always alone. I tell you, nobody ever sat in a machine with me until 1932, when one of Roscoe Turner's fliers took me over San Francisco Bay and Oakland to see some old friends of mine in Alameda.

I think I spent four or five minutes in *Saint Geneviève* on the ground. So then I was given the *Grasshopper* to take up and put down.

Some of the men would go and get classes on the motor and the carburetor and all that. But I didn't—if I had I wouldn't have known what they were talking about. All I wanted to do was to fly.

I didn't make too many hops in the *Grasshopper*. We had little thirty-two-horsepower Anzani motors in those planes, so you know you couldn't go very fast or very high. Then the third plane was what we called the *Goat*. It was made out of white spruce and pine and bamboo, and the wings were cotton fabric put through some process to tighten the fabric and stiffen it. My time on that plus a little bit on the first two planes was thirty-two minutes when I was ready to try for my license.

We had an official timekeeper from the Aero Club of America —I think his name was Mr. Phillips—and he kept records of every student on the field. He clocked you from the minute your wheels started to run until the minute you got back, and sometimes my time was three minutes, sometimes five minutes, but it totaled thirty-two minutes when Mr. Houpert said I was ready to qualify for my license. Five minutes, two minutes, three minutes —whatever the time was, when the wind wouldn't come up too strong I'd keep on going.

It was just one month to the day that I learned to fly. I started on the thirteenth of July, and on the thirteenth of August I got my license. That was just one month, and in that one month I was in the plane exactly thirty-two minutes. It was just so wonderful for me to be in the plane and be able to manage it, because I always used to say, "Oh, if I were only a bird." I used to live in Central America and watch those big buzzards flying, and I thought, "Oh, how beautifully they fly!"

When it came to qualifying for your license, they put a great big piece of white muslin on the ground and you had to land within a hundred twenty feet from that, one way or the other. Harriet Quimby landed right on the dot. She made a beautiful landing. Mine wasn't so good, but it passed. I think I landed about a hundred feet from the white muslin, but still, I was within the requirements.

Then they had two pylons—I don't know the distance, but they weren't very far apart—and we had to go around those pylons at two hundred feet altitude. Now, you know, that wasn't very high. Four times around the pylons, two sets, and that was that. Then you got your license. Oh, it was lots of fun!

My flying career didn't last awfully long, because in those days—well, to put it this way: it was man's work, and they didn't think it was woman's work or that a nice girl should be in it. There were a few fliers that thought we had as much right as they, but most of them didn't. "Why don't they leave it to us?" was the attitude. . . .

I was the first woman to fly in Mexico City. That was my first real big flight. Of course, I had flown in Shreveport, Louisiana— that's where I had an awful fall. Then in Wichita I had another fall. That one could have been very serious. People had never seen a machine in the air in Wichita and there was quite a crowd. It was late afternoon, because the wind had been up all morning and they didn't think we'd be able to fly, but we did anyhow. So they had a line, a police line, and big cables to hold the crowd back. They were right in line with the way the wind was.

When they saw me coming down, they thought that the minute my wheels touched I was going to stick there without rolling. Well, the plane didn't do that. I saw that line right in front of me, and I thought, "Oh, if I can't do something, I'm going to mow right in there." So I just nosed my plane down, just as much as I could, and cut off the spark. I let the wheels touch, and I brought it right back up, but it wouldn't go—only took me over the crowd, and then it burst into flames. Mr. Houpert and the mechanics started for me in a dead run.

They pulled me out. My gas tanks had burst. They were on either side of where I sat on a little chair. I wasn't strapped in. I didn't even have a strap! These two tanks burst their moorings and away we went. The gas and oil exploded and got over me . . . but they pulled me out. My hair had come out from under my cap and so on, and my gloves were kind of burnt and every-thing . . . but it was nothing, I was ready to go up again. . . .

Matilde Moisant

After that, the most exciting flight I had, and one I enjoyed so much, was this. You see, the church people on Long Island didn't want flights on Sunday. One Sunday, the son of one of the richest bankers in Paris was at our house for dinner. He said, "Mademoiselle Moisant, you say that you fly the Moisant monoplane with a fifty-horsepower Gnome motor?"

I said, "Yes."

He said, in his half French, half English, "*Pardon*, but really, I don't believe it."

I said, "That's your privilege. But why don't you believe me?"

"Well, I don't think a woman can," he said. "I've never seen a woman fly a plane with a motor that big, and I don't think she can."

We left the table. The church people had called for the arrest of anybody who took up a plane on Sunday. So Fred said, "Tild, if our guest doubts your word, will you fly your plane if I get it out at the field?"

I said, "Sure."

He said, "All right, when we get through dinner, we'll get in the car and go."

The planes were at a different field that day, because we had been flying in a meet, and my brother had big locks on all our hangar doors. So Fred said, "Now, listen, I don't want you to make a fool of yourself, nor of me. If you want to back out, now's the time, but don't back out after I get that door open."

I said, "I won't," so he went to open the door. He had his mechanics there. A police officer came up and said, "You can't take out your machine."

"Why not?"

"We have an order that nobody is to fly on Sunday."

Fred said, "I can't see why. It is my property."

"Well," he said, "I'm sorry, but I can't let you open the door."

"All right," said Fred, "if you won't let me open the door, I'll have my mechanics break the locks, that's all. I have a right to go in there, and I have a right to do what I want with my property."

Well, anyhow, the officer said to my brother, "I'll tell you what—if you promise your sister won't fly, I'll let you take it out."

Fred said, "I promise nothing. Either you open that peaceably or I will see that it's opened."

Anyway, they opened the door and a mechanic took the plane

out to the field. I got in, and I said to Mr. Houpert, "Now, listen, Mr. Houpert, I won't give this usual signal, but you watch my head, and when I go like that, you give word to the men at the tail to let her go." I said, "I'm not going to land here, but I'll circle twice, then I'm going to dip, just as if I were going to land, but I'm going up again, God willing, and I'm going to go and land on our own field. Then you get in the car and take everyone over to our field."

There were four officers on motorcycles there. I got in the machine and one of the officers came up and said, "Listen, young lady, don't forget, if you fly that plane I'll arrest you when you come down."

I said, "Well, I haven't flown it yet, have I?"

He said, "No, but if you do . . ."

But of course we had it all arranged. So I circled twice, and came down about ten feet off the ground, and then away I went. They told me afterwards that when I dipped the officers said, "Now get ready to catch her when she gets out of the machine, as we're taking her to headquarters." Of course, they didn't know that the fun was going to be at the other field.

When I dipped and went away our French friend, who knew what I was going to do, said, "Say, Monsieur Officer, if you want to arrest her, you'd better get wings on your motorcycle!"

We all went to the other field. Fred started over there, too. You know, I was just so happy to be flying that I never thought about the officers on the field any more, never thought that I was making a scene of any kind. I went and landed on our field, and I made a nice landing. Fred came running up to me, and so did Mr. Houpert, and they said, "Jump out, quick! The officers are here. They want to arrest you!"

Then it all came back to me. One of Fred's friends was there in a Fiat car, and he said, "Get your sister in this. First put her in my car, and then we'll cover her and pass her right to your car, and you can take her to New York."

That was all right with Fred. They got me under cover in the friend's car and we started for New York. I said to this man, a friend of my brother's, "Where are you taking me, and what am I running away for?"

"Well, you know, they want to arrest you for flying on Sunday," he said.

"I haven't done anything that I shouldn't do," I said. "The plane is my property, I'm not flying for money, I'm not flying commercially, I'm flying for fun."

He said, "They have a warrant to arrest anybody that flies on Sunday."

I said, "I'm not going to run away. Stop the car. I never ran away from anything and I'm not going to run away from this." So he said, "Well, it's up to you."

The road had a parkway in the middle, and the officers were on one side and we were on the other. We stopped. Four officers got off their motorcycles, crossed over and came to me, and one of them said, "Well, Miss Moisant, first we want to congratulate you."

"What, on your wanting to arrest me?"

"No, for having enough nerve to take your machine up." See, they were soft-soaping me, and I wasn't being soft-soaped at all. "But," he said, "let me tell you something—you just come out of the car and come on with us, and it'll be all right."

I said, "I don't get out of this car."

"Well," he said, "we'll take you out."

Just then my brother came up. He got there just in time. They were just ready to pull me out of the car, and Fred came up. "Now, listen here," he said. He pushed his way through—there was quite a little crowd already—and he said, "Now, listen, anyone who lays a hand on her, it's as much as his life is worth."

There were two or three who said, "Yes, Mr. Moisant, we have some clubs here, we'll fix them if they touch her."

They said, "We don't want to make any fuss, Mr. Moisant. Come on, let's all go to town and see the sheriff and everything."

He said, "I'll tell you what I'll do. We can all go back to my field and then we'll talk it over."

So when we all got back on his property, he turned around and said, "Now, where's your warrant for her arrest?" They said, "We haven't got a written one, but we were told to arrest anybody who flew on Sunday." At that point he told them, "Now, listen here, if you officers don't get off of my property I'm going to have *you* arrested for trespassing."

That was that. That's the only time that my sister didn't go when I was flying. That Sunday she said, "No, I'm staying home." When we came back, and she heard about it, she was mortified.

"Now your picture will be in the paper," she said. "You've disgraced the family."

"Well," I said, "you know I always was a tomboy."

The next day we all went to the sheriff. He said, "What did Miss Moisant do?"

"She flew on Sunday."

"Did she fly for money?" he said.

"No."

"Were there any prizes?"

"No, she just did some flying."

"I'm going to tell you something," the sheriff said. "Instead of wanting to arrest her, you'd better go and beg her pardon for annoying her, because she's got just as much right to fly her airplane as you have to ride a motorcycle or anybody to drive an automobile."

The next day there was a picture in the newspaper of the cutest little witch you ever saw, sitting on a broom, and waving to the officers.

"Now," I said to my sister, "Lou, I didn't disgrace you too much, did I?"

Part of the problem of women learning to fly was simply that of what to wear. For centuries, women's fashions seemingly had been designed to prevent them from stepping out of their limited lives and into more active competition with their men. At the turn of the century skirts dragged the floor, corsets contorted the female figure into grotesque S-curves and exaggerated hourglass shapes, and frills and ruffles weighted everything down and lent the costumes of the period a distinctly overdecorated look. Only a few months before Harriet Quimby and Matilde Moisant learned to fly, a great breakthrough occurred. Skirts were raised enough to show off a well-turned ankle. But this radical—some thought it scandalous—development was far from the ideal costume for making a flight in the open, cockpitless planes of that time.

So the ladies improvised and made fashion headlines while they pioneered in the new science of flying, as this contemporary fashion report notes:

What to wear in the air no longer puzzles the birdwoman. Each woman flier has settled the matter to her satisfaction, and while the costumes may differ in detail to suit the individuality of the wearer there is sameness in the general outline.

The accepted toggery is a two-piece suit consisting of a blouse and knickerbockers and trouserettes. The headgear differs according to the feminine ideas. It may be an automobile cap or a becoming hood of some soft material.

Mlle. Dutrieu, the French airwoman and the pioneer of her sex in the air, set a new fashion in flying clothes on her first appearance in this country at the Nassau Boulevard aerodrome. Her drab colored costume of cravenette serge caught the feminine eye as she swung across the flying field to give the spectators an idea of what a birdwoman looks like aground.

Her two-piece suit consists of a blouse and a divided skirt, with a suggestion of the harem. The two garments are joined by a black patent leather belt and a Norfolk jacket effect is obtained by an arrangement sewed on the upper part of the skirt, which falls gracefully over the feet when she walks and with a button and strap is secured around her ankles before she mounts her Farman biplane.

The masculinity of her appearance is somewhat relieved by a small pair of patent leather boots topped with white. She wears an ordinary automobile cap.

Mlle. Dutrieu is always corsetless when she soars. She says this affords freedom of movement and lessens the danger in case of a fall. Neither of the American fliers, Miss Quimby and Miss Moisant, takes this precaution.

Miss Harriet Quimby's plum colored satin costume is perhaps more picturesque than that of Mlle. Dutrieu. It has a blouse and knickerbockers with a monk hood attached. The knickerbockers have the inside seams closed by rows of buttons which when unfastened convert the knickers into a walking skirt. The blouse is cut with the long shoulder seams and fastens under the arm. Miss Quimby wears high top leather boots.

She says her next costume will be plain knickerbockers, as she always wears a long coat when she is aground and there is no need of a skirt.

With the exception of the hood and the material the costume of Miss Moisant is practically a duplicate of the one worn by

Miss Quimby. It is made of a heavy tan colored cloth and inter-
lined with silk, while Miss Quimby reverses the materials. Small
patches of black net are inserted over the part of Miss Quimby's
hood that covers the ears, so that she can keep in touch with the
workings of her engine.

With her cameolike face, her plum-colored flying suit and
her glamorous connection with *Leslie's Weekly*, Harriet Quimby
was inevitably the romantic leading lady of the air. The news-
papers called her "the Dresden China aviatrix" and followed
her career in great and glowing detail. Unnumbered readers of
Leslie's Weekly thrilled to her first-person accounts of "How a
Woman Learns to Fly," "How I Won My Aviator's License,"
"The Dangers of Flying and How to Avoid Them," and "An
American Girl's Daring Exploit," the latter an account of Miss
Quimby's most famous flight, the first by a woman across the
English Channel.

After earning her license, Harriet Quimby made her first exhibition flights in the New York area, then went to Mexico with
Matilde Moisant in December, 1911, to fly at the inauguration of
newly elected President Maderos. There the thought of flying the
Channel first crossed her mind. "The more I thought of it, the less
formidable the feat seemed to be," she said later.

In March she sailed to England and made a deal with the
London *Mirror* to underwrite her expenses. She arranged to use a
Blériot monoplane similar to the planes she had been flying back
at the Moisant field, and by early April movie cameramen were
on location to record the historic moment, a crew of *Mirror*
reporters was at sea on a tugboat just off the Dover coast, and
Miss Quimby was ready to go. She planned to reverse Blériot's
1909 route and fly from England to France, because "the Dover
cliffs were higher." Whether this was merely a feminine whim or
whether she felt it might be easier to start high and sort of coast
downhill to the beaches of Calais she never fully explained.

There were many similarities between Miss Quimby's experience crossing the Channel on April 16 and Louis Blériot's flight
three years earlier. She too was held back by poor weather, then

Harriet Quimby gets a triumphant welcome on a French beach after becoming the first woman to fly the English Channel.

set out early one morning and was plagued by bad visibility on what was otherwise a fairly uneventful trip, as she related in *Leslie's Weekly:*

At three-thirty Tuesday morning we were called, had our hot tea and got into our automobiles and at four o'clock were at the flying grounds. There was no wind. Scarcely a breath of air was stirring. The monoplane was hurried out of the hangar. We knew that we must hasten for it was almost certain that the wind would rise again within an hour. Mr. Hamel, whose courtesy and consideration I shall always remember, jumped into the machine and was off for a short "try-out" of the engine and to report atmospheric conditions. He found everything satisfactory and hurried back, making one of the beautiful and easy landings for which he is famous.

The sky seemed clear, but patches of cloud and masses of fog here and there obscured the blue. The French coast was wholly invisible, by reason of moving masses of mist. The wind had not come up yet. The smooth grounds of the aerodrome gave me a chance for a perfect start. I heeded Mr. Hamel's warning about the coldness of the channel flight and had prepared accordingly. Under my flying suit of wool-back satin I wore two pairs of silk combinations, over it a long woolen coat, over this an American raincoat, and around and across my shoulders a long wide stole of sealskin. Even this did not satisfy my solicitous friends. At the last minute they handed me up a large hot-water bag, which Mr. Hamel insisted on tying to my waist like an enormous locket.

It was five-thirty A.M. when my machine got off the ground. The preliminaries were brief. Hearty handshakes were quickly given, the motor began to make its twelve hundred revolutions a minute, and I put up my hand to give the signal of release. Then I was off. The noise of the motor drowned the shouts and cheers of friends below. In a moment I was in the air, climbing steadily in a long circle. I was up fifteen hundred feet within thirty seconds. From this high point of vantage my eyes lit at once on Dover Castle. It was half hidden in a fog bank. I felt that trouble was coming, but I made directly for the flagstaff of the castle, as I had promised the waiting *Mirror* photographers and the moving-picture men I should do.

In an instant I was beyond the cliffs and over the channel. Far beneath I saw the *Mirror's* tug, with its stream of black smoke. It was trying to keep ahead of me, but I passed it in a jiffy. Then the quickening fog obscured my view. Calais was out of sight. I could not see ahead of me or at all below. There was only one thing for me to do and that was to keep my eyes fixed on my compass.

My hands were covered with long Scotch woolen gloves which gave me good protection from the cold and fog; but the machine was wet and my face was so covered with dampness that I had to push my goggles up on my forehead. I could not see through them. I was traveling at over a mile a minute. The distance straight across from Dover to Calais is only twenty-five miles, and I knew that land must be in sight if I could only get below the fog and see it. So I dropped from an altitude of about two thousand feet until I was half that height. The sunlight struck upon my face and my eyes lit upon the white and sandy shores of France. I felt happy, but could not find Calais. Being unfamiliar with the coast line, I could not locate myself. I determined to reconnoiter and come down to a height of about five hundred feet and traverse the shore.

Meanwhile, the wind had risen and the currents were coming in billowy gusts. I flew a short distance inland to locate myself or find a good place on which to alight. It was all tilled land below me, and rather than tear up the farmers' fields I decided to drop down on the hard and sandy beach. I did so at once, making an easy landing. Then I jumped from my machine and was alone upon the shore. But it was only for a few moments. A crowd of fishermen—men, women and children each carrying a pail of sand worms—came rushing from all directions toward me. They were chattering in French, of which I comprehended sufficient to discover that they knew I had crossed the channel. These humble fisherfolk knew what had happened. They were congratulating themselves that the first woman to cross in an aeroplane had landed on their fishing beach.

Less than three months after this triumph, Harriet Quimby was dead, the victim of a bizarre accident that sent her plum-color-satin–covered body plummeting into the mud flats of Boston Harbor.

It happened this way. Miss Quimby returned to America on May 12 and signed up to fly at an exhibition in Boston during the first week in July. She brought a two-seat Blériot back with her and agreed to take the manager of the meet, William A. P. Willard, father of aviator Charles Willard, on a flight out to Boston Light and back in the new airplane as part of the show. Claude Grahame-White had made this trip two years before when he first came to the United States, but it was about 20 miles over water and still seemed quite dangerous to the spectators who gathered to watch Miss Quimby go the same route. But she reassured them, saying, "A water landing is all right in a Blériot unless you come down head first. In that case, the heavy motor at the extreme forward end of the machine would drag the monoplane deep into the water and sink it. But if it comes down

The battered body of Harriet Quimby is brought ashore after accident over Boston Harbor.

'pancake' the broad wings would float us for two hours or more.

"But I am a cat and I don't like cold water," she said and then was on her way.

Her trip out to the lighthouse was uneventful. Blanche Scott was also on hand for the Boston show and was flying at the same time as Harriet Quimby, giving the five thousand spectators the unusual experience of seeing two women aviators in the air at the same time.

On the return trip, the Blériot, painted pure white and dazzling in the late afternoon of a lovely summer day, sped back over the harbor wobbling slightly in a gusty 8-mile-per-hour breeze. She circled the field once, soared out over the bay once more, then began to let down. Suddenly, there was an upward flash of the tail and the airplane seemed to stand almost on end in the air. For an instant it poised there and then began a swift plunge downward. Willard's body was thrown completely out of the plane at this point, followed almost immediately by Harriet Quimby's. Before the horror-struck gaze of the big crowd the bodies hurtled end over end and struck the shallow water about 200 feet from shore. The airplane, ironically, righted itself after the two fell out and glided gracefully into the water on an even keel. When it struck it nosed over, but it was later discovered to be virtually undamaged. Both victims were found terribly crushed when they were extricated from the mud of the shallow bay into which they had plunged deeply.

"If they had been strapped in, the accident would not have happened," said Glenn Martin, who had also been flying at the meet. "When going at a terrific speed, the machine on striking a 'hole in the air' will drop suddenly and lift one from his seat. I wear straps in my aeroplane, and even then I am thrown violently up against them by such drops."

Lincoln Beachey had a different theory. "They were going eighty or a hundred miles per hour," he said. "Miss Quimby was coming down from some five thousand feet with full power on. She was a light, delicate woman and it could easily have happened that the terrific rush of air was too much for her and that she became weakened and unable to control her levers."

Also on the scene was Ruth Law Oliver, another young woman who was just beginning her flying career—in fact, her husband had just purchased her a new Wright Model B and had had it shipped to Boston so that she could take her first lessons while the meet was going on. Harriet Quimby made a vivid impression on the fledgling aviatrix, who is still living in San Francisco, and years later she recalled the day:

I didn't know Harriet Quimby really at all. But I know that she had been a correspondent for *Leslie's Weekly* in New York. At that time, she was one of the few women that drove an automobile, and she had a little red Ford roadster. They tell about her going to Mineola Field to fly.

I do recall the modesty of those days. She wore what I considered a beautiful suit, made of satin, and high black, laced kid boots, and a little cap. But when she came out of the hangar to make her flight they had a little flight of steps arranged so that she could walk up the steps and step into the plane. She came out of the hangar with a long cape over her, and at least a half a dozen of her girl friends all standing around her, to shield her from the sight of the people. She climbed up, and stepped into the plane, and dropped the cape to her friends, and took off. Well, it was the prettiest thing. It was so modest. She was a very delightful girl to see. I was always sorry that I had not known her. And an excellent flier—she took that plane off like a bird, went out over Boston Harbor to Boston Light.

On the way back, the passenger just went out of the plane. We were not belted in or fastened in in any way, at that time. I was sitting there looking—we were waiting for me to go up and take a flight. He went up in an arc, out of the plane, as though he had jumped. It looked as though he had stood up and jumped, and came down. At the same time, after his weight was gone, which balanced that type of plane at that time, the plane just turned over in a nose dive, upside down—and she fell out. They fell in the water, just at the edge of the exhibition field, which was at the edge of the bay, on their way back, just before she reached the field. It was said by some at the time that the manager, who faced some financial difficulty with the meet, had jumped out. It's hard to believe, because he should have known that without his weight in there, the plane would be overbalanced.

Well, anyway, she got killed, so no more flying was done until the next day. But I can always figure out a reason. I had considered the purchase of a Wright biplane, because after study it seemed to me that they'd had the greatest success. The Wright brothers were the first to succeed in flying. So the fact that she had been killed in a monoplane didn't scare me. I figured it was the monoplane's fault.

Like a meteor she had burst into the sky with breathtaking brilliance, then, just as suddenly, she was gone and the sky seemed vastly emptier after her passing.

1911:   ii

It was Sunday in mid-September, 1911, and out at the race track at Sheepshead Bay, Long Island, the day was flawless: warm and sunny, with puffy little white clouds in a blue sky. Some two thousand people watched as a young lady from Memphis self-consciously poured a bottle of grape drink over the landing skids of a brand-new Wright biplane. She dubbed the plane the *Vin Fiz Flyer* in honor of the grape drink.

Then the pilot came forward, tall, taciturn and with a distant look in his eye. He accepted a four-leaf clover from another lady in the crowd, climbed into the seat of his fragile-looking craft, lowered his goggles, lit a cigar and waved to his helpers to start the engine. The plane's two wooden props came to life and scattered spectators who had crowded too closely around the machine. The *Vin Fiz* gathered speed over the race track infield and gracefully took to the air. For better or for worse, Calbraith Perry Rodgers was on his way across the country from New York to the Pacific Coast.

Eighty-four days later, Cal Rodgers landed on the sand at Long Beach, California, taxied to the water's edge and washed his wheels in the Pacific Ocean. He was the first man to fly across the United States, and he had flown farther than any man in the world. But it had been a rough trip. Cal was on crutches by the time he made Long Beach. His plane had been wrecked and rebuilt so many times that only the rudder, the engine drip pan and a strut or two remained from the original machine that took off from Sheepshead Bay.

En route Rodgers had five disastrous crashes which demolished his plane. He had seven takeoff and landing accidents which required major repairs. His engine quit in flight six times. Things got so bad at one point that a rumor began circulating that the special train accompanying Cal carried a coffin just in case.

But, with his cigar clenched between his teeth, Cal Rodgers persevered. In doing so, he not only became America's first transcontinental flyer, but he also set a record for determination and sheer guts which has never quite been equaled. And as far as the public was concerned—the thousands who saw him along the way and the millions more who followed breathless accounts of his trip in a score of newspapers—Cal's 4,000-mile odyssey was the biggest aviation adventure of the year, perhaps of all time. It certainly was the high point of aviation in those early years.

Rodgers had made his public debut as an aviator just a month before at a big, wild exhibition in Chicago that saw one world record set, two inexperienced pilots killed and nine days of crowd-pleasing flying by a galaxy of the world's best airmen. Twelve Wright pilots were there, including Brookins, Coffyn and Welsh, but their machines seemed a little antiquated (one newspaper referred to them as "old ice wagons"). The Curtiss crowd showed up as daring and aggressive as always. The spotlight this time was on Lincoln Beachey. He flew like a madman when he was down near the grandstand, then, by strapping on a ten-gallon tank and simply climbing until his gas ran out, he coaxed his Curtiss pusher to an altitude record of 11,642 feet. He then glided down to a perfect dead-stick landing. Among the more interesting new faces at the meet was Thomas Sopwith from England, who took turns flying a Wright biplane and a Blériot monoplane. Sopwith, who later built the legendary Sopwith Camel of World War I fame, recalls that it was John Moisant's Paris-to-London flight in 1910 that got him interested in flying. "I was incurably bitten by the aviation bug then and there and never recovered," he says.

Few people at Chicago gave Cal Rodgers more than passing notice until the end of the meet, when it was found that he had won the grand prize by staying airborne longer than anyone else. Flying day after day without attracting much attention from the grandstands, Rodgers had put in a total of more than twenty-four hours in the air, and he collected $11,285 in prizes as a result. When this was announced, the crowd was astonished and many people were heard to ask, "Who is Rodgers?"

Meanwhile, a Wright-trained pilot named Harry Atwood had stopped off in Chicago while en route from St. Louis to New York on a record-breaking cross-country trip. Atwood pushed on and landed on Governor's Island on August 25, having covered some 1,265 miles in nine days. This fine flight, accomplished without mishap or serious difficulty, reawakened interest among American aviators in the $50,000 prize offered by William Randolph Hearst in the fall of 1910 to the first person to fly from coast to coast in thirty days or less. Hearst's offer was good for one year only; to win the $50,000, the transcontinental flight had to be completed before October 10.

By the end of the first week in September, eight pilots had formally entered the race for the Hearst prize. Cross-country champ Harry Atwood was one of the first to sign up. So was Cal Rodgers. Robert G. Fowler, one of the best students graduated recently from the Wright school, made daring plans to cross from west to east in a Wright biplane via the 7,000-foot Donner Pass in the Sierra Nevada Mountains. From Boston came word that Earle Ovington would also try for the prize in a Blériot monoplane. Cocky little James J. Ward, a former jockey, entered the contest with a Curtiss biplane. The three other entries were not serious contenders and dropped out without flying.

Atwood too would later abandon the race without starting, because he could not get financial support. Ovington got going so late that he had no chance at the prize. Even so, he tried to take off from New York, but crashed immediately and quit right then and there. That left three: Fowler, Ward and Cal Rodgers.

Fowler was the first to get under way. On September 11 he took off from San Francisco's Golden Gate Park and flew 129 miles to Auburn, California, at the foot of the high mountains. A big six-footer who neither smoked nor drank, Fowler was a well-known West Coast automobile racer who held the current auto speed record from Los Angeles to San Francisco. He was also hopelessly optimistic. "I have planned for twenty flying days," he said. "My average is set at 175 . . . but I hope to have a couple of days of five hundred miles or more."

The following day, as Fowler followed the Southern Pacific Railroad track up through the mountains toward the Donner Pass, his rudder-control cable snapped. By using brute force on the wing-warping lever, Fowler managed to prevent his plane from plunging to earth completely out of control. But he couldn't find a safe landing place as he spiraled down, and he crashed in some trees near the village of Alta, California. Fowler was not seriously injured, but his plane had to be rebuilt completely and twelve days passed before he could take to the air again.

Meanwhile, Jimmy Ward readied his Curtiss biplane on

Governor's Island. On September 13 he got off to a good start, but almost immediately became lost over the maze of railroad tracks leading out of Jersey City. The wind was gusty that day and it gave Ward a hard time. "It kept me so busy with my machine that I could only look down once in a while," he said.

Ward had arranged for a special train to accompany him on his trip. It was to serve as living quarters for him and his party and also as a repair shop and source of spare parts for his plane. But Ward missed the tracks his train was on as he passed Jersey City and didn't find the train until late afternoon. As a result, he spent the night in Paterson, New Jersey, only 20 miles from his starting point.

On the day that Ward set out, Cal Rodgers loaded a new, custom-made Wright racing plane aboard a train in Dayton, Ohio, and departed for New York. The new Wright biplane was known as the Model EX. With a wing span of 32 feet, the single-seat EX was slightly smaller than the Wright Model B, which was the standard production model at the Wright factory at that time. The EX had a four-cylinder, 35-horsepower water-cooled engine which gave the plane a top speed of 55 miles per hour. There was no throttle on the engine; and though some adjustment in engine r.p.m. could be made by advancing the spark, there were really only two speeds to the EX engine: wide open and stop.

Though the EX was the latest thing from the Wright factory, its control system remained unchanged and seemed a little primitive in 1911. The left-hand lever made the aircraft climb or descend by flexing a big elevator plane in the tail. A similar lever on the right warped the wings and caused the craft to bank. A hand lever at the top of the right stick controlled the rudder. There was no windshield, the single seat was hard and had no seat belts, there were no armrests, and while the EX was said to be a sweet plane to fly, it was nevertheless a physically exhausting proposition and terribly uncomfortable.

Cal Rodgers looked as if he could take the punishment, however. He was thirty-two years old, six feet four inches tall, and weighed close to two hundred pounds. He learned to fly at the Wright school in Dayton in June and showed such aptitude that he was allowed to solo after only an hour and a half of instruction. He prided himself on his physical stamina and was thus the ideal man to capture the endurance prizes in Chicago.

Reporters meeting Cal in New York when he arrived on Friday, September 15, found the big, handsome young man shy and difficult to talk to. Cal, it seems, was partially deaf and was sensitive about this among strangers. Already this physical impairment had made him abandon a boyhood dream of a military career and a way of life that had become almost traditional for the men in his family as far back as the Revolutionary War.

As a Rodgers, and as a Perry, Cal was related to some of the country's most illustrious and adventurous military men. Captain Oliver Hazard Perry, the hero of the Battle of Lake Erie in 1813, and Commodore Matthew Calbraith Perry, who opened Japan to the West in 1854, were ancestors. A grandfather, Rear Admiral Christopher Raymond Perry Rodgers, had served with distinction in the Union Navy during the Civil War and was later superintendent of the Naval Academy. Cal's father was an Army captain who served with the 15th Cavalry against the Indians in the Southwest. He was killed by lightning while on patrol just six months before Cal was born.

Cal spent his last day in New York attending to final arrangements for his trip. The Armour Company of Chicago had agreed to back him financially if he would advertise Vin Fiz, a new grape soft drink that the meat packers were promoting. Armour was to pay Cal five dollars for every mile flown with the Vin Fiz advertisement lettered on the wings and tail of his plane. The company also arranged and paid for a special three-car train that followed Cal all the way to California. As his part of the deal Cal agreed to pay for all fuel, oil, spare parts and repair of his plane.

Sunday, September 17, the day of Cal's departure from Sheepshead Bay, found Fowler still stuck in California with a wrecked aircraft. Ward was stalled for repairs in Owego, New York. His engine had failed on takeoff the previous day and he had piled into a barbed-wire fence.

Cal's start on his long journey was magnificent, "the most

Rodgers posed confidently for publicity photos before he left Sheepshead Bay, Long Island.

daring and spectacular feat of aviation that this country or even the world has ever known," as one newspaper reported. After leaving the race track at Sheepshead Bay, he circled Coney Island dropping Vin Fiz advertising leaflets. Then he thrilled Flatbush residents by skimming over Brooklyn at an altitude of 800 feet.

He crossed the East River at the Brooklyn Bridge, passing over the battleship *Connecticut*, which was steaming upstream toward the Brooklyn Navy Yard. At that moment a reporter for William Randolph Hearst's New York *American* had a strange, fleeting vision. He wrote: "From the aeroplane, flying so true and free, to the sluggish battleship below confined forever to its narrow element . . . was the space of an age that may spell the doom of the battleship for all time."

The residents of blasé old New York were impressed as he crossed the heart of Manhattan. "Thousands of persons from windows, housetops, sidewalks and streets witnessed the most inspiring sight of their lives when Rodgers, at a height of more than half a mile, sailed across the city," says one account in the New York *American.* "That a man was in control of the dazzling white machine with its glints of gold and silver when it caught the full rays of the declining September sun, and that he was flying directly over the city with its death-trap of tall buildings, spires, ragged roofs, and narrow streets gave a new and never-to-be-forgotten vision to all who were fortunate enough to see him."

For once, Cal's engine ran perfectly and he didn't have to worry about an emergency landing in the streets of New York. He followed Broadway up to Madison Square, then turned west toward New Jersey, where he planned to fly over the special train which was waiting on the Erie Railroad tracks.

Cal's special train consisted of an engine and three cars: a white "hangar car" which was decorated with the Vin Fiz advertisements and which carried a second airplane, an automobile, spare parts, supplies and baggage; a day coach which was used as a lounge and observation car; and a buffet-Pullman car in which Cal, his wife Mabel, his mother, his cousin Lieutenant John Rodgers (who later became a famous Navy pilot), his chief mechanic Charles Taylor (on loan from the Wright factory), and other members of the party lived for the next few weeks.

Profiting from Ward's confusion over the Jersey City railroad yards, Cal arranged for his crew to mark the Erie tracks with strips of white canvas. He had no difficulty picking up his train and, following it north, he flew as far as Middletown, New York, on his first hop.

A crowd of nine thousand people awaited Cal in Middletown. Some five hundred autos had been parked in a circle to mark off a landing area at the Middletown fairgrounds, but the crowd just wouldn't stay out of the way. "I had to herd them up before they would clear a space," Cal said. "But I came down so easily it didn't knock the ashes off my cigar."

All in all, it had been a most satisfying day. "No man ever had

263

a truer machine and a more perfect engine than I did today," said Cal. "There was not a miss of the cylinders and not a swerve of the machine." Rodgers had left Sheepshead Bay around 4:30 p.m. and had covered the 84 miles to Middletown in 105 minutes. Said Cal, "It's Chicago in four days if everything goes right."

It actually turned out to be Chicago in twenty-one days, three crashes, and a thunderstorm. Cal's troubles began on the next morning when he tried to leave Middletown. As he took off, his undercarriage struck a willow tree at the end of the field. The plane faltered, then recovered momentarily. Cal could see that he was too low to clear some power lines looming ahead, so he cut his engine. The plane hit a hickory tree, tipped over and plummeted straight down into a chicken coop. Cal landed on his feet in a tangle of wire, wood, fabric and feathers, his head bleeding from a vicious clout he had received on the way down. Somehow he managed to hang on to the cigar he had lit just before takeoff. But his beautiful plane was demolished.

The citizens of Middletown immediately pitched in to help Cal rebuild the *Vin Fiz*. The armory was thrown open for him and the mangled aircraft, and replacement parts from the special train were hauled there for reconstruction. The Middletown Electric Railway offered Cal $1,000 to help defray his expenses, and the aviator and his wife were overwhelmed with invitations from the hospitable Middletonians. Under Charlie Taylor, Cal's mechanics worked around the clock and put the plane back together in forty hours.

While Cal was stuck in Middletown, Fowler was still held up in California. Ward, who also followed the Erie Railroad through New York State, continued to have problems with his engine. After repairing the damage done at Owego, Ward flew on to Corning, where he made an emergency landing after his engine ran out of oil and stopped in flight.

By Wednesday, September 20, Ward was ready to go again, but he made only 11 miles after leaving Corning. A hose connection on his radiator worked loose and sprayed him with hot water. He landed in a pasture, fixed the loose connection, but then smashed his undercarriage and bottom wing trying to dodge the crowd of cows and people which had gathered to see him off.

On learning of Ward's troubles, Rodgers sent him this tele-gram: "Too bad old man. Sorry to hear you are down again. Grit like yours is bound to kill the jinx and win. A gray kitten came into my car this morning and chased the hoodoo. Hope to take the air this afternoon. Very best wishes. C. P. Rodgers."

It was the following afternoon, however, before Cal could get away from Middletown. Then for a while it seemed as though Cal's gray kitten really had vanquished the hoodoo. Cal flew from Middletown to Hancock, New York, covering 95 miles in 78 minutes for a ground speed of 74 miles per hour. There were some minor problems, but the day's run was exhilarating. In setting down his thoughts about the hop for the New York *American*, Cal gives us one of the finest surviving impressions of flying in those early days:

I was above the air currents going faster than the wind and the engine went on singing a sweet song. I lit a fresh cigar and let her go.

An airman cannot tell too much about the country he goes over. There are no signs up where he is and little towns come so fast that a new one seems to begin before an old one ends. All I could see was a ribbon of silver below me coiling around heavily wooded mountains. There was a glint now and then of the tracks, but the river was my guide until I got to Lackawaxen. I had been looking out for that place because the Lackawaxen River shoots off to the left of the Delaware and it has a branch road too.

As I neared there I began to look and I soon picked out the strips of white canvas stretched on the right track. I swung a little there and we were off again, going as fast as ever.

Town followed town until I picked up Callicoon by the long strips of canvas on a broad level field. I made a quick study of my engine and although I could tell the water was going fast, I made a jump for Hancock, twenty-five or twenty-six miles away. I seemed to be right up on the town when plop! out flew a defec-tive spark plug. I cut out the cylinder and then rather than have overheated machinery, I shot down to the first field I saw ahead of me.

There was nothing the matter with that field except that at one end there is a tract of soft ground. I lit perfectly and was slowing down when one of the skids hit this soft spot, stopped, and slewed the machine. There was a snap of breaking timber and my right skid had gone. There was nothing to do but wait for the train.

I had an amusing experience in the meantime. There were two men digging potatoes in that field and evidently they wanted to get them in out of the wet. I believe they looked up when I came down within fifty feet of them but I don't know. I went over to them and asked where I was and one of them told me between grabs at the potatoes. Of course the crowd came, seemingly out of the mountains, but those two men kept at it.

On the next day, Friday, September 22, Jimmy Ward's engine failed once again and he crash-landed at Addison, New York. In Chicago, the odds were now five to one that Ward would kill himself before he got to Buffalo. Under these circumstances it wasn't difficult for Ward's wife and his manager to convince him that his luck was too bad to continue; so the plucky little jockey dropped out of the race for the Hearst cross-country prize.

Cal Rodgers, meanwhile, was having an exasperating day. He left Hancock a few minutes after 11 A.M., following the Erie Railroad tracks as usual. But he turned the wrong way at a rail junction and, having no compass, wandered many miles off course into Pennsylvania before he discovered his error. When he landed to get his bearings he was confronted with a new hazard:

The crowd as usual came up out of the ground. They told me I was in Scranton, forty-five miles from where I ought to be. I had a hard time trying to save my machine. The crowd went crazy. There wasn't a name on my plane when I started this morning, but in ten minutes, there wasn't an inch free from pencil marks. They didn't mind climbing up to get a good spot. They liked to work the levers, sit upon the seat, warp the planes, and finger the engines. I nearly lost my temper when a man came up with a chisel to punch his monogram on an upright.

The crowd was basically friendly, though, and after Cal shooed them away from the plane, they got him some gas. A local chauffeur and a fireman turned the props for him and started the engine. By mid-afternoon Cal was back on course. Around 6 P.M. he landed for the night at Elmira, New York.

The next day found both Rodgers and Fowler airborne. The latter, after being grounded twelve days for repairs, again headed up the steep slopes of the Sierra Nevadas. Fowler figured he needed to climb to an altitude of 8,500 feet in order to navigate safely the tricky gusts and treacherous downdrafts in the 7,017-foot Donner Pass. On Saturday, September 23, Fowler spent two hours and twelve minutes climbing to 6,500 feet, then just couldn't seem to get any higher. "It is no use," he said when he landed. "I spent twenty minutes at one place climbing three hundred feet." But, as we shall see, Robert Fowler was not a man to give up easily.

Rodgers, meanwhile, had a close call taking off from Elmira. He struck some telegraph wires just as he lifted off, and settled abruptly back to earth. The damage was not serious, but it delayed his departure for six hours. The rest of the day wasn't much better. Halfway to Canisteo, New York, the spark plug that popped out on him two days earlier again worked loose and Cal had to hold it in with one hand and fly the plane with the other. He finally got disgusted and landed at Hornell, near Canisteo, at 3:27 P.M. When he touched down, his left skid snagged something. The plane slewed violently, throwing Cal out of his seat and smashing the left wing. Cal was not hurt—and accidents of this type had become so commonplace by now that his mechanics were able to repair the damage quickly. They had the plane ready for takeoff by the next morning.

Cal got away from Hornell without incident the following day shortly after ten o'clock. He landed at Olean for an hour's rest, then pushed on again. Ignition trouble once more forced him down and he landed on a farm in the Allegany Indian Reservation near Salamanca. "The landing was perfect," Cal later related. "The next minute an Indian came running across the field. 'Big bird,' he said. 'Biggest bird ever saw.'"

Cal had now passed the point where Ward had given up, and was way ahead of Fowler in the race across the continent. He was anxious to keep moving and tried three times that afternoon to take off from the field on the Indian reservation. The third time, he piled into a barbed-wire fence and that was that. The *Vin Fiz* was demolished for the second time.

On the same day, Fowler was making what was to be his final attempt to get over the Donner Pass. It was a study in frustration. After takeoff Fowler climbed higher and higher on favorable winds. Between the Cisco and Tamarack stations on the Southern Pacific line he reached 8,000 feet. He could see Summit Station near the highest point on the pass, and he was all set to ease over the hump into Reno. But his engine boiled over at the last minute, and Fowler had to turn back. He hung around Emigrant Gap, California, for a few more days, hoping for favorable winds. But they never came and he abandoned his attempt to get over the mountains. Fowler, however, wasn't completely licked yet and was soon making plans to set off across the country via a southerly route out of Los Angeles.

By Wednesday, September 27, the *Vin Fiz* was repaired again and ready to go. But the weather turned bad, and Rodgers had to wait until Thursday before resuming his flight. When he did leave Salamanca on the twenty-eighth, it was with a sigh of relief. "Seeking a place of departure in that part of the country is like hunting for gold, a very uncertain thing," Cal said. Salamanca was his last stop in New York State, and with the Allegheny Mountains behind him Cal could look forward to flying over some relatively level country where the air would be smoother and safe landing fields easy to find.

He followed the Erie Railroad across the northwest tip of Pennsylvania and on into Ohio on Thursday and had his best day's flight to date. Said Cal: "I kept going to Akron, the smoke of which I made out ten miles away. When I got within about three miles of the city and made out hills everywhere in the dusk, I swung about and made for a field. It was so dark then that I could not see whether there were ditches or furrows, but I had to take it. I lit on hard, smooth turf and stopped without a single break." He spent the night in Kent, Ohio, after covering 204 miles that day.

The following day Cal was grounded because of bad weather. On Saturday he got an early start and logged another 200-mile day. "When I was sailing above Akron it was as enjoyable as any day I have had on the race for the Hearst prize," Cal said. "I could light cigars with ease at any stage of my flight." He made stops for rest and fuel at Mansfield and Marion, then was forced down when his engine stopped running just across the Indiana line at the little town of Rivare. Cal's "hoodoo" was still with him; his engine quit because of a clogged fuel line.

The weather was threatening the next morning, but Cal took off anyway. He was caught up almost immediately in the roiling fury of a thunderstorm. This was the first time in history that an airplane pilot had penetrated a thunderstorm and lived to tell about it:

I turned to the northwest pointing along the Erie ready to buck the gale which was steadier up there. I noticed right ahead of me a full grown rainstorm coming right at me. I saw the milky water falling and the cloud weaving . . . the only thing left for me was to try and run around it.

I turned and scooted to the east and rounded to on the outer edge of the cloud outside the rain only to find another one sweeping down on me. I had to turn and run away again, and this time I saw to the northwest a third big cloud bearing down on me. There was a space between the two clouds and I made for it. It was clear enough but I had forgotten the thunder and lightning. That was their little playground.

The first thing I knew I was riding through an electric gridiron. I didn't know what lightning might do to an aeroplane, but I didn't like the idea so I swung her and streaked it for the east only to run bang up against a big rain cloud in active operation. I seemed to have run into a cloud convention.

If you have been out in a hailstorm you know how that rain cut my face. I had taken off my goggles for fear that I might become blinded by moisture, and I took off my gloves and covered what I could of the vital points of the magneto. It was a cold and painful situation.

I looked for my engine to stop on me any minute and began searching for a place to alight. I couldn't find one because a big cloud had quietly rolled in under me and the earth had disappeared. It was lonesome. I might be a million miles up in space. I might be a hundred feet from earth. I breathed better when I sailed over the edge of the cloud and saw the misty land beneath me.

It was raining but even that seemed friendly compared with the whirling mists that make up a cloud. I saw a little village off to the right and another just under me. I had to find a windbreak. Luckily, I found one, a cup surrounded by woods, and dropped down, landed all right and climbed under my machine to get out of the wet.

Rodgers' third major smashup occurred at Huntington, Indiana, where he swerved to avoid running over some spectators.

I hadn't more than lighted a cigar when a couple of men came running out of the woods. They said I was near Geneva about 18 or 20 miles off my course. . . . I got away from there at 3:40.

Cal continued on to Huntington, Indiana, where he met his train and called it a day. The weather the next morning, Monday, October 2, was still unsettled, clear but gusty. Accounts of his attempted takeoff at Huntington are confused and Cal himself wasn't too certain about just what went wrong. Apparently he tried to take off downwind rather than buck the gusts. He couldn't gain altitude, and he hopped and skipped across the field, heading toward a group of spectators. Rather than plow into the crowd, he slewed his plane to the right, still desperately trying to become airborne. The plane passed between two trees and under some telegraph wires. The left wing snagged on a small rise, the plane crumpled, and Cal was thrown clear. He was uninjured, but it was a bad smash and his beautiful machine had to be rebuilt for the third time.

Tuesday and Wednesday were spent on repairs in Huntington. Cal flew to Hammond on Thursday, then was delayed by weather for two days. On Sunday, October 8, he flew into Chicago, where he exhibited his plane for a few hours at Grant Park. He had been en route now for three weeks exactly and had made only a little more than 1,000 miles. Cal estimated that he had been airborne twenty-three hours and thirty-seven minutes out of the past twenty-one days, and at this rate it was obviously impossible for him to reach California before the October 10 deadline on the Hearst prize. A Chicago reporter asked him if he was going to quit at this point. "I am bound for Los Angeles and the Pacific Ocean," Cal replied. "Prize or no prize, that's where I am bound and if canvas, steel, and wire together with a little brawn, tendon, and brain stick with me, I mean to get there. The fifty-thousand-dollar prize, however, seems to be practically out of the question. But anyway it doesn't matter much. I'm going to do this whether I get five thousand dollars or fifty cents or nothing. I am going to cross this continent simply to be the first to cross in an aeroplane."

As if to prove his resolution, he left Chicago in the late afternoon and headed southwest along the Chicago and Alton Railroad tracks to a small town between Lockport and Joliet. He flew all the way to Springfield the next day without incident. On Tuesday, October 10, Cal got an early start from Springfield and turned west with a strong tail wind. He bypassed St. Louis because the city reneged on a $1,000 offer to have him give an exhibition. By nightfall he reached Marshall, Missouri, halfway across the state. He flew over 200 miles that day and at times made good a ground speed of better than 70 miles per hour. Cal had now traveled 1,398 miles since leaving New York and had broken Harry Atwood's record.

On Wednesday, Cal flew into Kansas City, Missouri, giving the city "an aerial thrill the like of which it never had experienced before," according to the Kansas City *Star*. Cal was the first aviator to fly over the city and he did a beautiful job of it. He flew up the Missouri River at 700 to 800 feet, then hedgehopped over downtown Kansas City. Schools were let out so that children could see him pass. He landed before a crowd of ten thousand at Swope Park shortly before noon. Later he flew to Overland Park, just outside Kansas City, Kansas, for the night.

The weather turned bad and for the next two days Cal was grounded at Overland Park. His crew took advantage of the delay to work on the *Vin Fiz*, as Cal was still having trouble with loose spark plugs. On Saturday, October 14, he took off from Overland Park and headed south along the Missouri, Kansas and Texas Railroad tracks. He sped across the state of Kansas in a few hours and finally came to earth at Vinita, Oklahoma, flying half an hour after sunset in the gathering dusk.

The next day Cal was weatherbound at Vinita. On Monday he was off again. He stopped at Muskogee, where a huge state fair was in progress. He landed before a crowd of thousands at the fairgrounds race track at 9:15 A.M.

Said the Muskogee *Daily Phoenix:* "To those who saw Rodgers alight and step from his machine, there came a sensation as if they had just seen a messenger from Mars."

Cal didn't tarry in Muskogee. The flight was going well now

and he seemed anxious to push on as hard and as fast as he could. He flew from Muskogee to McAlester, Oklahoma, before nightfall, then made it to Fort Worth, Texas, the following day, a record distance for Cal of 265 miles. On Wednesday, October 18, Cal put in an appearance at the Texas State Fair at nearby Dallas. During the flight to Dallas a curious eagle came up to inspect the *Vin Fiz*. To Cal's alarm, the eagle made a head-on run at the plane, then veered off at the last minute.

Cal left Dallas the next day. "Amid tumultuous applause from an eager crowd of 75,000 persons, Cal P. Rodgers, sea-to-sea aviator, glided gracefully down the infield of the State Fair race track at 1:50 P.M.," reported the Dallas *Morning News*. "After hovering over the Fair Grounds for fifteen minutes in the most thrilling exhibition of aerial navigation ever seen here, he headed his biplane south and started again on his long journey to the Pacific Coast."

That afternoon he flew on to Waco, where a purse was made up for him by the Young Men's Business League. On the following day he flew to Austin, where he also received a purse. He left there around 4 P.M. after circling the dome of the State Capitol building. Seventeen miles south of Austin his engine failed and he glided to a safe landing in a farmer's field near the town of Kyle. After the special train arrived, chief mechanic Charlie Taylor inspected the engine and found that a piston had "crystallized." He replaced the engine with the spare one carried aboard the train.

A day was lost at Kyle due to repairs and high winds. Then on Sunday, October 22, Cal flew to San Antonio. By now the strain of the trip was beginning to tell. He had lost fifteen pounds since leaving New York, and his leathery windburned face looked "gaunt," according to a reporter for the San Antonio *Express*.

Rodgers spent a day in San Antonio resting and tuning his aircraft. He left shortly after noon on Tuesday, October 24, picked up the Southern Pacific tracks, and flew 132 miles to Spofford, Texas.

The next morning Cal had his fourth serious accident. It was just plain bad luck. As Cal took off from Spofford, his right propeller struck the ground. The plane swerved out of control and lurched to the left, splintering both props, demolishing the undercarriage and crumpling the wings. Said Cal philosophically, "These wrecks are part of the game and are to be expected, but of course are unwelcome."

His crew was extremely proficient by this time and had the plane ready to go by the next morning. He flew on to Sanderson, Texas, crossing the Rio Grande River into Mexico three times en route. He was delayed at Sanderson a day because of high winds. Then on Saturday, October 28, he pushed on to the town of Sierra Blanca. He reached El Paso on Sunday, October 29.

Cal averaged 142 miles a day across Texas on the days that he was able to fly. His "hoodoo" was still with him, but somehow the problems that caused such agonizing delays prior to Chicago could not be coped with more easily. He smashed his skids attempting to take off from Sanderson, for example, but was able to repair them in two and a half hours and still get in the best part of a day's flying. En route to El Paso the water pump on his new engine began to leak. In making the emergency landing at Fort Hancock he smashed another skid. Three hours later all the damage was repaired and he was on his way.

After a day's layover in El Paso, Cal set off across the desert. On Tuesday, October 31, he flew 222 miles to Willcox, Arizona, pausing on the way at Deming, New Mexico, to repair a broken magneto spring and again at Lordsburg to refuel.

The next day Rodgers flew into Tucson, Arizona, where his approach was watched through a telescope at the University of Arizona by that indomitable cross-country flier, Robert Fowler. Fowler had left Los Angeles on October 19. The two men chatted briefly, then Rodgers was off again. Fowler too kept pushing eastward and finally reached the Atlantic coast at Jacksonville, Florida, on February 8, 1912, 112 days after leaving Los Angeles.

After leaving Tucson, Rodgers went on to Maricopa, Arizona, where he spent the night. On November 2, he put in a brief appearance at Phoenix, then literally flew on until his gas ran out. He was forced to land at Stoval Siding, a small one-man Southern Pacific station 60 miles east of Yuma. When his train caught

When transcontinental contender Bob Fowler couldn't fly at one point, he tried making a few miles on a railroad handcar.

up with him it was too late to continue. So Cal and his party spent the night on the desert.

By now the end of his odyssey was in sight. But the troubles that had plagued Cal all the way across the continent suddenly seemed to intensify in a last effort to thwart him.

After leaving Stoval Siding early on the morning of Friday, November 3, Cal flew on into California. Four miles beyond Imperial Junction on the Southern Pacific line, as he flew over the Salton Sea, the number-one cylinder in his engine exploded, driving metal shards into his right arm. He glided down for a perfect landing next to the Southern Pacific station at Imperial. It took a doctor over two hours to remove the fragments of the engine from Cal's right arm.

The engine was hopelessly wrecked by the explosion; so

Charlie Taylor had no choice but to put in the old engine which had been removed at Kyle, Texas, and overhauled. Cal set out again on Saturday and got as far as Banning, California, before he gave up. His spark plugs had come loose on him, and the radiator had begun to leak. It was just like old times again.

The next day, with only 75 miles to go before reaching his official destination, Cal left Banning and was soon forced down by a broken gasoline line. He finally reached Pasadena at 4:08 on the afternoon of Sunday, November 5. He had been en route forty-nine days since leaving New York, and had covered 4,231 railroad miles in three days, ten hours and four minutes of actual flying time, an average speed of 51.5 miles per hour.

Cal landed at Tournament Park and was literally mobbed by ten thousand wildly cheering people who rushed onto the field when he landed and swarmed around the plane. He was escorted

After 49 days and 4,231 miles, Rodgers finally made it to Pasadena and a hero's welcome.

from the *Vin Fiz* by policemen who had to punch the crowd back with their nightsticks. Cal was wrapped in an American flag, driven around the field, then taken to the Hotel Maryland, where he celebrated by drinking a glass of milk and eating some crackers.

By this time there wasn't much romance left in flying, as far as Cal was concerned. "I am glad this trip is over," he said. "I am not in this business because I like it, but because of what I can make out of it; personally, I prefer an automobile with a good driver to a biplane. But someone had to do this flying and I decided it might as well be I.

"My record will not last long," he went on to say. And he ventured the opinion that "with proper landing places along the route and other conditions looked after, the trip can easily be made in thirty days or less."

Despite the sense of finality to his arrival in Pasadena, Cal did not consider his trip over until he reached the Pacific Ocean. On Sunday, November 12, he left Pasadena and headed for Long Beach. Halfway there he crashed in a plowed field while attempting an emergency landing. For the fifth time, the *Vin Fiz* was demolished. Cal was hauled from the wreckage bruised and unconscious. The next day he revived, sat up in bed, smoked a cigar and talked to his family and a few friends.

"I don't know what may have caused it," he said. "Something may have broken or I may have temporarily lost control. I can't say. Anyway I know I hit the ground a mighty hard whack. But it's all in the ball game. I am going to finish that flight and finish it with that same machine."

Cal's ankle was broken in the crash and it was almost a month before he was well enough to be up and around again. On Sunday, December 10, he hobbled through an alfalfa field near Compton, climbed aboard his beloved plane, tucked his crutches behind him, and took off for Long Beach. He landed on the sand and wet his wheels in the ocean as a gigantic crowd of fifty thousand people cheered him from the Long Beach boardwalk. His historic flight was finally over.

There is not much more to the story of Cal Rodgers. He was

With crutches prominently displayed on his lower left wing, Cal Rodgers ended his transcontinental odyssey by washing his wheels in the Pacific Ocean at Long Beach.

broke now; he had lost the $50,000 Hearst prize, of course, and had spent every penny of the money paid him by the Armour Company to keep the *Vin Fiz* going. For a few weeks more he was a hero honored by everyone across the land. He received a gold medal from the Aero Club of America and drew big crowds whenever he made exhibition flights.

But Cal seemed a little lost. He wanted to fly to San Francisco, but never got around to it. And he spoke vaguely of starting his own aircraft factory, but no plans materialized. On the afternoon of April 3, 1912, Cal took off for a quick spin around Long Beach. While flying out over the water a few yards from the beach, his plane hit a flock of seagulls and plunged out of control into the ocean. Cal was immediately pulled from the wreckage by some swimmers, but it was too late. His neck was broken and he died a few feet from the spot where he had made history only four months before.

1915

As was the case with so many things, the Wright brothers' instincts were sound when they offered their invention first to the United States government for military purposes. Though the narrow-minded chieftains of the U. S. Army missed the point the first few times around, the airplane was a natural weapon of war and it wasn't long before it made its combat debut.

The airplane's first military missions were flown in 1911 during the Tripolitanian War, one of the many preludes to World War I. In this conflict, Italy wrested control of what is now the North African nation of Libya from the Ottoman Empire. Blériot airplanes were used by Italian forces for reconnaissance and scouting behind enemy lines. A more fateful development took place in the Balkan Wars of 1912–13 when Bulgarian aviators dropped small bombs on the Turkish-held city of Adrianople. They didn't do much damage, but they cast a long, dark shadow over the future.

The gathering clouds of war were an obvious stimulant to the development of the airplane in Europe. While Wright and Curtiss planes that hadn't changed much still dominated the American scene, new names such as Deperdussin and Nieuport in France and Bristol and Roe in England were beginning to crowd the old-timers. In 1913, a streamlined Deperdussin monoplane that was years ahead of its time won the Gordon Bennett race with a speed of 200 kilometers (124.28 miles) per hour and made most American planes look like antiques. It demonstrated clearly the line which aircraft design was later to follow so successfully, although structural weaknesses and inadequate materials delayed complete acceptance of the streamlined monoplane for a while.

Germany, under the leadership of Ernst Heinkel and other talented designers, was beginning to catch up rapidly with the rest of the world. Meanwhile, in the Netherlands, a young engineer whose planes would later write history for Germany made his first flights in 1910 and was on his way. This was Anthony Fokker, who moved to Germany before hostilities broke out.

When the war began in Europe in August, 1914, Germany had between 800 and 900 combat aircraft, while the air forces of Britain and France totaled less than 1,000. Military aviation was shamefully neglected in the United States during these crucial years, and when the United States finally entered the war in April, 1917, the U. S. Army had fewer than 300 aircraft, while the

While American aircraft design lagged behind, French builders at an early date were making surprisingly streamlined and modern-looking planes, such as this 1913 Deperdussin racer.

Navy and the Marine Corps were down to fifty-four, none of them suitable for combat operations. America, apparently, was more interested in the last and most magnificent burst of exhibition flying that had yet been seen.

The excitement centered around the shows put on by Lincoln Beachey toward the end of his career. He did things with an airplane that were believed impossible, and while others were struck down from the sky for daring to challenge the immutable laws of gravity and aerodynamics, Beachey somehow survived— at least for a while. He was the first American to "loop the loop." He was also the first pilot in this country to fly upside down and live to tell about it.

To Orville Wright, Lincoln Beachey was simply "the greatest aviator of all." Beckwith Havens remembered him as "a little bit of a fellow with a pugnacious jaw" who rented safe-deposit boxes in towns all around the country just to keep his money away from an ex-wife who always seemed just one jump behind him. "There was no stunt flier in the world but Lincoln Beachey—no comparison between Lincoln and the rest of them," his older brother Hillery once said, and no one ever seriously challenged his remarks.

The Beacheys came from San Francisco and, like so many early aviators, Lincoln got his start with balloons and dirigibles. He was taught to fly dirigibles by Thomas Baldwin in 1905, then barnstormed for several years with his own gasbags. He made the first airship flights over Washington, where he landed on the White House grounds on one trip and paid a call on Mrs. Theodore Roosevelt. He also performed in Montreal, Mexico City, New York, St. Louis and Philadelphia. In this last city he made some spectacular night flights with searchlights on his dirigible.

By the time Beachey appeared at the Dominguez Field Meet in January, 1910, he was sharp enough as a dirigible driver to beat veteran Roy Knabenshue in a race around the track, if "race" is the proper word to describe the spectacle of two primitive airships moving in the same general direction at approximately the same time of day. It was at Dominguez Field that Curtiss and Paulhan put on such a good show and it must have been obvious to Beachey that the time had come for him to make the transition to an airplane.

For someone who was later to achieve such fame as an aviator, Beachey had a surprisingly difficult time mastering the airplane. His first effort came with a homemade monoplane which he built after the Dominguez Field Meet and tried unsuccessfully to fly at Indianapolis when the Wright team made its debut, in June, 1910. Later that month, Beachey appeared at an exhibition at Minneapolis with both dirigible and monoplane. He made several flights with his airship, but the plane was still a failure and was finally demolished when he ran into a fence with it on one of several unsuccessful attempts to take off.

Beachey next started hanging around with the Curtiss exhibition team, working as a mechanic and plane handler, bumming hops whenever he could.

But he seemed unable to learn how to land a plane without smashing it up. "He broke up several of Curtiss' planes in Los Angeles in the winter of 1910–1911," according to his brother. "It got so that Curtiss was afraid to look at him. Just turned away." In spite of this ineptitude Curtiss somehow sensed that the young—Beachey was then twenty-three—dirigible pilot had what it took to become a good flier eventually. He sent Beachey to the Curtiss flying school that had been set up at San Diego's North Island and soon after that Beachey was on his way.

His first exhibition tour took him to Florida and Cuba in early 1911, then back north through South and North Carolina, Tennessee, Maryland, and finally to the nation's capital again, where he circled the Capitol dome and the Washington Monument. He rapidly developed a very distinctive style of flying which electrified the crowds that gathered for the show. In contrast to the sedate Wright pilots, Beachey never seemed to fly straight and level, but was always twisting and turning and bucking up and down. He usually concluded his act by climbing to about 5,000 feet, then pushing his rickety Curtiss biplane over into a vertical nose dive or "death dip," as it came to be called. With fabric rippling and guy wires whining in the wind, he held the dive until it seemed that he must crash. Then, at the last instant, he would pull out and touch down right in front of the grandstand.

As he went along from show to show, he added some trimmings to his standard act. "I've seen him come down from six thousand feet, straight down," Hillery Beachey said in an interview tape-recorded for Columbia University, "and take both hands off the wheel and hold them out and let the plane come out of it by itself. I've also seen him make a vertical spiral coming down, the first roll of this kind ever made."

When it came to flying in and out of tight places, there was no other pilot who could approach Beachey's skill and precision. While many of his colleagues preferred race track infields for their flights, Beachey liked to take off and land on the track itself in front of the grandstand, no matter how narrow it was nor how strong the wind might be blowing in the wrong direction. When trees lined the track, he ducked under their branches; he wasn't disturbed by telephone poles and wires and seemed to dart in and out among them like a dragonfly; and at times, ladies swooned and strong men fell to the ground when he made low passes over their heads.

One of Beachey's most famous tight-squeeze flights took place in June, 1911, on a swing through the Northeast. Flying out of Buffalo, he announced his intention to go over Niagara Falls in his airplane. Beachey later said it was the most thrilling flight of his career—and perhaps it was a bit more exciting than he intended. Taking off in a light rain shower, he climbed to 2,000 feet, then came roaring down at the brink of the falls. He circled twice down low to give the crowd of 150,000 an extra thrill, then plunged over the falls into the gorge below. He emerged from the mist at the foot of the cascade dripping wet but still flying, then got blasted by the wash from the outlet of the power tunnel which shoots out from the rocky precipice near where he recovered from his dive. But he staggered on and under the bridge 400 yards downstream from the base of the falls. The space he flew through was 168 feet high and barely 100 feet from side to side. When almost in the spray of the whirlpool rapids, he pointed toward the cliffs on the Canadian side, pulled up, barely squeaked over the edge of the gorge by a few feet and plunked

Hands-off stunting just a few feet above the ground never failed to awe the crowds that came out to see Lincoln Beachey.

down. It was easy enough to go over the Falls, but climbing back out was another matter, and neither Beachey nor anyone else has tried the same stunt since.

Beachey was one of the more dapper aviators of the era and customarily flew in an expensively tailored pin-striped business suit with high starched collar, two-carat diamond stickpin in his tie, and a checkered golfing cap which he wore backwards to keep it from blowing off. He was also one of the more enigmatic of the early pilots. Despite his flamboyant appearance and daredevil flying, he usually disappeared right after a show to avoid the crowds of fans, interviewers and autograph seekers. Liquor affected him more than people did—"One glass of champagne, and he'd be tight," recalled Beckwith Havens—so he didn't drink much. But he made good friends among his colleagues and fellow pilots and there always seemed to be at least one young lady in every town he visited who claimed to be his fiancée. It was almost inevitable that some of his flying exploits would soon begin to assume the proportions of legends. One episode Hillery Beachey always liked to tell about took place in 1912:

Curtiss and Wright had both sold planes to the Army and one of their specifications was that they had to make a figure eight in a certain amount of space. They were flying the Wright plane a little shorter than the Curtiss plane and Glenn Curtiss asked my brother to go down there and show them how they could fly. So Lincoln went to Washington and took his hands off the wheel and flew a smaller figure eight with no hands than anybody had ever flown before. The next day he got a letter from the Army and they asked him not to fly an airplane at an Army airfield again. Why? Well, they were afraid the Army fliers might try to emulate him and kill themselves. It was just too much for them.

Flying with no hands was not particularly difficult in a Curtiss plane. The banking of the wings was controlled by a yoke which fitted around the pilot's body, and the main control column could be held steady between the pilot's legs. But the public didn't know these fine points, and when Beachey roared down the track just a few feet off the ground and spread his arms way out as he passed the grandstand, it seemed as though he was doing the impossible.

Beachey probably flew more exhibition dates in 1911 and 1912 than any other pilot in America. He appeared in at least twenty-three states, the District of Columbia, and Cuba, and made the first flights ever seen in Puerto Rico. But the greater the show that Beachey put on, the harder it was for other pilots to satisfy the crowds at their exhibition dates. People were coming to expect more and more dangerous stunts, and as a consequence many exhibition pilots were getting killed when they pushed themselves and their planes beyond their limits in an attempt to put on a good show. Beachey began to be blamed for many of the fatalities—it got so bad that some newspapers referred to fatal accidents as "pulling a Beachey"—and this bothered him terribly. The death of Curtiss pilot Eugene Ely at an exhibition in

Georgia in late 1912 was a particularly heavy blow. Ely, the man who made the Navy's first carrier landing, was a superb pilot in Beachey's estimation and a good friend. When Mrs. Ely publicly accused Beachey of murdering her husband by encouraging him to fly dangerously, Beachey decided it was time to quit. "I am through with flying," he said at a banquet. "You couldn't get me in an airplane again at the point of a revolver. I am convinced that the only thing that draws crowds to see me is the morbid desire to see something happen. They call me the 'Master Bird-man,' but they pay to see me die."

For a while after his "retirement" Beachey went into vaudeville and toured the country telling about his flying experiences. It wasn't much of an act and before long Beachey forgot his solemn resolve to stay out of airplanes. Beckwith Havens remembered the moment Beachey changed his mind:

Beachey went into vaudeville and even played the Palace here in New York. It was a dismal little act—he'd just walk out on the stage and talk about his flying. But he was so worried about how so many people were getting killed in airplanes at that time, and when they began to blame it on Beachey he resented it so much that he said he'd never fly again.

One day when he was playing at the Palace I had a lunch date with him at the old Knickerbocker Hotel. I had just read in the paper that morning about a fellow in France looping the loop. Nobody had ever done that before. So when we started having lunch, I asked him, "Did you see about this fellow in France looping the loop in an airplane?"

"He did what?" said Beachey.

"He looped," I said.

"Doggone," he said. "I don't know how many times I've been over on my back trying to get into some of those little fields in a dive, but I never thought to try to make a loop!"

Soon after that he went up to Hammondsport, got Curtiss to build him another airplane, and took up looping.

The world's first loop was performed by a little-known pilot named Adolphe Pégoud in a Blériot monoplane on September 1, 1913. Pégoud did it the hard way—by going around the outside.

Adolphe Pégoud

His method was to climb up several thousand feet, throttle his engine back and push his nose over. As he went down he continued to hold his control column forward until he was upside down. He added power on the bottom of the circle, then, while still inverted, flew up the other side of the circle. He got to the top and was level again just about the time he ran out of speed.

This is an extremely difficult maneuver and it says a lot about the strength and quality of the Blériot airframe that it could do an outside loop without shedding its wings. There was no plane available in the United States at this time which could have withstood the same stress.

Now Beachey's reputation was at stake. Here he was, billed across the land as "the World's Greatest Aviator," and he had been upstaged by a Frenchman he had never heard of. He hurried to get back in the air and reclaim his title.

The new plane he had ordered from Curtiss was ready to be tested in Hammondsport in early October. It was smaller than the standard Curtiss biplane, was specially braced to withstand the maneuvers Beachey contemplated and had a powerful 90-horsepower Curtiss engine in it. But with all the extra weight and drag added by the acrobatic reinforcements, it proved too much for Beachey to handle the first time he took it up. While attempting a landing he struck the top of a Navy tent, killing a young woman who had climbed up for a better view and seriously injuring her sister. This caused Beachey to lose complete control of the landing and he wrecked the plane, without, however, getting hurt himself.

The plane was redesigned, completely rebuilt and sent to Curtiss' West Coast headquarters at North Island, San Diego. After just a week of practice, Beachey was ready for his first attempt to do the loop. He made it look easy—with no difficulty at all he did three loops in succession over the Polo Grounds at Coronado on November 25. Beachey's loop was different from Pégoud's. He started out the same way, by pushing over to gain speed, but then, instead of continuing to push over until he was on his back, Beachey pulled up in an "inside" loop and was on his back at the top of the circle rather than at the bottom. The plane fell through naturally on the other side of the circle and ended up in a conventional dive which Beachey pulled out of with little difficulty. It was an easier maneuver than Pégoud's outside loop and could be controlled with more precision. This enabled Beachey to fly it at a much lower, and more hair-raising, altitude.

By the end of 1913, Beachey had done almost three dozen loops at various West Coast exhibitions. It was like old times. The crowds were huge wherever he went and the newspaper accounts were breathless and colorful.

On the last day of December, 1913, he once again demonstrated his complete mastery of flying in tight places by taking off and flying *inside* a large convention hall in San Francisco. Here is the way a reporter for the San Francisco *Chronicle* recounted this extraordinary feat:

Lincoln Beachey, San Francisco's aviator of upside-down fame, demonstrated indoor aviation yesterday afternoon in the world's largest frame building, Machinery Palace, on the Exposition grounds, and had one of the narrowest escapes of his career as a birdman when his high-powered biplane crashed into the end of the building. The damage to the aeroplane was nominal, however, and Beachey was unscathed except for the terrific force of the collision.

The machine had traversed about half of the 900-foot length of the exhibit palace, going at a speed of about 60 miles per hour, when Beachey alighted gracefully on the floor and sped toward the north end of the building. Owing to the wet condition of the floor the single brake on the forward wheel of the machine was practically without effect, and the momentum of the craft snapped the cloth streamers held by attendants to retard the machine as though they had been only gossamers.

The several hundred spectators who braved the hard rain to witness this most unique of all of Beachey's feats held their breath for the moment as the aeroplane tore through the last barrier of cloth and sped on toward what seemed the goal of destruction. The crash of the machine echoed through the great building and after a moment of suspense some one cried out that Beachey was safe. This was confirmed almost at once when Beachey was seen to clamber out and walk about his biplane inspecting it and making an inventory of the damage to it.

Beachey was the least excited person in the building and he declared he had gotten much worse jolts on collisions with fences and other out-of-doors obstacles. Notwithstanding Beachey's assertion, however, the force of the impact was so great that two planks an inch thick on the north wall were broken.

Aside from the accident those in charge of the exhibition declared the flight a big success.

But the pressure to top himself was as relentless as always and soon Beachey was thinking of new ways to awe the crowds. In April, 1914, he made a quick trip to France and bought two 80-horsepower Gnome rotary engines which promised to keep running better when upside down than the stationary Curtiss engines. Meanwhile, Hillery Beachey and Lincoln's mechanics Art Mix, Al Hofer and Warren Eaton were in Chicago building a special looping biplane.

The *Little Looper,* as the new plane came to be called affectionately, was probably the finest aircraft built in the United States up until this time, from a structural point of view. It was tiny—its wing span was just a shade more than 25 feet and it weighed only 775 pounds with Beachey aboard. The Gnome rotary engine looked tremendous in this small plane, but everything was in perfect balance and Beachey had no difficulty maintaining control upside down, right side up, slow or fast— and the *Little Looper* could hit speeds up to 85 miles per hour and climb at an impressive rate of 1,125 feet per minute.

Beachey painted his name in big, bold letters on the top of the upper wing so that it would be visible to the crowd whenever he flew inverted, and soon added another stunt to his bag of tricks. This was a vertical-S maneuver and it demonstrated, even more than the loops, how complete Beachey's mastery of acrobatic flying was with the new airplane. The vertical-S was a combination of outside and inside loops. The top half of the S was made by pushing the nose over all the way until the plane was flying upside down. Sometimes Beachey would then fly inverted for

For thrills and excitement, nothing in America in 1914 could rival the races—such as this one at Davenport, Iowa—that Lincoln Beachey staged with Barney Oldfield and Eddie Rickenbacker.

some distance. The bottom half of the S came after this stretch of inverted flying and was accomplished by pulling back on the control column to get the nose going down in a dive, then pulling out of the dive in the normal upright way. The bottom half of this maneuver was similar to the split-S that most modern student pilots learn during the course of their instruction.

And there were even more tricks, some of them pure showmanship. Occasionally Beachey dressed as a woman and pretended to steal an airplane and take off with it. With his long skirt billowing and his big hat flapping, he would career across the sky imitating someone who didn't know how to fly, barely averting disaster after disaster in the nick of time. Another popular feature consisted of races with famous automobile drivers such as Barney Oldfield and Eddie Rickenbacker. Auto and airplane were pretty evenly matched in those days and it was usually the layout of the track that determined the victor. If the track had a long straightaway, the airplane usually won. But if the track was circular, or had very short straight stretches, the automobile could usually pull ahead because of its shorter turning radius at high speeds.

The 1914 season was Beachey's busiest and most successful. By the end of the year, it was estimated that Beachey had looped 1,000 times before seventeen million people in 126 cities. His fee was $500 for the first loop at an exhibition plus $200 for each loop after that. His terms: cash in advance, and it was not at all unusual for him to pick up $1,500 for a six-loop day's work.

As the year wore on and Germany began its sweep across Belgium into France the newspapers turned their attention toward more serious matters, and Beachey's headlines became fewer and fewer. While many months would pass before America entered the war, the atmosphere was changing, nevertheless, and it was obvious that the carefree days in which the airplane was born and brought to maturity were almost over. But as far as Beachey was concerned, there was still time for one more fling, and the Panama-Pacific International Exposition, scheduled to begin in San Francisco in February, 1915, seemed like a good opportunity to grab the headlines again.

So Beachey returned to his home town and put Warren Eaton to work building a radically different new airplane for stunts at the exposition. Meanwhile, Beachey put on a New Year's Day show at San Francisco with the *Little Looper* in which he swooped down on a mock battleship in the bay in a demonstration of aerial "bombing." The target was planted with dynamite and other fireworks, which were detonated in a spectacular flash of fire and smoke as Beachey passed over. Work continued on the new airplane, which was to make its debut after the formal opening of the exposition. When it was rolled out for its first test flights at a beach south of the city, it was quite a surprise, for the new machine was a trim, racy-looking monoplane that was the most advanced design that had been produced so far in the United States. The plane was flown a few times, then dismantled and put away, giving rise to speculation that something was wrong.

Beachey opened the exposition with a looping show on February 21, 1915, and continued to make daily exhibition flights in the *Little Looper*. However, fair officials talked Beachey into exhibiting his new monoplane, and after further tests with the *Little Looper's* reliable and powerful Gnome rotary engine, Beachey unveiled the monoplane at the fairgrounds on March 13, looping it three times before rain called a halt to the day's flying.

The next day was a Sunday and a crowd of fifty thousand lined the field to see the monoplane take off with the great pilot at the controls. He made two brief hops that afternoon, then headed out over the sunny bay to try some stunts. He climbed to 5,000 or 6,000 feet so that all could see and made several graceful, effortless-looking loops. Then he began his vertical-S maneuver. The plane's behavior in the top half of the S was normal, but when Beachey pulled back into the bottom half the monoplane went into a screaming, uncontrollable dive in which it hit a speed of 250–300 miles per hour, according to other aviators who saw the flight. As Beachey tried to pull out of the dive, there was a loud, sickening crack as first the left and then the right wing snapped and folded upward around the body of the plane. It hit the bay with a great splash and sank immediately.

Beachey's last flight began with a takeoff before a tremendous throng of people at the fairgrounds in San Francisco.

The wreckage was located quickly by a Navy diver from the battleship *Oregon,* which was anchored in the bay. Thirty-five minutes after the crash the wreckage was raised by a crane on another ship and Beachey's body was removed and wrapped in canvas by sailors from the *Oregon.* Thousands of people watched in silence from the shore and many removed their hats when Beachey's body was lifted up.

There was an official investigation conducted for the Aero Club of California by aviator Robert Fowler and others who saw the accident. Their report concluded that Beachey didn't realize how fast he was going in the unfamiliar airplane, yanked his controls too hard when he tried to pull out and strained the airframe far beyond the limits of its strength.

Though most people didn't realize it yet, an era was ended. A few lesser-known stunt pilots continued to give exhibitions after

Beachey's death, but the exciting and, at times, almost unbelievable early period in aviation was really all over now. The great pioneers—the Wrights, Curtiss, Blériot, Santos-Dumont, the Voisins—had moved off the center of the stage, and while they were still active in the business of making airplanes (except for Wilbur Wright, who had died), their flying exploits had been surpassed by the exhibition pilots, who, in turn, found the public's gaze turning, after Beachey's death, to a new generation of aviators. The new crowd seemed terribly young and wet behind the ears and they wore cavalry boots and white silk scarves instead of business suits and high starched collars. They performed for a far different audience and the stakes were a lot higher, for now there were two kinds of enemies—the natural ones which had been there all along and the man-made terrors of war. But in time they too would prove themselves worthy successors to a proud heritage.

It is interesting to note that the period of time that elapsed between the Wrights' first powered flight and the end of this first great era in aviation was about the same as the time between Sputnik I and the first man on the moon—less than twelve years. We take pride in our technological sophistication these days, but apparently, if the history of flight gives a valid perspective, we progress no more rapidly and are no more inventive than at the turn of the century.

The magnitude of our ambition has grown. We reach for the stars now. But I believe that the great leap that carried aviation in a dozen years from the sand dunes of the Carolina Outer Banks to looping the loop over San Francisco Bay demanded at least as much of the human spirit as the leap from Sputnik I to the moon. We live in an age when everything, good or bad, that the human mind conceives seems possible to achieve. The Wrights and the men and women who took to the air immediately after them lived in a far different world—a world that was well satisfied with its own goodness and extremely impatient with those who tried the new things. The early aviators had to be a little larger than life to dare what they did, and they paid a heavy price for failure.

The early aviators who survived were frequently damaged and scarred beyond the physical knocks they took. Santos-Dumont died a suicide in 1932, haunted by visions of crashes and air attacks. Glenn Curtiss turned his back on aviation in bitterness over patent suits and legal wrangles and plunged into Florida real-estate speculations until his death in 1930. Orville Wright never married and he became more and more of a recluse in Dayton after Wilbur's death in 1912. Orville died in 1948. Blanche Scott was married briefly, then divorced. Pretty, vivacious Matilde Moisant never found a husband.

Yet there were always new people who would accept the risks. Unknowingly, the torch was passed on the day that Lincoln Beachey died. For among the crowd that helplessly watched his awful, fatal plunge was a young man named Eddie Rickenbacker who would soon come to symbolize, more than anyone else, the spirit of the next crowd of pilots to occupy the stage.

But memories of the early days linger on. Fifty years after Beachey's death almost to the day, a group of middle-aged men met for brunch on a quiet Sunday morning in San Francisco. Then they drove to a pier down on the waterfront. They brought with them a floral wreath, which they dropped reverently into the bay. The sea was calm and peaceful and the wreath slowly drifted out to the spot where Beachey died.

It is doubtful whether the death of any other early pilot has ever been commemorated with such a touching and eloquent gesture as this one by San Francisco members of the American Aviation Historical Society. But it is not enough. Those of us who fly today cannot ever pay adequate tribute to the ones who gave so much in the early years.

Acknowledgments

To recapture the excitement of the early period of aviation I have attempted to bring the reader up close to events and personalities by means of eyewitness and first-person accounts insofar as possible. I am deeply indebted to innumerable nameless newspaper writers whose vivid reporting has contributed so much to my attempts to re-create the mood of those early years. I have also relied heavily on the extensive tape-recorded interviews of Hillery Beachey, Ross Browne, Frank Coffyn, Beckwith Havens, Matilde Moisant, J. T. C. Moore-Brabazon and Ruth Law Oliver which were conducted by the Columbia University Oral History Office and underwritten by the American Heritage Publishing Company. Finally, this book would not have been possible without the assistance of many people: Paul Garber, chief historian at the Smithsonian Institution's National Air and Space Museum for many years; my "Paris team" of Austin Briggs, Jerry Trippe and Peter Watkins; my wife, Lorna, who really got this book moving with her research into countless files of old newspapers; and the following individuals and institutions:

Aerospace Studies Institute, Maxwell Air Force Base, Alabama
Aerospace Studies Institute Liason Office, Silver Spring, Maryland
Air Force Historical Foundation, Bolling Air Force Base, D.C.
American Aviation Historical Society, Los Angeles, California
Lord Brabazon of Tara
Brigadier General Thad A. Broom (Retd.), Washington, D.C.
Mrs. Ross J. Browne, New York, New York
Cessna Aircraft Company, Wichita, Kansas
Douglas Aircraft Company, Inc., Santa Monica, California
Colonel Arthur C. Goebel, U.S.A.F. (Retd.), Los Angeles, California
Mr. and Mrs. Beckwith Havens, New York, New York
Library of Congress, Washington, D.C.
Lockheed Aircraft Corporation, Burbank, California

Martin Marietta Corporation, Baltimore, Maryland
Mrs. Elizabeth Mason, Columbia University Oral History Office, New York, New York
Marvin W. McFarland, Library of Congress, Washington, D.C.
Mrs. Alexander McSurely, Arlington, Virginia
Musée de l'Air, Paris, France
National Air and Space Museum, The Smithsonian Institution, Washington, D.C.
National Archives, Washington, D.C.
The National Cash Register Company, Dayton, Ohio
Mrs. Ruth Law Oliver, San Francisco, California
Edward V. Rickenbacker, New York, New York
Mrs. Mabel Rodgers-Wiggin, Center Moriches, New York
San Diego Aerospace Museum, San Diego, California
Sir Thomas Sopwith, King's Somborne, Hampshire, England
E. D. Weeks, Des Moines, Iowa
Mrs. A. Christiane West, Alexandria, Virginia
John A. Weyl, Los Angeles, California

I am grateful for permission from several publishers to quote from the following works:

The American Heritage History of Flight, by the editors of *American Heritage.* American Heritage Publishing Co., Inc., New York, N.Y., 1962.

Claude Grahame-White, by Graham Wallace. Putnam & Company Ltd., London, 1960.

"Coast to Coast in Twelve Crashes," by Sherwood Harris. *American Heritage,* October, 1964.

"Early Flying Experiences," by Major General Benjamin D. Foulois, U.S.A.F. (Retd.), *Air Power Historian,* April, 1955.

Bell and Baldwin, by J. H. Parkin, University of Toronto, Toronto, 1964.

Men, Women and 10,000 Kites, by Gabriel Voisin. Putnam & Company Ltd., London, 1963.

The Papers of Wilbur and Orville Wright, edited by Marvin W. McFarland. McGraw-Hill Book Co., Inc., New York, 1953.

Santos-Dumont, by Peter Wykeham. Putnam & Company Ltd., London, 1962.

The following works also provided valuable background:

L'Aviation; ses débuts—son développement, by Ferdinand Ferber. Berger-Levrault & Cie., Paris, 1908.

"Glenn H. Curtiss' First Off-Water Flight," by George E. A. Hallett. *Aerospace Historian,* Winter, 1966.

The Curtiss Aviation Book, by Glenn H. Curtiss and Augustus Post. Frederick A. Stokes Co., New York, 1912.

Experiments in Aerodynamics, by Samuel P. Langley. Smithsonian Institution, Washington, D.C., 1902.

"Histoire de l'aéronautique," by Charles Dollfus and Henri Bouché, *L'Illustration,* Paris, 1942.

The Invention of the Aeroplane, 1799–1909, by Charles H. Gibbs-Smith. Taplinger Publishing Co., Inc., New York, 1966.

Langley Memoir on Mechanical Flight, by Samuel P. Langley. Smithsonian Institution, Washington, D.C., 1911.

My Fifty Years of Flying, by Harry Harper. Associated Newspapers Ltd., London, 1956.

To Ride the Wind, by Henry Still. Julian Messner, Inc., New York, 1964.

Vehicles of the Air, by Victor Loughead. Reilly & Britton, Chicago, 1909.

The Wright Brothers, by Fred C. Kelly. Harcourt, Brace & Co., New York, 1943.

Picture Credits

Index

[Page numbers in italics refer to illustrations.]